NO GOD
BUT ONE
ALLAH OR JESUS?

ALSO BY NABEEL QURESHI

Seeking Allah, Finding Jesus

Answering Jihad

NO GOD BUT ONE

ALLAH OR JESUS?

A FORMER MUSLIM INVESTIGATES
THE EVIDENCE FOR ISLAM
AND CHRISTIANITY

AUTHOR OF THE *NEW YORK TIMES* BESTSELLER
SEEKING ALLAH, FINDING JESUS

NABEEL QURESHI

ZONDERVAN®

ZONDERVAN

No God but One: Allah or Jesus?
Copyright © 2016 by Nabeel A. Qureshi

This title is also available as a Zondervan ebook.
This title is also available as a Zondervan audio book.

Requests for information should be addressed to:
Zondervan, *3900 Sparks Dr. SE, Grand Rapids, Michigan 49546*

Library of Congress Cataloging-in-Publication Data

Names: Qureshi, Nabeel, author.
Title: No God but one : Allah or Jesus? / Nabeel Quereshi.
Description: Grand Rapids : Zondervan, 2016. | Includes bibliographical references.
Identifiers: LCCN 2016019945 | ISBN 9780310522553 (softcover)
Subjects: LCSH: Islam—Relations—Christianity. | Christianity and other religions—
    Islam. | Islam—Doctrines. | Christianity—Doctrines.
Classification: LCC BP172 .Q7185 2016 | DDC 261.2/7—dc23 LC record available at
    https://lccn.loc.gov/2016019945

Published in association with the literary agency of Mark Sweeney & Associates, Bonita
Springs, Florida 34135.

Cover design: Brian Bobel
Interior design: Kait Lamphere

Printed in the United States of America

16 17 18 19 20 21 22 23 24 25 26 /DHV/ 15 14 13 12 11 10 9 8 7 6 5 4 3 2

This book is dedicated to David Wood,
a great friend and total doofus.

CONTENTS

ACKNOWLEDGMENTS

Great heart and countless hours of effort have been invested into this book. I am deeply indebted to the Zondervan team for their encouragement in spite of the many bumps and turns along the way. I would particularly like to thank Madison Trammel for his ever-present support, Jesse Hillman for strategic perspectives, Brian Phipps for his longsuffering patience, and Stan Gundry for his vision in making this book a reality. Thanks is also due to Mark Sweeney for his insight, wisdom, and loyal friendship.

I would also like to thank the many people who had a hand in making this book better: Richard Zetter, Richard Shumack, Matthew Thomas, John Njoroge, Shawn Hart, and Betsy Duncan. I must thank my darling bride, Michelle, for her loving encouragement despite the many days I had to spend away from her to write. I would also like to thank my beautiful daughter, Ayah, for being born in the middle of this project, filling my life with color and joy.

Last, and certainly not least, I would like to thank the Lord God for giving me the impetus and means to pour myself into this effort. I pray it would all be for his glory and his people. Amen.

PREFACE

Dear Reader,

I truly thank you for taking the time to read this book. For me, and for millions of others like me, the subject matter of these pages is far more than information. It is the full engagement of heart and mind in search for the true God and true Life. What I share is a summary of fifteen years of research that wrenched my heart and transformed my life.

You might have already read the account of my journey from Islam to Christianity, *Seeking Allah, Finding Jesus*. That book is the heart of my story, detailing the relationships, emotions, and spiritual struggles in my search for God. *No God but One: Allah or Jesus?* is the mind of my story, examining the religions and their claims. In the course of this book, I hope to elucidate two overarching matters in particular: that the differences between Islam and Christianity have great implications, and that the evidence of history strongly supports the Christian claims.

"GOD," "ALLAH," AND "YAHWEH"

Before beginning, the title of this book could use some explanation. Both Islam and Christianity are monotheistic, believing there is "no God but one," but they differ fundamentally on who that God is: Allah or Jesus.

There are at least four common uses of the Arabic word *Allah*. First and foremost, it is used to refer to the Muslim concept of God as described by Islam. This should not surprise anyone. The second use is to simply mean God in a generic sense; so, as with the English word *God*, Allah need not imply any specific religion. But the last two uses may be surprising: Many Arabic-speaking Christians do use *Allah* to mean the triune Christian God, and sometimes Christians use the term just to refer to the first person of the Trinity, the Father.

To further complicate matters, Christians often do not clearly distinguish between persons of the triune God. Thus they can confuse their Muslim friends by saying something like, "Jesus is God," and in the next breath, "Jesus is the Son of God." Although both statements are technically accurate doctrine, they will only cause confusion by switching between uses of the word *God*. Their Muslim friends might respond to this by saying, "So is Jesus his own son?" And they would be right to ask for clarification.

In this book, I will attempt to pay close attention to the way I use these words. The term *Allah* will refer specifically to the Muslim conception of God, the term *Yahweh* will be used when I intend to refer specifically to all three persons of the Trinity, and the term *God* will be used when the occasion calls for a generic use or intentional ambiguity. The terms *Father*, *Son*, and *Spirit* will be used to refer to the specific persons of the Trinity. Finally, if this paragraph is difficult to understand, I am really glad you are reading this book. Please spend extra time in part 2.

THE CHALLENGE OF SEMANTICS

One of the greatest troubles in religious discussions is how we define our words. When some people say "Islam," they essentially mean the religion that a Muslim friend practices. But what a friend does can look very different from what an imam in Saudi Arabia does, so how do we decide which of them more accurately represents Islam? There are many branches and sects that purport to follow Islam, so how can we know whether they are actually Muslim? Do we just assume that everyone who identifies as a Muslim is representing Islam? If so, how do we handle the assertion that terrorist groups like ISIS do not represent Islam when they clearly claim to be Muslim?

This problem is more difficult than it appears, but to prevent our terminology from becoming a moving target, we have to at least circumscribe a definition. I think a religious group ought to be defined through a historical lens. What was it that gave the group its own identity and set it apart from other groups at its inception, according to its traditional narratives? In the case of Muslims, their defining act was assenting that Muhammad is a prophet and exclusively following his teachings as revelations from Allah. In this book, we will consider all who do the same to be Muslims. We will consider Islam to be the teachings of Muhammad in that early period of identity formation.

Using the same reasoning, at their inception, Christians distinguished their identity from their Greco-Roman context by the belief in the God of the Hebrew Bible; yet they were distinct from other Jews because, on account of Christ's resurrection, they believed Jesus himself to be the God of the Hebrew Bible, at least in some sense. Thus, those who hold to the monotheism of the Hebrew Bible while also following the divine, risen Jesus I consider to be Christians. Christianity would then be constituted by Jesus' teachings as understood in that early period of identity formation.

FINAL THOUGHTS AND CLOSING PRAYER

This book has been a dream of mine for about a decade. I have met thousands of people who desperately seek God and are caught between the polemics of Islam and Christianity. I do not claim to be unbiased, but I have been on both sides of this debate, and I know how taxing it can be to try to wade through all the arguments. It is my prayer that this book will reach many who are in the throes of their search, and I pray it will lead them to the altar of the one true God. If that is you, know that I have prayed and shed tears for you, and that this book is written for you.

If you are reading this book mostly to learn and not out of a personal struggle, please pause now and pray for those who are struggling between Islam and Christianity, striving to know God. Pray that he will meet them, and that he might equip you to be a part of their journey.

Now to Yahweh, the God of the Universe, who is able to do immeasurably more than all we can ask or imagine, I pray. I commit this book to You,

Lord, that You might be made known and glorified. I ask that You rescue lives and transform this world. May many come to a saving knowledge of You and a relationship that fills Your heart and theirs with joy. It is in the name of Jesus I pray. Amen.

FATIMA'S DILEMMA

R epent! Otherwise you have blasphemed!"

Her brother had seethed with rage, his words still echoing in Fatima's mind. *Repent! You have blasphemed!* They were laced with threat: The penalty for blasphemy was death. Had she really blasphemed? She had not meant to. It had been a heated argument, and she accidentally blurted out some words . . . but what now? How could this have happened? She was struggling to think clearly. Her very life was in jeopardy.

Lifting her face from her hands, Fatima glanced at her computer. It was where she had confided her most private thoughts and inner struggles, where she could discuss new ideas and share opinions with compassionate ears. Her computer was her window to friends and freedom.

But today, it had betrayed her. As a result, she had been locked in her room for hours and feared for her life. Her brother could return at any moment, and unless she repented, it could be the end. She had to think. She had to think quickly and clearly.

Despite the treachery, her computer remained her only recourse. As she had done so many times before, she returned to her laptop to help her process. Logging onto an Arabic forum, she began a post.

Time stamp: 5:15 a.m., July 24, 2008
Author: Rania

She had been signing on for years as "Rania," but the forum knew her well. They knew that she was really twenty-six-year-old Sara Fatima al-Mutairi, a spirited young woman, a passionate teacher, a patriotic Saudi, and a recent convert to Christianity.

Born in the province of Qasim, Fatima's family came from a distinguished Bedouin tribe and had raised her in accordance with their ancestral religion of Islam. Desiring a devout daughter, her mother had enrolled her in a Quran school at a young age, and Fatima began to take her Islamic faith very seriously. She started learning the Quran, scrupulously covering her hair with her *hijab*, and even fasting twice a week. She began to outstrip her family in religious zeal, avoiding television and secular music, and ultimately giving up friends on account of her fervor.

Fatima's mother grew concerned. She desired a faithful daughter, not a fanatical one. This was not the Islam that she knew. Regretting her decision, she took Fatima out of the Quran school and enrolled her in the state system.

Over the ensuing years Fatima's life normalized, yet she maintained a passion for her religion. She engaged in online debates with agnostics and apostates, defending her beloved prophet and religion from their attacks. In the course of these dialogues she investigated Islamic history and theology carefully, confident her faith would stand up to scrutiny. Yet during these debates she realized, amid anguish and despair, that she could no longer follow Islam. She stopped eating for several days, fell into depression, and became an atheist.

But something told her this was not the answer. She began her search for God anew, this time calling out to him for help. It was then that she came across the Gospels, particularly the gospel of Matthew. It captivated her. She read it four times, being most moved by the Sermon on the Mount. After months of deliberation and investigation, she accepted its message. The Christian community with whom she connected advised her to keep her new faith a secret, as leaving Islam in Arabia incurs the penalty of death. This was difficult for Fatima, passionate and outspoken as she was, but she hid her conversion from all, keeping her private thoughts on her computer and conversing with her Christian community only online.

It was to this online community that she now returned, in her moment of critical despair. After a brief thought, she titled her post and continued:

> **Time stamp:** 5:15 a.m., July 24, 2008
> **Author:** Rania
> **Title:** I am in big trouble
> **Body:** The peace of our Lord and our God and Jesus the Messiah. I am in big trouble. My family has started to doubt me because of a religious argument this evening with my mother and brother . . .

Her brother. Fatima did not need to explain to the forum how dangerous an argument with him could be. Fatima's brother had a similar start in the same family, but his story progressed very differently. His fervor for Islam had only grown since childhood, and he had become a fanatic. Ultimately he joined the "Commission for the Promotion of Virtue and the Prevention of Vice," Saudi Arabia's religious police, dedicated to enforcing a stringent version of Islam upon its citizens. Although many Muslims take issue with the Commission in specific and Saudi Arabia's dogmatic version of Islam in general, the religious stringency attracts zealous young men like Fatima's brother.

Fatima's fingers flew across the keyboard, the words now pouring out of her as she recounted the harrowing events of the evening. She explained that, in a moment of weakness, she had complained about her lack of religious freedom in Islam. When her family pressed her to explain herself, she had blurted, "The way of the Messiah is purer than the way of the Messenger, and there is a great difference between them!" Her brother flew into a rage, threatening, "Repent! Otherwise you have blasphemed!" Even though Fatima tried to apologize, he broke into her room, took her computer, and started searching through her files. There he found Fatima's journals, her Christian confessions, and even a picture of the cross.

His darkest suspicions were confirmed. A sharp malice flooded his eyes. He left her, giving her four hours to consider what she had done.

Repent! You have blasphemed!

As she came to the end of her post, she made a simple request: "His glance frightened me. I do not trust him. Pray for me, please . . ."

Four hours had passed. Her brother would return at any moment. She had to choose: Would she repent and embrace Islam, or would she stand firm in her Christian faith, potentially at the cost of her life? Which would it be, Islam or Christianity?

ISLAM OR CHRISTIANITY?

For Fatima, absolutely everything hinged on that question. No matter the strength of her convictions, when faced with the threat of death, she probably had a moment of considering how certain she really was: *Is the way of the Messiah truly all that different from the way of the Messenger? Can we really be confident that one religion or the other is true? Even so, is the truth worth dying for?*

Every year, millions are faced with Fatima's dilemma: to follow Islam or Christianity, to worship Allah or Jesus. Like Fatima, unless the seeker lives in a nominal or secular environment, the stakes are high: It can cost a seeker her family, her friends, her job, and potentially her life. For such seekers, it is not simply a matter of believing whatever seems right. They need to be sure, and they need to be sure it is worth the sacrifice.

For me, it has been a decade since I decided to leave Islam, and the fallout of my decision haunts me every day. I knew it would, well before I ever converted, but I also knew that I was sure. I was sure that Islam and Christianity are not just two paths that lead to the same God, but two very different paths that lead very different ways. I was sure that I had excellent historical reason to believe the gospel. I was sure that, though I loved Islam, I could not ignore the problems that crippled its foundations.

But most of all, I was sure that following the one true God would be worth all trials and all suffering. I had to follow the evidence and the truth, no matter the cost.

I left my religion of twenty-two years and became a follower of Jesus in 2005. In 2009, after graduating from medical school, I decided to leave medicine in order to share what I had learned about the gospel, the message of Christianity. I sincerely believe that this message has the power to transform hearts and change the world. The God it proclaims is unlike any other, and it is an unfathomable honor that we get to be a part of his story and introduce people to him.

While sharing this message, I often come across two kinds of people: Christians who enjoy criticizing Islam, and Muslims who want to argue but do not want to learn. I am not writing this book for either of them. I am writing for people who—like Fatima and I did—need the answers to these questions:

- What are the differences between Islam and Christianity?
- Can we be confident that Christianity or Islam is true?
- Is the truth worth dying for?

It took me four years to answer these questions, and they remain so important to me that I have studied them for another decade beyond. This book is my brief answer. After I share my findings, we will see how Fatima answered the same questions and discover the outcome of her story.

WHAT ARE THE DIFFERENCES BETWEEN ISLAM AND CHRISTIANITY?

In August 2005, I came to the most painful realization of my life: I no longer believed Islam. I had no recourse left and could no longer delay the eventuality I had been fighting for years.

As a child, I was raised to love Islam. I enjoyed memorizing chapters of the Quran and reciting them in my daily prayers. I looked forward to fasting every year with my family during Ramadan, thrilling in the early morning prayers and the communal suppers in the evening. I eagerly anticipated celebrating each Eid with my extended family. My entire life revolved around Islam, and I was proud of my Muslim heritage.

Ironically, it was my confidence in Islam that brought my faith to the breaking point.

Shortly after starting my undergraduate studies in 2001, I challenged a Christian friend at my university to consider the truth of Islam. Using reasoning that I had heard at mosques and from Muslim authorities, I argued that Islamic doctrines were verifiably true, whereas Christian doctrines were verifiably false. His responses led to research and investigation that ultimately spanned four years. What I discovered time and time again was that Christian doctrines held firm whenever they could be tested historically. The arguments against Christianity I had trusted my whole life were flawed and poor, and Christianity stood strong.

But it was what happened next that shook my world and rattled me to the core. My friend used the same critical standards I had used against Christian doctrines to challenge Islam. Under the weight of this consistent scrutiny, the foundations of Islam crumbled.

By the summer of 2005, I realized that I no longer believed the *shahada*, the Muslim proclamation that "there is no God but Allah, and Muhammad is his messenger." Proclaiming the *shahada* is the minimal requirement of a Muslim, and I simply did not believe it. I desperately wanted to believe it, because everything I loved was found in Islam:

my family, my friends, my culture, my traditions, my heritage. Leaving Islam meant sacrificing everything I knew and devastating the people I loved most.

At the same time, Christianity held no allure for me. My family were not Christians, I had just three Christian friends, my only experiences visiting churches had left a poor taste in my mouth, I thought Christmas and Easter were pagan traditions, and I really had no idea how I could fit in as a Christian. I did not want to believe in Christianity at all.

But I realized that it was too late: I already believed Christianity was true, and I could not be a Muslim because I could not honestly proclaim the *shahada*. The only question left was whether I would take the final step and move forward in faith. It is one thing to have found compelling evidence and quite another to act in faith on that evidence, especially when the cost is virtually unbearable.

On August 24, 2005, when I could resist no longer, I bent my knee to Jesus and proclaimed my faith in him. Soon after, my family was shattered, and the next year of my life was by far the most harrowing I have ever endured. I was now an outsider, both to my family and to all my friends in the Islamic community. It was just weeks before I received my first death threat. Ten years later, I still get the occasional death threat, I never regained my old friends, and my family has never been the same. I feel the painful fallout of my decision every day.

So when I hear people say that Islam and Christianity are basically the same, I have to try to restrain my incredulous response. Are Islam and Christianity the same? My parents certainly do not think so, nor do any of the dozens of friends I lost. This cliché is a slap in the face to the hundreds of thousands of converts who have left Islam for Christianity and vice versa.

Not only are these religions different, but the differences have far greater ramifications than I realized when I converted. I knew that the historical doctrines of the two religions were different, but doctrines do not exist in a vacuum. They work together to impact the way we see the world, which in turn changes who we are.

For example, the Muslim conception of God, whom we will call *Allah*, has different characteristics from the Christian conception of

God. Of course, the most obvious is that Allah is not triune, whereas the one Christian God subsists in three persons: the Father, the Son, and the Holy Spirit. The concept of God's personhood is so disparate between Islam and Christianity that the basic Christian axiom "Jesus is God" registers as blasphemy to the average Muslim. Although both religions teach that there is no God but one, merely beginning to consider God's personhood demonstrates that they disagree significantly about what he is like.

And what we think God is like has a tremendous impact on how we see the world he created. Why did God create humans: to share intimacy with them or to test them? What does he think about people: are they his servants or his children? How does he want us to live: focusing on love or focusing on law? What does he tell us about the afterlife: to anxiously anticipate unknown judgment or to have joyful faith in his grace? The Islamic view of God and the Christian view lend themselves to different answers, and how we answer these questions changes how we see ourselves, other people, and the world around us.

Both Muslims and Christians believe that there is no God but one, but is he Allah or is he Jesus? I can tell you from personal experience and in all sincerity: How we answer this question has the power to change who we are.

PART 1

SHARIA OR THE GOSPEL?

TWO DIFFERENT SOLUTIONS

CHAPTER 1

THE WAY TO LIFE

As a young college student, I was proud to be a voice for Islam in the great chorus of religious perspectives at my university. The diversity of thought was beautiful because it existed in an environment where critical thinking was encouraged. As we presented our ideas and views, others were free both to challenge our perspectives and to gain insights from them, and we were all sharpened by the critical engagement. Tolerance meant always accepting people, without always accepting their ideas.

So it was that in the midst of challenging a colleague's most dearly held beliefs that we became best friends. David Wood was on the debate and forensics team with me at Old Dominion University, and when I saw him reading a Bible, I did not hesitate to question its reliability and preservation. Due to our mutual passion for God and truth, we connected instantly, even though our views strongly clashed. We found ourselves in such constant disagreement over fundamental matters that we often signed up for classes together just so we could sit in the back of the lecture halls and argue.

But when the circle was broadened and other viewpoints were brought into the discussion, there was a surprising trend that emerged. The first time it happened was when an agnostic teammate named Marie overheard one of our arguments and joined the discussion. David and I found ourselves side by side, in agreement with one another against her views. The second time it happened was when a Buddhist friend named Zach presented his grounds for being Buddhist, and David and I both disagreed with him for the same reasons. Whenever we engaged people from other worldviews, the discussions highlighted the similarities between Islam and Christianity.

There's really no question that Islam and Christianity are close to one another on the broader religious spectrum. They are both monotheistic, the largest two faith communities in the world, and they share many similarities. Each teaches the doctrine of an eternal, all-powerful, all-knowing God who is sovereign over the universe. It is God who created mankind out of one man and one woman, yet mankind turns away from him. Each teaches that one day there will be a resurrection and final judgment. Before then, it is of paramount importance for us to seek God and follow him.

But the similarities between Islam and Christianity run even deeper, beyond the trappings of monotheism: Both lay claim to Abrahamic lineage; both teach that God has sent messengers, human and angelic, to steer people back to him; both teach that God has inspired divine scriptures to guide man; both teach that Satan is a deceiver that misleads the unwary; and both teach that believers ought to sacrificially care for each other and proclaim the truth to nonbelievers.

Perhaps the most surprising shared feature is reverence for Jesus. Both Islam and Christianity teach that Jesus was born of a virgin and that he was the most miraculous man who ever lived. Both the Bible and the Quran teach that Jesus cleansed lepers, healed the blind, and even raised the dead. Indeed, both books teach that Jesus is the Messiah, and Muslims await his return, as do Christians.

So there's no question that there is much in common between Islam and Christianity. It would be biased to ignore this, especially considering that the gamut of worldviews runs from atheist to pantheist, as David and I witnessed at our university.

THE WAY TO LIFE: A LAW OR A PERSON?

But the many similarities do not mean that the differences are not significant. Humans and chimpanzees share 95 percent of their DNA, but the remaining 5 percent is incredibly important! So it is with Islam and Christianity. There is much shared DNA, but the two are phenotypically quite different.

Where the difference matters most is in the ultimate message of each religion. According to Islam, the way to paradise is sharia, a code of laws to follow that will please Allah and earn his favor. *Sharia* is literally translated "the way." According to the Christian message, the gospel, the way to eternal life is Jesus. He said, "I am the Way, the Truth, and the Life; no one comes to the Father except through me" (John 14:6). In Islam, sharia is the way, and in Christianity, Jesus is the way.

How is it that the way to life in one religion is a law, whereas in the other faith it is a person? To understand, we have to compare sharia and the gospel.

CHAPTER 2

COMPARING SHARIA AND THE GOSPEL

THE ISLAMIC WORLDVIEW

The word *Islam* means "submission," and the plain message of Islam is exactly that: Humans should all submit to the sovereign will of God. Allah, having predestined the universe, made mankind with the express purpose of worshiping him (Quran 51.56). To guide humanity, Allah sent prophets to all people to lead them out of ignorance (Quran 4.163–165).

It is important to note here that the concept of *prophet* in Islam does not mean the same thing that it does in the Bible. Prophets in Islam have a higher status than all other people, being men chosen by God to lead mankind. The Quran uses the term to mean a divinely appointed leader, not necessarily one who prophesies.

Adam is considered the first prophet, but also mentioned in the Quran are Noah, Abraham, Ishmael, Isaac, Jacob, Job, Moses, Jonah, Aaron, Solomon, David, and of course, Jesus (e.g., Quran 4.163). Since these people all submitted to Allah, they practiced submission (i.e., Islam). Thus they are considered people who submit (i.e., Muslims). All who followed these prophets in submitting to Allah are also considered Muslims, even if they were born ages before Muhammad.

Allah revealed his guidance to each prophet as the people needed it and as they could bear it. For example, Moses' people needed to rebel against the Pharaoh, so Allah revealed "eye for an eye, tooth for a tooth." But Jesus' people needed to be peaceful, so Allah taught them to "turn the other cheek." Both Moses and Jesus, as well as other prophets, were given divine scripture. Angels dictated Allah's revelation to them, and the revelation was written down as Torah, *Injil (gospel)*, and other books (e.g., Quran 5.46).

Tragically, people did not faithfully follow the prophets that Allah sent to them. So in his mercy, Allah sent Muhammad and gave him the Quran. Thus, Allah gave mankind the final, perfected religion (Quran 5.3). Islam is therefore the culmination of Judaism, Christianity, and all other world religions, which started off in line with Islamic teaching. All people still following these religions after the arrival of Muhammad are either misled or rebellious, and no religion will be accepted from them on the day of judgment except Islam (Quran 3.81–85).

It is there, at the day of judgment, that one finds the major impetus to follow Islam. The Quran emphasizes that on that day, all people will be held accountable to Allah for their sins (Quran 6:164; 17:15; 35:18; 39:7; 53:38). This is an understanding firmly entrenched in the Muslim psyche: Though God may be merciful and absolve us of our sins, no one else can intercede. Muslims must live as good a life as they can to approach heaven, and hope for God's merciful judgment to secure their salvation.

THE ISLAMIC SOLUTION: SHARIA

However, Islam teaches that the fundamental problem of mankind is ignorance, that man needs to be guided in order to live good lives. Once people learn what to believe, *aqeeda*, and how to live, *sharia*, they will earn the pleasure of Allah.

In regards to right belief, the emphasis is on the Islamic conception of monotheism: Allah is not a Father, and Allah is not a Son (Quran 112). He is an absolute unity, a monad. The other basic components of *aqeeda* have already been mentioned above: belief in the prophets, belief in divinely inspired books, belief in angels and the unseen, belief in the day of judgment, and belief in Allah's predestining sovereignty. Together, these are called the *Six Articles of Faith*. There is much, much more to Islamic belief, but this is the core.

Right practice in Islam is learned through Islamic Law, called *sharia*, which is understood as "the way to water." Especially for a desert people, the concept is powerful: Following sharia is the way to life itself. Sharia dictates virtually every aspect of a devout Muslim's life, from what foods to eat, to proper forms of currency, to exact words to recite during prayers. Of all Islamic practices, five are paramount: proclaiming the Islamic motto, the *shahada*: "There is no God but Allah, and Muhammad is his Messenger"; praying the five daily prayers; fasting during the month of *Ramadan*; giving alms; and undertaking a pilgrimage to Mecca. Together, these are called *the Five Pillars of Islam*.

Both *aqeeda* and sharia are ultimately grounded in the life and teachings of Muhammad. He is the embodiment of Islam, and this is why Muslims are expected to follow him as the perfect exemplar. His actions and his sayings in life are recorded in a vast body of literature, collectively called *hadith* literature. So important are the hadith that, after the Quran, they form the second rung of sharia.

Given the breadth of teachings in the Quran and the incredibly wide scope of hadith literature, discerning sharia is a task for the learned. Muslim jurists study the vast traditions and legal precedents before making official judgments, called *fatawa* (plural of *fatwa*). These men are technically called *fuqaha*, but they are often included under the umbrella term for a Muslim leader, *imam*. Collectively, the consensus of these scholars is called *ijma* and is understood to be the third major component of sharia.

Finally, we are at a place to understand the message of Islam. Sharia is more than just Islamic law. It is the answer to mankind's ignorance and, if followed, will result in a life of peace with Allah and an abundance of his blessings. Sharia is derived from the Quran, exemplified in Muhammad's life, and explained by imams. On the last day, if we have obeyed and done well, Allah may grant us mercy and allow us into heaven where we will have an eternal reward.

So in sum, when it comes to salvation in Islam, sharia is literally "the way," and submission to God's will is our primary expression of worship.

THE CHRISTIAN WORLDVIEW

In the beginning of the Christian worldview is the one God, Yahweh. He exists as three persons who love each other perfectly. Thus, the one God is love in his very essence. Out of this love, God created mankind in his image, that God might love man and man might love God.

It is important to note that this concept of love is often misunderstood by Muslims due to the various ways the word *love* is used in English. The specific concept of love we are discussing is often called *agape* love. It is not the kind of love we envision in a romantic relationship; it does not imply much emotion at all. The Bible gives a beautiful description of this love in 1 Corinthians 13, but it is essentially this: a selflessness that delights in others. That is who God is, almighty yet most humble, the center of the universe yet selfless. He created mankind so he could delight in us, and we in him, with selfless love.

But in order for this love to be valuable, it must be voluntary, so God gave man the choice to love him or reject him. When man disobeys God, it is tantamount to rejecting God. In rejecting the Source of Life, we bring death upon ourselves. This bears repeating: The result of sin is death because it is a rejection of the Source of Life.

That's why, in the Christian worldview, sin against God is more than just doing something wrong. It is rebellion against the Sustainer of the universe. It is the most destructive force in the cosmos, the ultimate root of every pained heart, every broken family, every pointless war, every heinous genocide. Sin spreads through generations like a malignant cancer, and it razes civilizations like a plague. The effect of sin is cataclysmic. Like taking a sledgehammer to a mirror, sin shatters the image in which man is made. When Adam sinned, the image of God in man was irreparably broken.

This is the Christian worldview: Sin has ravaged our souls and the entire world. There is no way for us to un-sin. We cannot simply do a few good deeds to unshatter our souls. There is nothing on earth that we can do. It would take a miracle, an act of God, to restore us and save this world.

THE CHRISTIAN SOLUTION: THE GOSPEL

But in the Christian message, there is good news. In Greek, the word for good news is *euangelion*, which in English is translated "gospel." And the good news is this: Even though we cannot get to God, out of his great love, God has come to us and made a way for us. God himself has paid for our sins and will eternally restore our souls. All we have to do is repent of our rebellion, have faith in what he has done, and follow him.

To pay for our sins, God—specifically the second person of the Trinity—entered into the world. Without changing his divine nature, God took upon himself a human nature. He was born as a human, but not of the broken lineage of Adam. He was born unbroken, the way mankind was intended to be, the way we will ultimately be when we are miraculously remade. He took the name *Jesus*, which means "God saves." With respect to his human nature he grew as a human, ate food as a human, suffered alongside humans, and ultimately died as a human. In all this he never sinned, so he was able to bear our sins. He lived the life we ought to have lived so he could die the death that we deserve to die. By dying on our behalf he took upon himself the sins of the world, so that whoever believes in him and accepts what he has done will have eternal life.

From the perspective of a human watching Jesus, it might have looked like just another man dying just another death. So to prove to the world that his death was not just another death but one that brings life to the world, and to prove that he was indeed the God he claimed to be, he rose from the dead. On the one hand, this was a sign to all who were skeptical that Jesus truly has supernatural authority and deserves to be heard. On the other hand, it was a symbol for those who believe in him that death has been defeated. Jesus has conquered it for us.

Those of us who wish to accept God's sacrifice on our behalf must repent of our sins and yield ourselves to following him. As we do, God—specifically the third person of the Trinity—makes our hearts into a holy temple and lives within us. He transforms us from the inside out. In other words, as we follow Jesus we become more like him, the unbroken man, and the Holy Spirit gradually begins the miraculous work of restoring our otherwise irreparable souls. Like Jesus, we are filled with a selfless love, and we begin to live for others instead of ourselves, just as God lived for us. Those who go further along the path of being like Jesus even reflect him in their willingness to die for others, just as Jesus was willing to die for us. They become more like God: selflessly delighting in others.

Finally we are at a place to understand the message of Christianity: The fundamental problem of mankind is sin, and we are powerless to save ourselves. The good news is that God loves us and makes a way for us by paying our penalty himself upon the cross. Jesus proved that he is the Author of Life by rising from death. We who repent and follow Jesus demonstrate our faith in him and his salvation, and God begins a transforming work in us. As we follow Jesus the Holy Spirit makes us more like him and sends us into the world to love mankind with the selfless love of God. We can even lay down our lives for others, as Jesus modeled for us. Our ultimate restoration will come to miraculous fruition when we are remade, unbroken, to live with him and love him for eternity.

So when it comes to salvation in Christianity, Jesus is literally "the way," and our love for God is our primary expression of worship.

CHAPTER 3

QUESTIONING GRACE

In 2013, I was given the honor of joining Ravi Zacharias International Ministries, a global team of Christian thinkers and evangelists. One of my first engagements was in Hong Kong with a charismatic Egyptian Muslim who had originally traveled east to pursue his dream of becoming a celebrity musician, but who ultimately became disenchanted with the music industry and found his peace in Islam. Since then, he had become a *da'ee*, a Muslim dedicated to preaching Islam.

He was very warm and hospitable, and even though our debate was impassioned, it had an encouraging and constructive tone. We embraced one another at the end of the dialogue and encouraged the audience to ask us questions before leaving. Soon after, two children approached me, a girl and a boy about twelve and ten years old, apparently sent by their mother. When they asked me their question, I could not help but smile, because I remembered asking the same question of Christians when I was their age, also urged on by my parents: "If God just forgives all Christians and none of them go to hell, why would any Christian do good when they can sin all they want?"

Now that we have considered the differences between the Islamic message and the Christian message, this question should be no surprise. In Islam, the reward for following sharia is heaven, and the deterrent for disobedience is hell. Why would anyone make the hard moral decisions if they were promised the reward regardless? Since the solution to man's problem in Islam is a law, the gospel's idea of a heart transformed by God is foreign to many Muslims—as it was to these children. The disjuncture between sharia and the gospel also leads to other common questions that Muslims ask Christians.

THE DOCTRINE OF ORIGINAL SIN

Since Islam teaches that every person must bear their own sin, Muslims often question the doctrine of original sin: How does Adam have anything to do with our standing before God?

Thankfully there is a bridge of understanding between Muslims and Christians here, as Muslims do believe that Adam was cast out of the garden when he sinned. Also, it is helpful to note that there are different views of original sin in Christian thought. The view that I found most helpful when I was still a Muslim points out that, when the dust settles, Muslims and Christians do not disagree on much here.

According to this view, the Bible teaches that no man is responsible for the sin of his father (Deut. 24:16; Ezek. 18:20), which means that people are not guilty of Adam's sin itself. When we are judged, we will be judged for our sins alone, but Adam's sin is where it all started.

Remembering the Christian view of the destructiveness of sin, when Adam sinned, it was as if his soul was pulverized. Even though Adam was created in the image of God, it was the shattered, irreparably distorted image of God that Adam's progeny inherited (Gen. 5:3). Since mankind inherited the broken image from Adam, all humans are broken and prone to sin. They are not judged for his sin, but because of his sin, we, his progeny, have all been born broken. Because of his sin, we all ultimately sin.

No matter our view of original sin, though, Christians believe that everybody does sin, and their own sin is enough to bring God's judgment upon them. With this, Muslims usually agree.

THE JUSTICE OF GOD: DEATH FOR THE SMALLEST SIN YET MERCY FOR THE GREATEST SINNER?

According to the basic principles of Islam, Allah will weigh good deeds against bad deeds when he judges us. In broad strokes, Muslims believe that someone who has sinned very little has little to worry about. For this reason they often ask why God would demand justice for even the smallest sin. As the *da'ee* in Hong Kong pointedly asked me during our debate, "Would it be just for a judge to sentence you to execution for jaywalking?"

This was a fair question, and when I was a Muslim asking the same question, I found that Christians often did not give satisfactory answers. Usually, they would point me to Romans 6:23, which teaches that "the wages of sin is death." My response would always be honest: "That's another reason not to trust the Bible. It does not make sense. Why give the death penalty for even the smallest of sin?" I was not surprised when the *da'ee* made the same challenge during our debate.

Nor was I surprised when he asked the corollary question: "How can God be just if he is willing to forgive serial killers and genocidal dictators? You're telling me Hitler could have gone to heaven if he had become a Christian?" It is an emotionally charged question, but one that deserves a thorough answer.

To fully understand, we need to remember two things: the nature of sin and the nature of God.

Remember that, according to Christian teaching, sin is not just doing something wrong. It is a rebellion against God, the Source of Life. Death is not a punishment for our actions as much as it is a consequence. God does not execute us for jaywalking; we get run over by a truck while jaywalking.

Regarding the nature of God, we need to remember that he loves us absolutely. Just as a perfect father would love his child no matter what the child does, so our heavenly Father loves us no matter what we have done. As an example, a father would love his son even if he were a thief. He might even turn his son over to the authorities to face the consequences of his crime, but it would be out of love and desire for ultimate rehabilitation. In the same way, God loves his children despite their sins, though he does allow them to endure the consequences of their actions on earth so that they might repent and change their ways. In all this he always loves us, because he is our perfect Father, and he is love.

But there are at least two sides to such love, and they often manifest at apparent odds with one another: mercy and justice. A father can love his criminal child by being merciful, but a father must also love his victimized child by demanding justice. Both mercy and justice are expressions of God's absolute love. This poses a dilemma: Where does God draw the line between the two? If he demands justice, where is the mercy for the criminal? If he offers mercy, where is the justice for the victim? He cannot draw that line arbitrarily because he is God. So where does God draw the line?

Magnifying this dilemma, God is also absolute. To illustrate, it is helpful to imagine a human judge that demands justice for every crime, never forgiving any. Though not merciful at all, he would be a very just judge. Now if God did not punish all sins, he would be less just than that human judge. Can we really believe that God's sense of justice could be potentially less than that of a human? Of course not. Similarly, if we can imagine a human judge that forgives every crime, he would be a very merciful judge, though not just at all. If God did not forgive every sin, he would be less merciful than that human judge. But God is the most merciful; his mercy cannot be outdone by a human.

What is the way out of this dilemma? Where does God draw the line between mercy and justice?

Herein lies the genius and infinitude of the love of God: He does not draw the line. He offers mercy to everyone who has ever sinned while also demanding justice for every sin ever committed. He does this by offering to bear the consequence of our sins himself. The consequence of our sins is death, and God is willing to die on behalf of all his children.

HOW CAN JESUS DIE FOR THE SINS OF MANKIND?

This is perhaps one of the most commonly asked questions in Muslim-Christian dialogue, and it is important to recall the Muslim impetus for the question: Islam emphasizes that each person will be responsible for their own sins. No human can intercede for another.

But here is another example where agreement is close at hand: Christians also believe, as Muslims do, that no mere human is in the position to bear another's sins. In order to come to that realization, though, I had to remember that Christians believe Jesus is God. Muslims believe that God is able to forgive sins, and that is exactly what Christians teach through the gospel: that God is the one forgiving the sins of mankind. His death on the cross is his reified act of mercy upon our sins. Instead of just forgiving us on the day of judgment in the distant future, he has paid for our sins at a very real point in time and space: in the first century, on the cross.

Another question follows closely: "Is it just for God to transfer sins? No one is able to bear the burdens of another, because that would be unfair." Here, it is helpful to note two things. First, people voluntarily bear the burdens of others all the time, and it is completely just. For example, when young adults want to obtain a loan from a bank but do not have any credit, they have to find a cosigner, usually a mother or father, to vouch for them. If they then fail to pay the loan, the burden falls on the parent who vouched for them.

In the same way, the gospel teaches that God, a good and loving Father, has vouched for us. When we stand guilty in judgment, our debt will be imputed to God, who has paid it.

Something else that is helpful to point out, though, is that the Quran actually does not teach that no one can bear the sins of another. Looking carefully at the relevant Quranic verses, all five of them teach that "no bearer of burdens can bear the burdens of another." It is not that no person can bear the sins of another, but that anyone who is already a sinner is in no place to bear the sins of others. Since Muslims believe that Jesus did not bear any sins, theoretically Islamic theology should be compatible with Jesus bearing the burdens of others.

WHAT REASON DO CHRISTIANS HAVE TO DO GOOD?

When the young siblings in Hong Kong asked me their question, I briefly considered the ways I could answer. Sitting down next to them, I nodded toward their mother and asked them a question in return: "Do you love your mom?"

Slightly taken aback, they answered emphatically, "Of course!"

Smiling, I asked them a simple question: "When she asks you to do something, like clean your room, what do you think would make her happier: if you cleaned your room because you love her, or if you cleaned your room because you were afraid she would punish you?"

Without hesitation, the sister answered, "Because we love her." And as the words left her lips, the realization was apparent on her face: obedience under the shadow of threat is hardly obedience at all, but compulsion. Christian obedience, devoid of threat and rooted in love, is what God truly wants.

I began to explain to her and her brother that when we respond to the gospel and live as children of God, our Father changes our hearts and makes us want to obey out of love. For the next few minutes they continued asking me questions in earnest, clearly unfinished when their mother whisked them away.

CHAPTER 4

DIAGNOSIS AND DELIVERANCE

In the spring of 2009, as I was graduating from medical school, I undertook a project working as a volunteer with a humanitarian organization called Physicians for Peace. They were doing excellent work around the globe, and the project that I chose to help with was geared toward educating young mothers in the barrios of Santo Domingo.

The Rio Ozama runs through the Dominican capital city, and its low-lying banks are home to thousands of metal shanties. Every year the rains cause the Ozama to swell into the crudely constructed shacks, and for weeks the occupants flee until the floodwaters recede, only to return to disease-infested homes. At the time, newborn mortality rates were high as young mothers often could not afford quality healthcare and were forced to watch their babies die. Physicians for Peace stepped in to equip key women in these barrios, whom we called resource mothers, to educate mothers of newborns on disease prevention and hygiene. Thanks to their work, newborn morbidity and mortality rates fell dramatically.

When I came on board, I found that the young mothers were facing an insidious disease that had not been diagnosed: depression. In their cultural circles, depression bore the stigma of being an imagined disease of unstable women. For my project, I trained the resource mothers to detect major depression and postpartum depression in the young mothers they were educating. Many of the resource mothers, especially those who were suffering with depression themselves, were surprised to hear that it was a real disease. They had always been told that depression was just in their heads and that they simply needed to "cheer up"; but no matter how hard they tried, the depression was real.

Clinical depression is an all-encompassing disease and can be harrowing if not diagnosed. These women had tried everything, but they never found relief because they did not know the real problem. When I finally spoke to them about the reality of depression, many of them broke down in tears, relieved to hear that their disease was real and that there was help for them.

I share this story because I believe the spiritual realm has this in common with the physical: If we misdiagnose what ails us, the treatment will not work, and we will continue to suffer. Islam diagnoses the world with ignorance and offers the remedy of sharia, a law to follow. Christianity diagnoses the world with brokenness and offers the remedy of God himself, a relationship with him that leads to heart transformation.

What is it that truly ails mankind, and is there a cure?

From my perspective, the gospel resonates with reality: People are broken in their hearts and souls, and no matter how educated or self-reflective we become, it does not appear that following rules will be enough to address the problem. The problem of mankind is deeper than what we do; it is embedded in who we are. Having spent some time working with the dejected and downtrodden, such as those whose lives have been ravaged by various addictions, I do not think ignorance is their problem. It is brokenness. Having seen families torn apart by abuse or anger, I know the answer appears to lie not in knowledge or following rules but in transformed hearts.

This leads me to a second observation: Mankind seems incapable of saving itself. In our natural selves, we perpetuate cycles of destruction. Our hearts are broken, so we break other hearts. We were abused, so we abuse in return. Our families were fractured, so we leave fractured families in our wake. When loved ones are killed, we kill in revenge. This is the way of humanity, and we need an otherworldly solution—something radical to break these cycles. We need God to save us.

The gospel is that radical solution. It teaches us that God gives us that otherworldly grace, forgiving us no matter what our sins. His love is extravagant: "Neither death nor life, neither angels nor demons, neither the present nor the future, nor any powers, neither height nor depth, nor anything else in all creation, will be able to separate us from the love of

God" (Rom. 8:38–39 NIV). He loves us, and we are forgiven. Our souls can rest in our loving Father and his all-embracing grace.

When we realize the depravity of our sins and the depths of our rebellion against God, it exceeds the mind's capacity to grasp this grace. What could we do to deserve such forgiveness? Nothing at all! He engulfs us with his infinite love and absolute mercy, though we cannot earn it.

It is into that overwhelming flood of grace that our hearts release their poison. When we have been forgiven so much, how can we hold our fellow man accountable for so little? In his love, our hearts are made new. We no longer begrudge, no longer desire revenge. Renewed by the restoration he has brought about in us, we desire to uplift the abused and restore the broken. He transforms our hearts, and we in turn are driven to transform the world around us.

And that leads me to my final point: The gospel is all about God and what God has done. God introduces life into the world, and when we rebel, God saves us. When we sin against God, God pays for our sins. When we sin against one another, God gives the grace of restoration. This message is all about him, not at all about what we can do or have earned for ourselves.

Not only does this free us from the anxiety of having to save ourselves, but it also frees us from the pride that comes with successfully following rules and assuming that we have won our own salvation. Being so unburdened by anxiety and pride, we are free to live for others.

So the gospel accurately diagnoses the problem of humanity, which is our own brokenness. Through his otherworldly, heavenly grace, he transforms us and frees us from our cycles of destruction. Through it all, he is at the center, disentangling us from pride and anxiety, helping us focus on others and not on ourselves. The gospel is not just an answer that works; it is the only answer that will work.

PART 2

TAWHID OR THE TRINITY?

TWO DIFFERENT GODS

CHAPTER 5

THE ISLAMIC INQUISITION

Although many challenge the notion that Islam was spread by the sword, there is no question that the sword featured prominently in Islam's early history. It was with the sword that Muslim armies swept North Africa and conquered Persia in the years immediately after Muhammad's death. The caliphs, Muhammad's successors, were soon after beset with high-profile assassinations: Umar, the second caliph of Islam, was slain by avenging Persians; Uthman, the third caliph of Islam, was besieged and then slaughtered by Muslim rebels; Muhammad's cousin Ali, the fourth caliph, was also assassinated by dissidents, but not before he had marched against the army of Aisha, Muhammad's young bride. That was the first Islamic civil war, often called the First Fitna, and on that day ten thousand Muslims killed one another on the field of battle. With the spilling of their blood were sown the first seeds of Shia and Sunni discord. The sword was ever unsheathed in these earliest years of Islam.

Following the age of the Companions of Muhammad, the Umayyad Caliphate governed the Islamic empire for a short ninety years until, through revolt and open war, the Abbasid Muslims took control and established a dynasty that lasted for 750 years. The reign of the seventh Abbasid caliph is fascinating, for it was he who imposed the *Mihna*, the Islamic Inquisition.

Al-Mamun became caliph in AD 813, after a struggle for power that ended in the beheading of the previous caliph, his brother. From the start, al-Mamun's rule was tumultuous, his allies few. Although he never embraced Shiism himself, he began ingratiating himself with the Shia. In AD 827, al-Mamun officially declared that Muhammad's cousin Ali, the paragon of the Shia and their first imam, was the best of all Muhammad's Companions. Even more striking than the move toward Shia sympathies was his alignment with Shia rationalism: He declared the Quran to be a created book.

This was a colossal proclamation, and to understand its immensity we have to consider the contemporary theological controversies in Islam. In those days, debates about the Quran raged among Muslim theologians over the doctrine of *tawhid*. *Tawhid* teaches that Allah is absolutely one; and the conclusion naturally arose among some thinkers that since Allah is *absolutely* one, he cannot have attributes. Attributes would curb his absolute unity, being things he has as opposed to things he is.

This conclusion of Islamic philosophy can use a little exploration. If God has attributes, he must always have had them, because he is unchanging. That would make those attributes eternal. If those eternal attributes are not a part of his essence, part of who he is, then something other than God existed alongside God from the beginning of time. The existence of eternal entities apart from Allah's essence was an affront to Muslim theologians committed to *tawhid*, the absolute unity of God.

Where this philosophical debate mattered most was on the issue of the Quran. It was understood that the Quran is the Word of God, his attribute of speech. Is the speech of Allah eternal? If so, something apart from Allah, his speech, would be eternal. It would exist in eternity past alongside Allah. Theologians who defended *tawhid*, like the Jahmiya and the Mutazili, saw this as blasphemous in light of Allah's absolute unity. It is clear why: It would mean there are two eternal entities, Allah and the Quran.

To establish their case from scripture, the rationalists referred to verses in the Quran that seemed to situate its contents in history. If the Quran refers to events in Muhammad's life, like the Battle of Badr, how could it be Allah's eternal speech? More convincingly, they cited 43.2 of the Quran, which says, "We have made it an Arabic Quran." If the Quran was made, how could it be eternal? Thus the rationalists argued that the Quran was created, and that it taught the doctrine of its own creation. Anyone who disagreed was an enemy of *tawhid*.

That is why when al-Mamun declared the Quran to be a created book, he justified his proclamation by saying, "He who does not confess that the Quran is created has no belief in *tawhid*." Those who believe in the eternality of the Quran, argued al-Mamun, are "the worst of the Muslims" and "the tongue of the devil." He instituted their inquisition.

Over the course of fifteen years and the reigns of three caliphs, Muslim thinkers in major cities who believed in the eternality of the Quran were interrogated, flogged, and threatened with execution because of their challenge to *tawhid*. One such man, Ahmad bin Nasr al-Khuzai, was brought before Caliph al-Wathiq, who questioned him about the Quran. When it became clear that Ahmad did not subscribe to its createdness but believed in its eternality, the caliph flew into a rage and personally decapitated him. Ahmad's head was taken to Baghdad and displayed publicly as a warning to others who might be tempted to make the same mistake.

Although such executions were not common, the victims of the *Mihna* included eminent theologians such as Ahmad ibn Hanbal, a founder of a major school of Sunni thought. Ultimately, it was the tenth Abbasid caliph, al-Mutawakkil, who abolished the *Mihna*. Less passionate about his theology, he simply forbade argumentation on the nature of the Quran.

Although the Islamic inquisition thus came to an end, the arguments about the Quran did not. Ultimately, the majority of Muslims espoused a view exactly contrary to the defenders of *tawhid*. Based on the position of a man named al-Ashari, the average Muslim today believes that the Quran is eternal despite the problem this creates for *tawhid*. And how did al-Ashari counter the arguments of the rationalists? How can the Quran be eternal without challenging the absolute unity of Allah? His response is famous: *bila kayf*, or "without how." In other words, there is no rational resolution; it is just true that the Quran is eternal and this does not contradict *tawhid*. In this proclamation al-Ashari emphasized revelation and tradition over reason and rationality, and his method has remained dominant among Muslim thinkers ever since.

Over time, and entirely without logical defense, al-Ashari's position on *tawhid* became the standard view, changing the history of Islam forever. His position is so firmly entrenched that, ironically, those who take al-Mamun's position today face persecution. In 1995 a highly respected Egyptian scholar named Nasr Abu Zayd was declared an apostate by sharia courts on account of his belief that the Quran is partially created. His marriage was officially annulled, he received death threats, and he was effectively forced into exile. However, in more tolerant Muslim environments like Turkey, debates about *tawhid* and the Quran continue unabated.

The *Mihna* is now but an obscure footnote in the annals of Islamic history. Most Muslims today do not realize that in the eyes of their forerunners, their beliefs about the Quran constitute a flagrant transgression of *tawhid*. Yet the debates of old echo into the present. If a Muslim is asked how belief in an eternal Quran does not challenge *tawhid*, they must still respond the way al-Ashari did over a thousand years ago: *bila kayf*. There is no rational response.

CONFIDENCE IN *TAWHID* AND SKEPTICISM TOWARD THE TRINITY

In my experience, devout Muslims are very proud of *tawhid*, their monadic conception of God. By contrast, they often see the Trinity as an indefensible, self-contradictory, polytheistic doctrine, especially since most Christians are unequipped to articulate the Trinity or explain how it is monotheistic. It is because of this relative confidence in *tawhid* that the Trinity is one of the most common topics of Christian-Muslim dialogue.[1]

As a practicing Muslim, I simply had no idea of the contradictory forms of *tawhid*, nor of how volatile intra-Muslim relations had been on account of them. I, and most Muslims I knew, simply thought that Islam's doctrine of God was clearly defined, unanimously agreed upon, and entirely unproblematic. In other words, we uncritically believed that *tawhid* was an impervious doctrine.

But the *Mihna* illustrates that Muslims have significant disagreements over *tawhid*, and there are multiple views in Islam. We have already explored the two views of *tawhid* in the *Mihna* that were contrary enough to cause bloodshed. A third, equally divisive view is that of many Sufis, called *wahdat al-wujud*. Literally translated "unity of being," this doctrine teaches that the entire universe is God. It is so offensive to some Muslims that they denounce Sufis as *kafir*, infidels, under charges of pantheism. By contrast, Sufi Muslims often believe that their knowledge of Allah is the most intimate and refined form of Islam. These are just three of the divergent views on *tawhid* that have been widely held by devout Muslims throughout Islamic history.

The average Muslim is not aware of this. Perhaps more than any other reason, my ignorance was why I was so confident in lodging criticisms against the Trinity. I would point out that the word *Trinity* is not found in the Bible and that the doctrine took hundreds of years to iron out. How could a doctrine so central to Christian theology have had such a long and complicated history? But because I had not studied the history of *tawhid*, I did not know that the exact same criticisms applied to Islam: the word *tawhid* is not found in the Quran, and the doctrine also took hundreds of years to iron out.

When we take a closer look at these two doctrines, we find that *tawhid* is similar to the Trinity in some other surprising ways, but as with our comparison of the Islamic and Christian worldviews, the differences are crucial. By the end of this section, we will see that the doctrine of *tawhid* is ultimately self-defeating, whereas the Trinity is not only coherent but also what makes us truly human.

CHAPTER 6

COMPARING *TAWHID* AND THE TRINITY

In 2003, while still in the throes of trying to convert my friend David Wood to Islam, I began watching debates with him. Out of the dozens of debates we watched, the Muslim debater for whom I had the most respect was Shabir Ally. He spoke warmly, had strong stage presence, and seemed very conversant with both Islam and Christianity. I had the privilege of watching him debate the following year in my hometown before an audience of nearly a thousand Muslims and Christians. I considered him the best Muslim debater in the world, and truth be told, I was a bit starstruck to see him live.

Had someone told me that I myself would debate him someday, I would never have believed it!

I received an invitation to debate Dr. Ally in the spring of 2015 at Wayne State University in Michigan. After much prayer and deliberation, I decided to agree, and I deferred to Dr. Ally for the topic. When I received his reply, my heart sank: He wanted to debate the Trinity.

Even though I had been a Christian for nine years and a full-time minister for five of those years, I still felt that the doctrine of the Trinity was at best something Christians could explain and defend; it was not a compelling doctrine and certainly not something to draw people's attention toward. But I had already agreed to the debate and allowed Dr. Ally to set the topic, so I could not back out now. As it seemed to me, I had stumbled into a debate with the best Muslim apologist in the world on the most difficult topic for Christians to defend. What was I to do?

There was nothing I could do except pray and study in earnest! So, joined by good friends and colleagues, I spent many hours with my knees on the ground and many hours more with my nose in the books. It was during that time, through prayer and study, that I discovered how magnificent the Trinity is, and how compelling it is when we trace it throughout Scripture and understand its implications. Studying the doctrine of the Trinity greatly increased my love for God.

It was also during those studies that I first came across the story of the *Mihna*. When I discovered it, I was shocked. An Islamic inquisition over *tawhid*? *Tawhid* had a developmental history? The insights I gained by studying *tawhid* more carefully have since given me much more confidence in presenting the Trinity to Muslims.

My first discoveries were the similarities between *tawhid* and the Trinity. Theologically, the debates about the Trinity among Christians unfolded in surprisingly similar ways as the debates about *tawhid* among Muslims. In order to understand this, it is very important to note that the Quran and Jesus serve as analogues in their respective religions. In the case of Islam, the Quran is the eternal Word of God, and in the case of Christianity, Jesus is the eternal Word of God (John 1:1–14).

This is more than a semantic coincidence. For Muslims, the expression of Allah in the physical world is the Quran, and for Christians, the expression of Yahweh in the physical world is Jesus. That is why each religion teaches their eternality: They are expressions of an eternal God.

But both of these doctrines were hammered into shape on the anvil of intrareligious debate. As we have seen, this posed a significant problem for Islamic theology, because *tawhid* has traditionally taught that there is no division within Allah. How can the Quran, something that is in some sense separate from Allah, be an eternal expression of Allah without jeopardizing his absolute unity? *Bila kayf.*

Christian theology, on the other hand, does not have a problem with the Word of God being an eternal expression of God that is in some sense separate from God, because it does not teach the absolute unity of God. It teaches that Yahweh is three in one.

But what does it mean for God to be three in one? Let's make sure we have a good definition of the Trinity before we examine why Christians believe it.

DEFINING THE TRINITY: DOES IT CONTRADICT ITSELF?

The Trinity is just like every other monotheistic doctrine in teaching that there is only one God. If we miss this, we miss everything! Christianity has always taught that there is only one God. Where Christian theology differs from other forms of monotheism is not on the number of gods, but on the concept of God's personhood. The doctrine of the Trinity teaches that the one God exists as three persons.

It is at this point that Muslims often level a charge of self-contradiction, but it certainly is not, and here is why: *person* is not the same as *being*. Your being is the quality that makes you *what* you are, but your person is the quality that makes you *who* you are. For example, we are humans. That is *what* we are. That is why we are called human *beings*. But *what* we are is not the same as *who* we are. If someone asks, "Who are you?" I should not respond by saying, "A human!" That answers the question of what I am, not who I am. Who I am is Nabeel; that is my person. What I am is a human; that is my being. Being and person are separate.

Unlike a human being, which has only one person, God has three persons. He is one being, Yahweh, in three persons: Father, Son, and Spirit. He's more than able to exist like that because he is God. If we say God must have only one person, like humans, then we are making God in our image. Who are we to limit God? It is up to God to tell us who he is.

That is where the discussion should really be between Muslims and Christians: on revelation, not on the conceptual plane of "Trinity versus *tawhid*," as if our reason alone can dictate or even decipher the nature of God. Based on their traditional teachings, Muslims and Christians should agree that God is greater than we can possibly conceive, more complex than we could ever hope to grasp. We are in no position to determine the intricacies of God's nature. If he were to inform us that he is one being in one person, we are obligated to believe him. If he tells us, "I am one being in three persons," who are we to say no to God? As believers in revelation, we must turn to divine Scripture to learn about God.

THE TRINITY IN THE BIBLE

Scripture is the reason why Christians believe God is triune. The doctrine of the Trinity is the best interpretation of the Bible. Just as the Quran does not systematically expound upon the doctrine of *tawhid*, the Bible does not expound upon the doctrine of the Trinity in any one place. However, there are five elements found repeatedly throughout the Bible's text that are best interpreted through the lens of the Trinity:

1. There is only one God (e.g., Rom. 3:30)
2. The Father is God (e.g., John 6:27)
3. Jesus is God (e.g., John 20:28; Rom. 9:5; 2 Peter 1:1)
4. The Holy Spirit is God (e.g., Acts 5:3–5)
5. These three are distinct persons (e.g., John 14:16–17)

So if there are three distinct persons that are God, but there is only one God, we are naturally led to the doctrine of the Trinity: one God who subsists in three persons.

A verse that indicates the unity of these three distinct persons is Matthew 28:19, which says, "Go and make disciples of all nations, baptizing them in *the name* of the Father and of the Son and of the Holy Spirit" (NIV). All three persons in this verse share one name, because they are one being.[1]

Now you may have noticed that the above verses are found in the New Testament. A common question that Muslims ask is, "If God is a Trinity, why do we have to wait until the New Testament to see it? Why did God not even give a hint of the Trinity before?" My answer often surprises them: He did, starting with the very first verse of the Bible.

Genesis 1:1 reads: "In the beginning God created the heavens and the earth" (NIV). If we look more closely at the word we translate "God," *Elohim*, we see it is plural. If we were to translate it literally, we would translate it "Gods." But the reason we do not translate it that way is because the verb in the sentence is singular. The word *Elohim* is plural, but the verse treats it as a singular noun. So, in the very first verse of the Bible, we see that God is in some sense plural, but in some sense singular. This fits the model of the Trinity perfectly: God is in one sense plural in terms of his persons, but in another sense singular in terms of his being. A monadic interpretation of God makes less sense of the verse.

Of course, if it were just this one instance, there would not be much of a case, but we find three indications of God's plurality in Genesis 1. The second is found in verse 26, where God says, "Let us make man in our image" (NIV). He refers to himself in the plural. Why would God call himself "us"? Some people respond that it is a plural of majesty; a king might refer to himself as "we," and indeed, Allah does this throughout the Quran. Such an explanation is anachronistic, though. Biblical Hebrew does not use the plural of majesty, and it is probable that such a literary device had not been invented yet. To say that the Bible is using a plural of majesty is to apply later manners of speaking and writing to the Bible, which is poor methodology. God is not referring to himself here with a "royal we." God is pointing out that, in some sense, he is plural.

Another indication of his plurality is found in verse 27, which reads: "And God created mankind in his own image, in the image of God he created *him*; *male and female* he created *them*." After emphasizing that God created mankind in his image, the Bible then says he created them male and female. That's not to say God has genders, but it is to say that there is plurality in his image. This is reflected in Scripture's use of *him* to refer to mankind, and then its switch to *them*. Mankind is in one sense singular, one humanity, but in another sense plural, composed of men and women. That is the image of God: both singular and plural.

So when we read the chapter carefully, we see that there are three indications in the very first chapter of the Bible that God is plural and singular. The Trinity is in the Bible from the very first verse, even multiple times in the very first chapter.

Before moving on, it is worth mentioning that the Trinity is implicit throughout the Old Testament. In Genesis 18, we find Yahweh coming as a man to speak with Abraham, informing him that he will destroy Sodom and Gomorrah. Then, in verse 19:24, the Bible says, "Yahweh rained down burning sulfur on Sodom and Gomorrah—from Yahweh out of the heavens." Yahweh appears to be both on earth and in the heavens, the person on the earth raining down sulfur from the person in heaven.

Lest it appear that this is not what Genesis is saying, Amos 4:11 confirms this interpretation: "'I overthrew some among you as God overthrew Sodom and Gomorrah . . .' declares Yahweh." Here, Yahweh refers to God in the third person. This makes little sense within a monotheistic framework unless we read the Old Testament through the lens of the Trinity.

Finally, an example of a passage in the Old Testament that features the deity of all three persons of the Trinity can be found in Isaiah 48:12–16. The clarity of the statement can be lost because of the many statements emphasizing the sovereignty of the speaker, but if we remove the intervening statements, the passage reads: "'I am he; I am the first and the last. Indeed, my own hand established the earth . . .' and now the Lord God and his Spirit have sent me." Here, the Alpha and the Omega says he was sent by the Lord God along with his Spirit. The next verse calls the speaker "Yahweh," "Redeemer," and "the Holy One of Israel." In this passage, Yahweh is sent by Yahweh and the Spirit of Yahweh, and this makes little sense unless read through the lens of the Trinity.

THE TRINITY AND *TAWHID* IN THE QURAN

Just as the Bible is the reason Christians believe in the Trinity, the Quran is the reason Muslims deny it. The clearest rejection of the Trinity in the Quran is 4.171. After denying the deity of Jesus, it says: "Do not say 'three.' (It would be) better for you (if you) stop. Only Allah is God. One."

But when we study the Quran more carefully, it appears the Quran is not actually denying the Trinity but rather polytheism, that Jesus is a second deity alongside God. For example, after denying that Jesus is God, 5.73 says, "Certainly they are infidels who say, 'truly, God is the third (of) three.' There is no god but one God." If the Quran envisions the Trinity as three gods, with Allah as one and Jesus as the second, who is the third? Apparently it is Mary, as is most clear in 5.116, where Allah says to Jesus: "Did you say to the people, 'Take me and my mother as two gods in addition to Allah'?"

So the trinity that the Quran denies is actually tritheism, three gods: Allah, Jesus, and Mary. At this point, some Christians argue the Quran gets the Trinity wrong, and this disproves the Quran. Muslims often argue in response that there very well may have been Christians that worshiped Mary, Jesus, and God as a trinity, and that the verses of the Quran are directed toward them. I choose to avoid this discussion, emphasizing instead that the Quran effectively denies polytheism, three gods, not the concept of a triune God as Christianity has traditionally taught.[2]

Throughout the rest of the Quran, Allah regularly says that there is only one God (e.g., 16.51; 47.19; 112.1), but always as a rejection of polytheism. *The Quran never rejects the possibility of one God subsisting in three persons.* The omission is noteworthy, as this had been the orthodox doctrine of Christianity for centuries before Muhammad and the advent of the Quran.

THE NINETY-NINE NAMES AND TRANSCENDENCE OF ALLAH

In addition to denying polytheism, the Quran expounds upon the transcendence of Allah, that he intentionally keeps himself removed from mankind. He remains behind a veil, as it were, speaking to humans only through angels. Verse 42.51 says, "It is not for any human being that Allah should speak to him except by revelation, or from behind a partition, or that He sends a messenger to reveal, by His permission, what He wills. Indeed, He is Most High and Wise."

This verse is instructive for two reasons. In the last sentence, "He is Most High and Wise," we find an example of the epithets the Quran uses to describe Allah, also called the ninety-nine names. The Quran tells Muslims to call upon Allah by any of his names (17.110), and Muslims often urge one another to learn these names to gain deeper knowledge of Allah's character.

Also instructive is the implication of Allah's transcendence: It is not for man to know him intimately. This is also reflected in his ninety-nine names, as there are no names that indicate Allah desires intimacy with man. The two possible exceptions are *al-Wali* and *al-Wadud*.

Some understand *al-Wali* to mean "the Friend," but really it means "the Patron," and it emphasizes the protection of Allah, not a relationship with him. The other word, *al-Wadud*, is more promising, as it does mean "the Loving" and is used twice in the Quran. But when we look more closely at the word, it seems an expressive idea is in view rather than a relational idea, as in "the Affectionate." This might seem like splitting hairs, but it is an important distinction. Only one of Allah's ninety-nine names could imply he wants intimacy with man, and looking carefully at this word yields nothing that necessitates a relationship.

Of course, it would help if we had more context for the term, but we find only two instances of the word in the Quran; and since they are epithets, surrounding words do not clarify the meaning. Considering the broader context is illuminating, however: In 11.90, *al-Wadud* is used to describe Allah just one verse after a warning, "Let not your dissension from me cause you to be struck," and in 85.14, it is only two verses after the warning, "Indeed, the vengeance of your Lord is severe." Neither occurrence inspires confidence that Allah wants an intimate relationship with humans.

Truly, nothing else in the Quran appears to indicate that Allah wants a relationship with humans. This is especially true of a father-child relationship, as the Quran specifically denies that Allah is a father (112.3), and in 5.18 it rebukes the idea of God's spiritual fatherhood: "The Jews and the Christians say, 'We are the children of Allah and His beloved.' Say (in response), 'Then why does He punish you for your sins?' Rather, you are human beings from among those He has created."

This verse is telling. When Jews and Christians suggest that they are children of God, the Quran says to castigate them and inform them that they are nothing but his creatures, as are all humans. We must also note that this verse actually does use the primary and best word for "love" in Arabic, *habb*, but it uses it to explicitly deny that people are God's beloved.

This may come as a shock to Muslims who grew up as I did, being taught that Allah loves us. It is a common teaching among Muslims, but it is not the teaching of the Quran. A verse that is often used to suggest that Allah is close to us is 50.16, which says that Allah is nearer to people than their jugular veins. What I was not taught, and what most Muslims I know are not taught, is that this verse is in the context of an extended threat: Allah is so close to you that he knows your subversive thoughts very well, and he throws doubters into hell.[3]

So indeed, as part of our understanding of *tawhid*, we need to include a balanced understanding of Allah's self-revelation. Allah intends man to pursue the relationship of a servant to his master, but not the relationship of a child with his father. Nothing in the Quran suggests that Allah desires intimacy with humanity. We are not his beloved—just one of his creatures.

REMOVED VERSUS RELATIONAL

There is an intrinsic reason why Allah does not desire a relationship with humans, whereas Yahweh does. On account of *tawhid*, Allah is a monad; he is not inherently relational. Yahweh, on the other hand, is three persons; he is inherently relational. The implications are far-reaching. When Muslims say, *"Allahu-Akbar,"* they mean "God is great," and Christians would agree with that.[4] Both Muslims and Christians believe that God is the greatest being in the universe. But if Allah is the greatest, and in his nature he is removed and does not desire a relationship, then Islam exalts the qualities of being removed and nonrelational.

On the other hand, if Yahweh is the greatest being, and intrinsic to his nature are intimacy and love, then Christianity exalts relationships and community. Remember from chapter 2 that the one God exists as three persons who selflessly love one another; love is therefore the central principle of God (1 John 4:8). It is out of that selfless love that he created this universe, and he expects it to function through love in reflection of him. That is exactly why the Bible teaches what it does: "'You shall love the Lord your God with all your heart and with all your soul and with all your mind.' This is the great and first commandment. And a second is like it: 'You shall love your neighbor as yourself'" (Matt. 22:37–38). Since God is the greatest being, relational and loving, relationships and love are the most important commandments for mankind.

According to Christian teachings, God is our Father. He loves us as a perfect Father, and he will always love us so. He wants us to have an intimate relationship with him, turning to him with our fears and failures, with our dreams and victories. He wants us to rejoice with him and in him. This is all because God is triune, and in his very nature he is love. This is all very different from the traditional doctrines about Allah in Islam.

CHAPTER 7

QUESTIONING COMPLEXITY

In the 1920s, a scientific discovery revolutionized the world forever. Until that time, physics had been considered one of the most unchanging, well-understood fields of scientific knowledge. Isaac Newton's principles had been proven sound again and again and again, for hundreds of years. Some nineteenth-century physicists, such as Pierre-Simon Laplace, even began to boast that science was now equipped to explain all movements in the entire universe, both past and future. Man, it seemed, had conquered physics.

But near the turn of the twentieth century, scientists started noticing cracks in their understanding of the world. In particular, the behavior of light did not always fit into Newton's box. Through the work of intellectual giants like Max Planck, Albert Einstein, Niels Bohr, and Erwin Schrödinger, physicists began to discover the hidden secrets of light. Combining the insights gained through the 1920s, Paul Dirac published his *Principles of Quantum Mechanics*, and the world would never be the same.

One of Dirac's students, John Polkinghorne, shares how Dirac explained the discovery to his students at Cambridge. "He took a piece of chalk and broke it in two. Placing one fragment on one side of his lectern and the other on the other side, Dirac said that classically there is a state where the piece of chalk is 'here' and one where the piece of chalk is 'there,' and these are the only two possibilities. Replace the chalk, however, by an electron and in the quantum world there are not only states of 'here' and 'there' but also a whole host of other states that are mixtures of these possibilities—a bit of 'here' and a bit of 'there' added together."[1]

In other words, something can be in two places at once in ways that are contradictory to reason. According to Polkinghorne, "Quantum theory permits the mixing together of states that classically would be mutually exclusive of each other. It is this counterintuitive possibility of addition that marks off the quantum world from the everyday world of classical physics."[2] This realization, a counterintuitive and apparently self-contradictory truth, is opening the door to twenty-first-century advances in technology that mankind could only have dreamed of before: technologies like MRIs, smartphones, and Blu-Ray players all owe their existence to quantum physics, and fields like quantum computing and quantum optics keep the future full of promise.

As a Muslim, I had been taught from childhood that the doctrine of the Trinity was not possible because it was too complex and even self-contradictory. But the more mankind probes the universe, the more we discover its dazzling complexity. As my eyes opened to the deeper truths of the world, I accepted that complexity does not somehow invalidate the Trinity. Why must we assume the Creator is any simpler, any easier to understand, than his creation?

I might suggest that the opposite must be true: By definition, we cannot comprehend God. If God created our minds, then he must be greater than their comprehension. Who are we to demand that he be simple enough for us to understand him?

But as we have seen, the Trinity is not contradictory. There is no contradiction in asserting that the one God exists in three persons. The common challenge from Muslims that the Trinity is unrealistically contradictory and complex is not a valid problem. Quite the opposite, as we have already learned through the story of the *Mihna*, the Islamic formulation of divine simplicity causes problems in explaining the eternality of the Quran. As we will learn now, the simplicity of *tawhid* has another flaw.

TAWHID, THE TRINITY, AND THE SELF-SUFFICIENCY OF GOD

Let us consider again the basic teaching of *tawhid*: God is absolutely one. This means that, in eternity past, before he had created anything,

Allah was alone. One person, all by himself. It was not until he chose to create the universe that Allah had anything to relate with. This is a significant theological problem because, through the ninety-nine names and otherwise, Islam teaches that Allah is a relational being. But if he had nothing to relate with before creating the universe, how could he be a relational being?

It is important to note that here I am using the word *relational* not in the sense of intimacy but in the sense of existing in relation to something else. For example, Islam teaches that Allah is *ar-Rahman* and *ar-Raheem*, the Gracious and the Merciful. Every devout Muslim knows this, because these are two of the most commonly invoked names of Allah. But these qualities imply that Allah is relational, that he is gracious *to someone* and that he is merciful *to someone*. He might have the potential to be gracious all by himself, but he cannot actually be gracious until there is something else to be gracious toward. The same is the case with mercy; something else needs to exist and receive his mercy for Allah to be intrinsically merciful.

So in order for Allah to actually be gracious and merciful, he has to first create the universe. In other words, Allah is dependent upon his creation in order to be Allah. He cannot be *ar-Rahman* or *ar-Raheem* until he creates the world to be gracious or merciful toward. *Allah's qualities are contingent upon creation.* Therefore it is irrational to say, as does traditional Islamic teaching, that Allah is intrinsically gracious or merciful or any other relational attribute, whether found in the ninety-nine names or not. If Allah is a monad, he needs his creation to be relational.

On the other hand, the doctrine of the Trinity teaches that the three persons of God have eternally loved one another with a selfless love. God has always been relational, always been loving. His mercy and justice are not contingent upon his creation, because they are the expression of his eternal love toward humans. That love was never contingent upon mankind's existence.

Because of tawhid, Allah depends on mankind in order to be Allah. Because of his triune nature, Yahweh is truly independent and self-sufficient.

So the simplicity of *tawhid* proves to be a fatal flaw for orthodox

Islam on two accounts: its inability to explain the eternal Quran, and the consequence that it makes Allah dependent upon his creation. Far from being self-contradictory, the complexity of the Trinity is what makes him logically consistent and self-sufficient.

A more apropos question that Muslims ask regards Scripture. Jews and Muslims agree that God is a monad, not three persons. Doesn't the Jewish understanding of monotheism come from the Bible, and doesn't it deny a Trinity?

THE *SHEMA*: "THE LORD OUR GOD IS ONE"

The most important Scripture for considering Jewish monotheism is the *shema*. It is the Jewish analogue of the *shahada*, and it is found in Deuteronomy 6:4. It reads, "Hear, O Israel: The LORD Our God, the LORD is one" (NIV). But we must be careful to understand the Hebrew and its nuances. In the first place, the verse can be translated: "Hear, O Israel: The LORD is our God, the LORD alone," as the New Revised Standard Version of the Bible translates it. But even if we translate it as "the LORD is one," what kind of "one" does the Hebrew refer to? An absolute unity, like *tawhid* teaches, or a composite unity, like male and female making up one mankind, as we saw in Genesis 1?

The word for "one" used in the *shema* is *echad*, and this is often the word the Old Testament uses to refers to a composite unity. To illustrate, let's revisit Genesis 1. Verse 5 says that evening and morning make one day. In other words, one day is a composite of evening and morning. Since the Scripture is referring to something that is one but made up of multiple components, it uses the word *echad*. In Numbers 13:23, a cluster of grapes is referred to as *echad*, since the one cluster is composed of many grapes. In Ezekiel 37:17, Ezekiel is told to hold two sticks together as if they were one; again, in Hebrew the word *echad* describes this compound unity. As a final example, referring back to the image of male and female, the Bible says that, through marriage, man and woman become one. The word the Bible uses to express two-in-one? Of course, *echad*. So when the *shema* says, "The Lord is *echad*," the Bible specifically uses that word, which allows it to mean a composite unity.[3]

Putting this together with our Scripture references from earlier in the chapter, the Bible tells us that there is only one God, Yahweh. The New Testament is clear that three separate persons are each God, but they are not each other. So we must conclude that the one God subsists in three persons. The Old Testament, starting from the first page, frankly suggests that God is multiple in persons, and the *shema* uses verbiage we would expect if Yahweh wanted us to know that he is one God in three persons.

JEWS AND THE TRINITY

When I mention these findings to Muslims, they often ask me why Jews do not interpret the Scriptures to say that the one God might have multiple persons or expressions. They are surprised when I respond that some did! One example is the Zohar, the famous and highly revered foundational text of Jewish mystical thought. While considering the wording of the *shema*, it says: "These three are one . . . So it is with the mystery of the threefold Divine manifestations designated by 'the Lord, our God, the Lord'—three modes which yet form one unity."[4]

But the belief that Yahweh was multiple in person or expressions goes beyond the mystical rabbis to the time of Jesus himself. Alan Segal, a Jewish scholar, argues that some first-century Jews held a "binitarian" notion of God.[5] Daniel Boyarin, himself an orthodox Jew and a scholar, argues that rabbis declared such notions to be heretical only in response to Christian theology, not before.[6] In other words, according to some notable Jewish scholars, views like the Trinity were present among Jews when Jesus was teaching in Israel. Only after Jews and Christians parted ways did rabbis declare such notions heretical, as a reaction to Christian theology.

CHAPTER 8

DO MUSLIMS AND CHRISTIANS WORSHIP THE SAME GOD?

In April 2015 I had an opportunity to encourage Christian students to reach out to their Muslim neighbors. It was a chapel service at a Christian college in upstate New York, and at the center of the mostly Caucasian audience was an Iraqi woman clearly distinguishable by her *hijab*, the headscarf that Muslim women commonly wear.

I have learned the hard way that, whenever I address an audience, I should try my best to present my message without offending people more than I have to. If people are going to find the gospel offensive, I would rather it not be on account of my presentation. So for the allotted hour, I was trying to read her reaction to my arguments and testimony, but she showed no reaction whatsoever. She simply listened. At least she was not obviously offended—so far so good!

At the very end of my presentation, a woman in the audience asked me a controversial question: "Do Muslims and Christians worship the same God?" My answer to this question had offended Muslims in the past, and I was worried it would do so again. But another thing I have learned the hard way is, when asked a question, I should try to answer it directly. So I offered a quick prayer in my heart and began.

I started by stating the obvious: Christians worship Yahweh, the Trinity, whereas Muslims worship Allah, a monad. This is not an incidental difference; Islam makes every effort to condemn the Trinity as blasphemy (4.171). The Quran rejects the relational aspects of God, saying that he is not a father (5.18) and he is not a son (112.3). It establishes its own doctrine of God, *tawhid*, in diametric opposition to the Trinity, and that doctrine becomes the central doctrine of Islamic theology.

Most people who say Christians and Muslims worship the same God are aware of this difference, but they treat it as relatively inconsequential. This is not a trivial difference, though; it has major implications. *Since mankind is made in the image of the triune God, love is woven into our very nature.* The Trinity gives us the most consistent, most powerful basis for being self-sacrificial and altruistic.

This is an important point to unpack. Of course, many people are very altruistic, regardless of their worldviews. A person does not need to believe in God to genuinely care for others, as secular humanists demonstrate. There are even people who do not believe in any kind of morality yet still desire to care for people. Ultimately, though, such ungrounded altruism is a sentiment, something a person just wants to do. Unless one believes in a transcendent basis for altruism, one's desire to care for people is unanchored and ephemeral, little more than a whim. According to this amoral worldview, nothing behooves a person to be kind. Even though someone might wish to be altruistic, in the next moment it would be entirely consistent with their worldview if they chose to be selfish.

Others believe in a morality that is essentially derived from evolutionary theory. People ought to take care of one another because the enterprise of life is to survive, and we ought to be mindful of other members of our species. Although this is a somewhat more grounded basis for altruism, it is ultimately still a weak foundation: Why should I, a thinking individual, subscribe to the enterprise of life? What if I do not want humanity to survive? Furthermore, is it really altruistic of me to care for others if my main purpose in doing so is to care for my own species, and by extension, to care for myself?

So atheistic altruism, though it may be sincere and practicable, is ultimately either sentimental or utilitarian and selfish. To root altruism more firmly, one needs to consider theistic models. In the case of Islam, Allah commands Muslims to take care of orphans, widows, paupers, wayfarers, and others. A Muslim can obey out of selfish purposes, such as a desire to avoid hell or obtain heaven, or he can obey out of a selfless desire to please God. So theism, as in the case of Islam, offers a more deeply grounded form of altruism.

But the Christian model of theism goes further still. Much further. Remember that the eternal love of God is intrinsic to who he is; each person of the Trinity loves the others selflessly. It was out of this selfless love that God created mankind. In other words, we were made in the image of a selfless, loving God, so in our very nature we are designed to be selfless and loving. When we are self-centered instead of selfless, we act against our very nature.

From the Christian perspective, people ought to be selflessly loving toward others not just because it is a good idea, not just because it helps our species survive, not just because it earns us a reward, and not just because it pleases God. People ought to be selflessly loving because it is who we are. Humans are made in the image of a selfless God; loving others is what makes us truly human.

No other worldview so deeply embeds into mankind the obligation to love and care for one another. As a foundation for altruism, nothing outstrips the Trinity.

So I answered the woman's question by emphasizing that Christians worship a triune God, and that this makes a great difference in how we see ourselves and the world around us. Shortly after my answer, the Iraqi woman approached me. With a thick Arabic accent, she thanked me for my talk, and with a thick American accent, I thanked her in return for listening so patiently. I asked what brought her to the Christian college, assuming it had been a Christian friend. Her answer gave me more than I bargained for.

She responded that, just five weeks prior, she had seen Jesus in a dream. He told her to go to a specific church in her town to learn the truth about him. At the church, a woman befriended her and shared the gospel with her. Without hesitation, she renounced her Islamic faith and accepted the good news of Jesus. Since that day, she had learned all she could about God, and when her friend found out I was speaking at the Christian college, she brought her along. It was her friend who had asked the question about whether we worship the same God!

So it turned out that the Muslim woman in the audience was not

Muslim after all, but a new Christian sister. Out of curiosity, I asked her friend why she still wore a hijab, to which her friend responded they were so busy discussing Jesus that they had not yet had the opportunity to talk about it! I was very glad to hear that answer. There is nothing inherently wrong with a headscarf, and focusing on it would be a waste of time in comparison with learning the truth about Jesus.

The question of whether Muslims and Christians worship the same God is complex, and there is much more that could be said.[1] Ultimately, when we understand the Trinity, we realize that the doctrine is not just a theological curiosity. It has far-reaching implications for how we ought to live and how we see the world, and it makes the Christian God categorically different from the Muslim God. It is what makes God relational, what makes his love eternal. It is how God can be in us through the Holy Spirit, while being over us as the Father, and suffering for us in the Son.

And it is the Son that most distinguishes the Christian God from the Muslim God. We need to learn about him not only in light of the Trinity but also in light of his life on earth. Now that we understand the doctrine of the Trinity, that the one God subsists as three persons, we will better understand what Christians mean when they say that the second of the three persons entered into this world as a human named Jesus.

PART 3

MUHAMMAD OR JESUS?

TWO DIFFERENT FOUNDERS

CHAPTER 9

THE COUNCIL OF NICAEA

The church held no political or military power in its first three hundred years, subsisting on faith and perseverance in the face of persecution. Christian martyrdom did not mean dying with sword in hand, but laying down one's life instead of one's faith. The words of Jesus were still fresh in their memory—"All who draw the sword will die by the sword" (Matt. 26:52 NIV)—and the young church fought no battles whatsoever.

Ironically, Roman efforts to kill were the midwife of the church. It was the Roman prefect of Judea, Pontius Pilate, who unwittingly aided in laying the foundation of Christian faith by ordering Jesus' crucifixion. A few years later, Nero heinously accused Christians of a crime he himself committed. The Roman historian Tacitus reports that Nero "falsely charged with guilt, and punished with the most fearful tortures, the persons commonly called Christians."[1] It was during this time of persecution by the emperor that Peter and Paul were executed. But by killing Jesus and the fathers of the church, the Roman empire galvanized the Christian spirit: Many welcomed martyrdom, that they might be given the honor of following their Lord and his apostles in suffering for the sake of God. Tertullian testified to this indomitable spirit with his famous words: "We multiply whenever we are mown down by you; the blood of Christians is seed."[2]

Christians faced these imperial or local persecutions episodically for almost three hundred years, and the night grew darkest just before the dawn. In February of AD 303, Emperor Diocletian ordered the destruction of a church and its Holy Scriptures, issuing edicts that the same be done to churches throughout the Roman Empire. The historian

Eusebius, an eyewitness to these events, tells us in his *Ecclesiastical Histories*, "Royal edicts were published everywhere, commanding that the churches should be razed to the ground, the scriptures destroyed by fire . . ." He goes on to say that the persecutions intensified in the coming days: "The first decrees were followed by others commanding that . . . those who refused (to offer sacrifices to Roman gods) should be tormented with countless tortures. Who could count at that time, again, the multitude of martyrs?" It was during this, the greatest and most sustained persecution of Christians by the Roman Empire, that a young man named Constantine rose to imperial office.

In October of AD 312, Constantine was preparing to fight an army twice the size of his. While leading his soldiers on a march on the eve of battle, Constantine, according to Eusebius, was dazzled by a vision: a radiant cross above the sun, with words written in the sky, "By this, conquer." The vision mystified Constantine, but that very night, Jesus appeared to him in a dream and told him to use the sign as a safeguard in all his engagements. So Constantine ordered his men to mark their shields with the Christian symbol. One can only imagine the soldiers' reluctance to bear the signs of a persecuted minority on their shields, but they complied. The next day, the soldiers won a decisive victory, and Constantine marched into Rome as its victorious Emperor.

After his supernatural encounter, Constantine immediately worked to reverse the persecutions of Diocletian. By issuing the Edict of Milan in AD 313, he granted freedom of worship for all religions, Christianity as well as other persecuted minorities. This was a watershed moment in the history of the church: Not only were Christians allowed to worship without risking their lives, but also they were allowed their Scriptures and the ability to openly assemble. Finally, for the first time since the crucifixion of Jesus, all Christian leaders could openly gather to discuss their Scriptures and doctrines under the patronage of the empire, without retribution.

THE COUNCIL OF NICAEA AND THE ARIAN CONTROVERSY

The first and greatest concern of the bishops, a concern shared by Constantine, was the growing division within the church on account of a man named Arius and the teachings he espoused. To deliberate over Arius's position, Constantine invited eighteen hundred bishops from throughout the Roman Empire, modern-day Spain to Syria, to convene at Nicaea in AD 325. Even though he offered to provide their transportation and lodging, only 318 had the ability to come. Some, such as the Bishop of Rome, were too advanced in age to attend, while others were physically incapable of making the journey due to disability from the persecutions or otherwise. Those who could come were described as "an assembly of martyrs" by church historian Theodoret. He describes Paul of Neo-Caesarea, a bishop from modern-day Turkey, as an example of one who "had suffered much from the cruelty of Licinius. He had been deprived of the use of both hands by the application of a red hot iron, by which the nerves that give motion to the muscles had been contracted and destroyed." Other bishops at the council, such as Paphnutius of Egypt, had their eyes gouged or their limbs dismembered. Yet they braved the long journey to Nicaea for the sake of attending the discussions.

These men had lived through the greatest persecution of Christians the church had seen, suffering torture and dismemberment rather than compromising their faith. These were the men now summoned to discuss the controversial teaching of Arius: "that the Son had a beginning, but that God was without beginning . . . He is neither part of God, nor of any subjacent matter."

The council gave Arius the floor, allowing him to share and defend his position. To clarify, Arius emphasized that he did believe Jesus was divine. As he had said in a letter to the Bishop of Nicomedia, Arius believed that the Son, "does not derive his subsistence from any matter; but that by his own will and counsel he has subsisted before time, and before ages, as perfect god, only begotten and unchangeable, and that before he was begotten, or created, or purposed, or established, he was not. For he was not unbegotten."

So Arius believed that Jesus was indeed a god, but not God. The

Father had "begotten, or created, or purposed, or established" Jesus before time and the creation of the universe; God had created a second god. When what Arius believed became clear, the council recognized his teachings as polytheism, and since the church had always taught monotheism, they deemed Arius a heretic. With 316 of the bishops in agreement, the council promulgated the Nicene Creed, the first ecumenical resolution of the church in history.

NICAEA IN POPULAR MEMORY

Seventeen hundred years later, the Council of Nicaea maintains a prominent place in popular memory, but the details are often misunderstood, as demonstrated by an encounter I had with a young Muslim in June 2010. David Wood and I attended an Arab festival in Dearborn, Michigan, because we heard that the event attracted more than two hundred thousand Arabs, and we figured it would be an excellent opportunity to talk to people about Jesus. So, donning a shirt that read "Jesus Always Loves You," I walked through the festival with David and waited for people to approach us with questions.

We had a stimulating day with many enlightening discussions. While on our way out, a group of teenagers stopped us and indicated they had questions. Being a youth pastor at the time, I was always encouraged by connecting with teenagers interested in matters of faith, but this was particularly heartwarming because they had an air about them that reminded me of my childhood: confident zeal for Islam and utter skepticism of Christianity. I was not surprised at all when one of the first questions they asked involved Nicaea. A teenager asserted that Nicaea was "the first time they decided Jesus was God."

I was actually impressed with him for correctly identifying the subject matter of the council. At the mosques I had attended as a youth, it was often repeated that Christians decided to take books out of the Bible at the Council of Nicaea and put other books in. I had challenged David with this assertion many years prior, but when we studied the council together, we discovered that it was entirely baseless. The books of the Bible were not even discussed at Nicaea. Since then I have noticed that, for whatever reason, people choose to situate all kinds of imagined church conspiracies at this council. So it was encouraging that the teenager got the subject matter right, but he got the context of the pronouncement completely wrong. This was not when the church finally decided that Jesus was God.

On the other hand, when the church was finally able to gather for an ecumenical council after three hundred years of intermittent persecutions, their very first concern was to put the cornerstone of their faith beyond dispute: "Who is Jesus?" All 318 bishops present agreed that Jesus was divine. No one suggested that Jesus was just a human. And when both sides had heard all the arguments, over 99 percent were in agreement that Jesus is no lower than God himself. Not just human, not just a prophet, not just a god, but God: "very God of very God."

There is a reason for the unanimous view: the belief that Jesus is "in very nature God" was one of the very first beliefs of the church. The gospel has always been purely about God and what he has done for mankind: He created them, he loved them, he lived among them, he saved them, he guides them, and his kingdom is at hand. One cannot understand the gospel without understanding this. The doctrine of Jesus' deity makes a tremendous difference in how the Christian faith works and what it means to follow Jesus.

In the same way as Jesus' deity is fundamental for Christian theology, Muhammad's prophethood is fundamental to Islamic theology. There is a reason Muslims have to affirm Muhammad's status as a prophet every time they recite the *shahada*. If Muhammad is not a prophet, orthodox Islam disintegrates.

When people gloss over Christianity and Islam as if they were the same, they overlook this fundamental fact: Jesus has a very different place in Christianity than Muhammad has in Islam. Deity is distinct from prophethood.

Apart from being exemplars for their followers, in virtually no way are Jesus' and Muhammad's positions parallel unless we conflate Islamic and Christian teachings. Let's carefully consider the Christian view of Jesus and compare it to the Muslim view of Muhammad so we can understand exactly how they are different and why it matters.

CHAPTER 10

COMPARING THE MESSENGER AND THE MESSIAH

I t has been a decade since I left Islam, and I have had some candid conversations with extended family members in that time. Amid the many abstract theological issues, I try to keep an eye out for the more visceral questions, as they tend to provide insight into where someone really stands. One such question that I am commonly asked is, "We respect Jesus, so why can't Christians respect Muhammad?"

In a sense, that is a fair question. Muslims rarely, if ever, say anything negative about Jesus, and I have heard Christians say very negative things about Muhammad. While I do agree that Christians ought to tread carefully when covering sensitive topics, this question is a classic example of inappropriately conflating the Muslim and Christian perspectives. From my experience, what Muslims generally "respect" is the Islamic understanding of Jesus, not the Christian understanding.

As an example, a family member who is particularly close to me once lamented that Muslims respect Jesus even though Christians do not respect Muhammad, yet in the very next breath he said that Jesus was "a weak and impotent God" if he died on a cross. When I objected that this was disrespectful to Jesus, he simply did not see it. It took a few moments to show him that, from my perspective, this was extremely offensive. He had a hard time understanding the offense, though, because he was so immersed in his own perspective.

What he needed in order to understand the Christian perspective was an account of who Jesus is from the very beginning.

A GOD WHO COMES INTO THE WORLD

As we saw in the previous chapter, the Quran explicitly says that Allah remains behind a veil, so Muslims conceive of God as a being who does not enter this world. Christians do not believe this, though, because their Scriptures teach exactly the opposite: The Bible repeatedly shows God coming among his people.

Starting with the third chapter of Genesis, the very beginning of the Bible, we find God walking in the garden where Adam and Eve were (Gen. 3:8). In Genesis 18, God appears to Abraham as a man and talks with him. In Exodus 34:5–6, God stood with Moses and walked in front of him. In Exodus 24:9–11, Aaron, Moses, and seventy-two elders all saw God at the same time and even dined with him. In an even more tangible experience, Jacob wrestled with God in Genesis 32:24–28. In Exodus 13:21, when the Hebrews needed guidance in the desert, God personally led them as a pillar of smoke by day and a pillar of fire by night. In another, rather important account, God commanded the Hebrews to make him a tabernacle, a place where he would descend and "dwell among them" (Ex. 25:8–9 NIV). After they built it, God filled the tabernacle with his glory (Ex. 40:34). These many appearances of God on earth are often called theophanies.

Another theophany in the Torah, Exodus 3:4, actually has parallels in the Quran. In this passage, God calls to Moses from a burning bush. The bush was burning on account of the very presence of God, which is why God says, "Take off your sandals, for the place where you are standing is holy ground" (v. 5 NIV). There was nothing about the ground itself that was holy, but the presence of God made it holy. God's presence in the bush is reflected in the Quran, 27.7–14. When Moses approaches the bush, a voice calls out from it, "Blessed is He *who is in the fire.*" The Quran also envisions Allah as physically present in the fire. That the ground was holy is reflected in 20.12, where God says, "Remove your shoes, you are in the holy valley of Tuwa." As in the Bible, there is nothing inherently holy about the valley; it makes most sense if it has been sanctified by the presence of God.

Regardless of how a Muslim might interpret the Quran, though,

Christians have traditionally interpreted the passages from the Torah as theophanies. Yahweh is a loving God who desires intimacy with his people, so he comes among them.

GOD PROMISED TO COME AS A CHILD

During the days of Isaiah the prophet, God informed his people that he was about to do something special: He would be born into this world as a child. In Isaiah 9:6, the Bible says, "For to us a child is born, to us a son is given, and the government will be on his shoulders. And he will be called Wonderful Counselor, Mighty God, Father of Eternity, Prince of Peace." Christians from the very beginning have understood this verse as being fulfilled in Jesus: God, having come to this earth repeatedly before, is announcing his coming incarnation. The Mighty God will be born as a child. This comes just a few chapters after Isaiah 7:14, which says, "The virgin will conceive and give birth to a son, and will call him Immanuel." Putting this together, Christians believe that hundreds of years before Jesus, the Hebrews were told that God would be born among them.

THE WORD BECAME FLESH AND TABERNACLED AMONG US

When God finally did come to live among his people, a new era began. The Scriptures for this era are called the New Testament. According to early church tradition, John, one of Jesus' three closest disciples, wrote an account of Jesus' life in the New Testament called the gospel of John. He begins his account by reminding readers of who Jesus was before his life on earth. John 1:1–3 are immensely important verses for understanding the Christian view of Jesus.

As we learned in the previous chapter, Christians believe the one God exists as three persons, and the second person is the Word. Just as the Quran is separate from Allah in one sense yet an expression of his divine knowledge and speech in another, so Christians believe that the Word is separate from God in one sense and a part of him in another. This is exactly the teaching of John 1:1: "In the beginning was the Word, and the Word was with God, and the Word was God "(NIV). The Word was *with* God (that is, separate from him in one sense); yet the Word *was* God (an expression of him in another sense).

The next verse teaches the corollary doctrine, that the Word is eternal. Again, just as Muslim theologians classically have taught that the Quran is the uncreated knowledge and speech of Allah, so the Bible teaches that the Word is eternal alongside the Father. "He was with God in the beginning" (John 1:2 NIV). From the very beginning, before time itself, the Word was present with God. It had to be, because it was an expression of God, who is eternal.

Also, just as Muslim scholars have traditionally taught that the Quran is best understood as Allah's knowledge or speech, so the term for "Word" in Greek is *Logos*, and it embodies two concepts: reason and speech. These two meanings are captured in the English derivatives *logic* and *dialogue*. When God created the universe, he used his divine reason and his speech. These are the ideas embodied in the notion that God the Father created the universe through the *Logos*, found in John 1:3: "Through him all things were made; without him nothing was made that has been made" (NIV). So the universe was made through the *Logos*, the Word—divine reason and speech.

Finally, departing from any parallel in Islamic theology, we find John 1:14: "The *Logos* became flesh and made his dwelling among us." The *Logos*, the Word who is God, became a human and lived with us. According to John the disciple, that is Jesus Christ. Jesus is eternal, and it was through him that the universe was created.

What is fascinating about John 1 is that it is full of theology from the Torah, emphasizing that this is not a new belief but a continuation of what God had done at the time of Moses and the prophets of old. One example is the wording John chooses in verse 14. When he says the Word "made his dwelling" among us, he literally says the Word *tabernacled* among us, reminding his Jewish readers of the theophany in Exodus 40:34 and what God had done in the time of Moses. His glory was once again coming to dwell among man as he did in the tabernacle, but this time by being born as a human.

This is the Christian view of Jesus: The God who created the universe, who walked with Adam, who talked with Abraham, who wrestled with Jacob, who stood with Moses, who dined with Aaron, and who led the Hebrews—that mighty God fulfilled his prophecy that he would be born as a human child to us. Jesus is "God with us," the second person of the Trinity, the eternal Word through whom the universe was created.

HE REALLY IS HUMAN

Before moving on, it is important to emphasize that Christians really do believe that God became a human. He was born as a baby, he ate food, he grew in wisdom and in stature, he wept, he suffered, and he died. He did not just appear like a human; he became one. But by the word *became*, Christians do not envision a change to God's nature. God never changed during any of the theophanies in the Torah, and he was not changing during his incarnation. Christians traditionally teach that God, rather than changing, was taking a human nature in addition to his divine nature. This doctrine is called the hypostatic union. When the Bible says that Jesus "grew in wisdom and in stature" or that Jesus died by crucifixion, Christians believe it is speaking with respect to his human nature, not his divine nature.

Christians have traditionally taught that everything Jesus did on this earth, he did as a human. He taught as a human teacher, he received prophecies as a human prophet, and his miracles were performed as a human empowered by divine authority. This is why he tells his disciple Philip that people can do the works Jesus had been doing, and even greater (John 14:12).

But though Jesus was a human, he was not of the lineage of Adam, who, we should recall from chapter 1, passed on his broken image to his progeny. Jesus, being born into the world by the Holy Spirit (Luke 1:35), was a human as humans were meant to be: unbroken. Since Jesus never sinned as a man, and since he also had a divine nature, he could forgive the sins of mankind by taking the penalty of sin himself. This is one reason why Christian theology would not work if Jesus were not God.

Also, since Jesus was never broken by sin, he lived a perfect life as an example of how all the rest of us ought to live it. Not an example in the sense of someone who made all the right choices, but an example in the sense of the perfect prototype, the one that all humans were made to be like.

PROPHETS IN ISLAM: MEN TO FOLLOW

Functioning as an exemplar is perhaps the only parallel between Jesus in Christianity and Muhammad in Islam, but even in this similarity, the mechanics are different. For Muslims, Muhammad is the perfect example not because he is the unbroken image in which we have been made, but because he is the most perfect instance of man, the greatest one who ever lived. Indeed, for some Muslims, Muhammad's greatness is legendary.

When I was ten years old, my mother enrolled me in a Sunday school course run by our local mosque in Norfolk, Virginia. The mosque itself was a Sunni mosque, but the teachers and students came from many branches of Islam. I had two teachers there, a Sunni teacher of general Islamic knowledge and a Shia teacher of Quranic recitation. For all practical purposes we believed the same things, which is why my mother could enroll me there; but there are certainly differences between the traditions, and at times I heard things there I had not heard before.

One day, my general Islamic knowledge teacher spoke on the nature of Muhammad. He emphasized that "Muhammad had many roles: prophet, merchant, general, husband, father, son, and more. In every role, he performed to perfection." So far so good. That was what I had always been taught. But then he said something new: "Muhammad never showed any emotional weakness. Had he cried and his tears fallen to the ground, the land would have become infertile!"

Although my parents highly exalted Muhammad, this was a step or two further than they had ever gone. Not all Muslims believe in this kind of superhuman status of Muhammad, but traditionally Muslims do see him as the greatest man who ever lived, and this account illustrates how lofty a position some Muslims ascribe to the Prophet of Islam.

Prophethood in Islam is more than just a role. It is a status. Prophets are understood to be greater than the average person, assigned by Allah to lead a people. For Muhammad to be considered the Chief of the Prophets is truly quite a claim. It was on the basis of this prophetic status that Muhammad established his authority and promulgated Islam. Since Allah had made him a prophet, the religion he taught was true and ought to be followed.

On the basis of their special status with Allah, Muslims popularly hold two beliefs about prophets: that all prophets are sinless, and that Allah would hear the cries of prophets in persecution and save them from death. However, the Quran seems to teach that prophets did sin (e.g., 28.15–16; 38.24–25; 47.19), and that they often were killed (e.g., 2.61; 3.183; 5.70). Accordingly, Muslim scholars tend not to agree with these common views, though they are not unanimous. Regardless, most Muslims do believe that Muhammad in particular was sinless, especially because Allah commands Muslims to follow him (33.21).

THE PROPHET AND SHARIA

Muhammad's status as the perfect exemplar is one reason Muslims have undertaken immense efforts to record his life. Within a few centuries of his death, over five hundred thousand accounts from the life of Muhammad were in broad circulation. As we learned in the first chapter, these accounts are called the hadith, and they record details of Muhammad's life ranging from anecdotes of his childhood to decisions he made as a general and statesman.

As my Sunday school teacher taught, Muhammad had a series of roles and performed them perfectly. So when Muslims want an example of the perfect husband, or the perfect statesman, or the perfect general, or the perfect merchant, they turn to Muhammad's life for exemplary guidance. The hadith record what Muhammad said and did in thousands of situations, and what he told the Muslim people to do in turn.

This is why, unlike the teachings of Jesus that focus on principles and heart transformation, the guidance in Islam comes in the form of particulars. Sharia reaches the Muslim people in the form of thousands of decisions made by jurists and scholars who are familiar with the traditions of Muhammad's life. It all comes back to the exemplary life of the prophet.

So the primary basis for accepting Islam is that Muhammad is a prophet of God, and the guidance that he brings, *sharia*, is interpreted largely from the records of his life as an exemplary leader. For these reasons, Muhammad's prophethood is foundational for Islam.

MISUNDERSTANDING THE CHRISTIAN JESUS AND THE MUSLIM MUHAMMAD

Some early orientalists, seeing so much emphasis on the person of Muhammad in Islam, labeled Muslims "Mohammedans." When I was a Muslim, this title riled me because it seemed to imply that we worshiped Muhammad. I now realize that it was simply a matter of careless projection: The focus of the Christian faith is entirely upon the one we worship, so it is appropriate to call followers of Christ "Christians." In Islam, although there is a tremendous amount of attention given to Muhammad, he is not the one Muslims worship, so it is galling to many Muslims to be called Mohammedans.

The same kind of misunderstanding occurs regularly in Muslim-Christian dialogue, when Muslims assume Christians worship a man. Since I became a Christian, many Muslims have charged me of willfully worshiping creation rather than the Creator, but that is because they carelessly project Islamic views upon Christians: that Jesus is just a man, and that God does not come into this world.

If Muslims and Christians could understand one another on these points, dialogue would be far more fruitful. Let's now take a look at common questions that can be clarified by what we have learned so far.

CHAPTER 11

QUESTIONING THE GOD-MAN

In the summer of 2012, I spent eight weeks in Oakland, California, studying Arabic through Middlebury College. I had just graduated from Duke University, where I had focused on the Gospels and the Quran for my master's degree. Even though my mother had taught me in my childhood how to recite Arabic, I could not use the language to communicate, so I knew that greater familiarity with Arabic would go a long way in my future graduate studies. I entered Middlebury just beyond the introductory level, which meant I would be prohibited from communicating in any language other than Arabic for the entire eight weeks. The program was so serious about this rule that we had to sign a contract the day we arrived. No English whatsoever, at any point, for two whole months. Not even during the evenings and weekends!

Until that time, I had not realized just how important language is for relieving stress. No jokes, no storytelling, very little fellowship—just a lot of hand gestures and listening to upperclassmen jabber away. It was a very trying time, but it forced us to quickly learn how to get by. Within a month, we were able to communicate with one another in what I am sure was horribly poor Arabic.

Thankfully, I had a friend near Oakland who was also a student of Arabic, and she regularly reached out to immigrants in the area. She asked me if I would be willing to meet a Muslim friend of hers from Saudi, and I gladly agreed. Anything to spend time with a friend and get away from the campus! That afternoon, I met a lively young student named Sahar. She told me about life as a woman in Saudi, including that the government required her to get her younger brother's permission so that she could study in America. When I asked what would have happened if he had refused, she replied, "He knows better than to say no to me!"

Soon the conversation turned to religious matters. Sahar indicated that she was resolutely Muslim and was not considering conversion, but she had questions about what Christians believed. After asking many questions, she at last asked me one that seemed to have been the most problematic for her. "How can you believe Jesus is God if he was born through the birth canal of a woman and that he had to use the bathroom? Aren't these things below God?"

This question is a very common one, but we should now be able to see why Muslims ask it: Allah does not enter into this world in Islam, whereas Yahweh has repeatedly done so. Allah remains behind a veil and sends messengers, whereas Yahweh is intimate and walks among us.

When we remember that Yahweh is different from Allah, and that Jesus is the second person of the Trinity, the answers to many similar questions become readily apparent.

HOW CAN GOD DIE, AND WHO WAS RULING THE UNIVERSE WHEN JESUS DIED?

These two questions were the first ones I asked David about Jesus' deity when I was a Muslim, and they are the most common ones that Muslims ask me now. Since Islam does not have a concept of divine incarnation, these are understandable questions. Truly, they are questions that Christians should ask themselves at some point, but they are not difficult to answer when we keep in mind what we have learned in this chapter.

When someone asks me, "How can God die?" I ask for clarification, because the question can be asked from multiple angles. Almost always the questioner says something along the lines of, "God is immortal, so he cannot die." To that, I respond with a question in turn. "I see what you mean, but let me ask you a question: When humans die, do our souls stop existing?" Of course, Muslims respond, "No, our souls do not die," to which I respond, "So even when we die as humans, it is the body that dies. It is not that we stop existing altogether. So it was with Jesus: He was killed with respect to his earthly body, but God did not stop existing."

Sometimes, though, by asking, "How can God die?" Muslims are essentially asking, "Who was ruling the universe?" There are many possible responses to this question, but the one I prefer is the simple one: the Father. This is why, if Muslims wish to engage in these kinds of questions, it is essential that Christians adequately explain the Trinity to them. The Father is not the Son, and the Father did not die on the cross.

IT IS UNJUST FOR GOD TO PUNISH JESUS FOR THE SINS OF MAN

This leads to another kind of question, one which even well-informed Muslims will ask. During the closing statements of my 2015 debate, Dr. Shabir Ally used the most caustic terms I have ever heard to challenge the gospel. He said that if the Father sent the Son to die for the sins of the world, then this was "cosmic child abuse." What kind of a Father is God if he punishes his son for the sins of others?

By this point, we should be able to readily see the problem with this assessment: Christians do not believe that God is punishing a random victim. Jesus is God. The Judge is himself voluntarily paying on behalf of the criminal. Against Dr. Ally's caricature, a more apropos illustration is shared by Brennan Manning in his book *Ragamuffin Gospel*.[1] In 1935, Fiorello LaGuardia, the mayor of New York, presided over a court case in which an old woman had been caught stealing bread to feed her grandchildren. Although LaGuardia wanted to offer her mercy, the shopkeeper demanded justice. LaGuardia judged her guilty and imposed a fine of ten dollars, but in the same moment he took ten dollars from his own wallet and paid the fine on her behalf. Acknowledging the woman's guilt, the judge himself paid the penalty and let her go free.

This is a beautiful illustration of mercy and justice, but if we tweak one minor detail it will accord better with the gospel: if LaGuardia had not just been the judge but also the shopkeeper from whom the woman stole. When we sin, we sin against God. He has to judge us guilty, but then he pays for what we have done. It all makes sense when we remember the Christian view of Jesus: He is God.

NO ONE HAS SEEN GOD

Many Muslims have asked me how Jesus could be God if the Bible says "no one has ever seen God" (1 John 4:12 NIV). It makes sense that Muslims would ask this question, interpreting John's epistle in light of *tawhid*, a monadic view of God. But John the disciple, the man through whom God authored this Bible verse, is also the author of the Gospel of John, and he interprets it for us in John 1:18: "No one has ever seen God; the only begotten God, who is at the Father's side, has made him known." In other words, when the Bible says "no one has ever seen God," it is referring to God the Father. Jesus, who is God and at the Father's side, has made him known. That is why Jesus is able to say to his disciple Philip, "Anyone who has seen me has seen the Father" (John 14:9 NIV). Seeing Jesus is seeing God, tantamount to seeing the Father.

So although no one has seen God the Father, people have seen God the Son. This means that every time someone in the Bible saw God, they were seeing the second person of the Trinity, Jesus. When we remember that Jesus is the second person of the triune God, this otherwise problematic verse is easy to understand.

THE MAJESTY OF A KING

Sahar's question to me that summer afternoon in Oakland intuitively captured a sentiment that I think many Christians can learn from: God is King of the universe, unimaginably holy, and it is far beneath his majesty for him to be born on this filthy earth. So I affirmed her question, but then asked her one in turn. "Sahar, let's imagine that you are on your way to a very important ceremony and are dressed in your finest clothes. You are about to arrive just on time, but then you see your daughter drowning in a pool of mud. What would you do? Let her drown and arrive looking dignified, or rescue her but arrive at the ceremony covered in mud?"

Her response was very matter of fact, "Of course, I would jump in the mud and save her."

Nuancing the question more, I asked her, "Let's say there were others with you. Would you send someone else to save her, or would you save her yourself?"

Considering this, Sahar responded, "If she is my daughter, how could I send anyone else? They would not care for her like I do. I would go myself, definitely."

I paused for a short moment before continuing, "If you, being a human, love your daughter so much that you are willing to lay aside your dignity to save her, how much more can we expect God, if he is our perfectly loving Father, to lay aside his majesty to save us?" She considered this for a moment, and the conversation moved on. As the dinner ended, my friend returned me to my immersion Arabic program, where the idea of drowning was perhaps a bit too real for me.

During my last week in Oakland, as the program was coming to a fruitful and merciful end, I received another text message from my friend inviting me out to dinner, this time to meet a new Christian from a Muslim background. When I arrived, I was met by a beaming Sahar! The message of God's selfless love had overpowered her, and she could no longer remain Muslim. A few days after our dinner, she had accepted Jesus as her Lord and Savior. Now it was time to rejoice with her, share stories about our amazing God, and point the way forward for her discipleship.

CHAPTER 12

LIBYA'S BEST FRIEND

In early December 2013, David Wood and I happened to be in Texas when the state was hit with a massive ice storm. The scene was surreal. Normally warm and sunny vistas were bleak and barren, and cars were sliding off the road as streets were covered in thick sheets of ice. The sky was an opaque gray, and confusion permeated the air as airports were cancelling flights and people were scrambling to find ways out of the state.

We had just left an In-N-Out Burger, where we had met with a young Pakistani woman who had recently left Islam and was seeking advice on reconciling with members of her family. Her struggles struck some raw nerves with me, and my spirit was burdened as we drove through the gloom and returned to our hotel. But upon entering the hotel lobby, I saw the headlines on a TV and my heart sank even lower: A young American teacher had just been gunned down in Libya.

It was a local news station reporting that Ronnie Smith, a Texan, had been out for a morning jog when gunmen in a black jeep targeted and killed him. The news reported that Ronnie had graduated from the University of Texas with a master's degree and was teaching chemistry in Benghazi. At this, my ears pricked up. Benghazi was a highly unstable, war-torn city where militias held more power than the government. Why would anyone go there to teach? I had a hunch, but I wanted to investigate and find out more.

Once I went online, my suspicions were confirmed. Ronnie Smith was a Christian who wanted to serve the Libyan people. He was a deacon at his church in Austin, and he took his faith seriously: Because Jesus was willing to die for those who sinned against him, Ronnie believed that following Jesus meant being willing to risk even his life to serve those who may even be his enemies. The gift that God had given him was to teach chemistry, so he decided to serve the Libyans as a teacher.

Fully aware of the danger, he and his wife moved their family to Libya in the immediate aftermath of its revolution, while the country was still in disarray. They decided to stay even after the notorious attack on the American consulate by a group called "Servants of Sharia," where the US ambassador, Christopher Stevens, and three others were killed. The Smiths stayed because they considered the lives of their neighbors and students more important than their safety.

One of those students, Yomna Zentani, told reporters how Ronnie impacted her and other students. "After everything that happened in Libya, we were losing hope and he was the only one who was supporting us, motivating us, telling us that as long as we studied everything would be okay. He was the silver lining. He dedicated so much of his time for all his students. He chose to come here and help us, and to risk his life."

RONNIE'S MOTIVATION

Even as I write this, tears are overwhelming me. I think of great men like Ronnie Smith and have to ask myself, How did Ronnie become like this? How did this man become so loving and self-sacrificial that he was willing to move even his family into danger to serve those who could never give him anything in return? Thankfully, I do not have to wonder. It turns out that Ronnie, in his response to a survey a few years before his death, recommended a sermon by John Piper titled, "Doing Missions When Dying Is Gain." About the sermon, Ronnie said, "Through sermons like these, God called me and my family to unreached peoples."

In that sermon, Piper impresses upon his congregation that Jesus "dies and he suffers for people all over the world in every nation." His followers are called to do the same if they wish to truly follow him. "The love offering of Christ is to be presented in person through missionaries to the peoples for whom he died . . . a presentation to the nations of the sufferings of his cross through the sufferings of his people." Christians ought to be ready to suffer alongside Jesus because their Lord suffered on the cross, and he intends for the entire world to be impacted by Christians following his model.

Quoting Hebrews 13:13 (NIV), "Let us, then, go to him outside the camp, bearing the disgrace he bore," Piper spends over half his sermon explaining that Christians who are called to follow Jesus have to be ready to suffer for the sake of the world. He shares stories of martyr after martyr who followed Jesus in reaching the world with his love. While studying the sermon, one example took my breath away in light of Ronnie's death: Piper spoke of Raymond Lull, a Christian who traveled to North Africa knowing he could be martyred for proclaiming the gospel to Muslims. As soon as Lull started preaching in Algeria, he was stoned to death. To this, Piper said, "What a way to go!"

This is the teaching that motivated Ronnie Smith and made him into the great man who served Libyans unto death: Jesus intends for us to follow him by reaching the world with his love, even if it kills us. When we consider the message of the gospel, all the pieces fall in place. God did not just tell us to love sacrificially; he is our Lord and exemplar, and so he first did it for us.

The Creator of the universe, God, surrounded by angels and worshiped in unimaginable glory, was willing to lower himself into this world and suffer for people so they could be saved and know his love. If he is the example for Christians, then Christians must be willing to leave any comfort and go anywhere so that people can know God's love and be saved.

God was willing to suffer for people who sinned against him, people who used the hands he gave them to crucify him. Not only did he tell his followers, "Love your enemies and pray for those who persecute you" (Matt. 5:44 NIV), he exemplified it. If he is the example for Christians, then Christians must be willing to self-sacrificially serve even their enemies, knowing full well that they may be killed for it.

The reason why Christians can follow Jesus boldly into death is because we are not worried about trying to save ourselves. The gospel is that God has already promised us salvation through his infinite mercy and grace. This is the synergy of Christian teaching: Christians can follow Jesus and die for their enemies because the gospel promises and enacts salvation, taking away all fear of death. This frees us to love everyone, friend and foe, enabling us to live according to the image in which we were made, the image of a God who is love in his very essence.

Combining these insights with what we learned in the previous two parts of the book, the gospel calls us to live and love without holding back, according to the image of the triune God in which we have been made, enabling us to follow Jesus, our Lord and perfect example, even in the face of death.

THE LOVE OF CHRIST: A MEGAPHONE TO THE WORLD

Ronnie Smith knew all this well, and when he left this world, he left it an example of a true Christian. What was most saddening as I read his story, though, was that few media outlets gave any clue as to Ronnie's motivation for being in Libya. Here was a vessel of Christian love, and few were highlighting the source. But days later, the spotlight was wrenched onto the lavish love of Christ.

One week after his murder, Ronnie's wife Anita wrote an open letter to the men who killed him. Its message was so transcendent, so other-worldly, that it stunned the world. She did not mince words.

To his attackers: I love you and I forgive you.

How could I not? For Jesus taught us to "Love our enemies"— not to kill them or seek revenge. Jesus sacrificed his life out of love for the very people who killed him, as well as for us today. His death and resurrection opened the door for us to walk on the straight path to God in peace and forgiveness. Because of what Jesus did, Ronnie is with Jesus in paradise now. Jesus came not only to take us to paradise when we die but also to bring peace and healing on this earth. Ronnie loved you because God loves you. Ronnie loved you because God loved *him*—not because Ronnie was so great, but because God is so great.[1]

Anita forgave the men who killed her husband. She forgave them because Jesus forgave us. She loves them because Jesus loves them.

Read that again: She said she loves them! She loves the men who ruthlessly took her best friend, who killed her husband of ten years, who left her infant son fatherless! How can she love those men? Shouldn't she want to exact retribution? Shouldn't she want to hunt them down and take from them what they took from her? This is a forgiveness and a love that makes no sense, that is unlike anything in this world. But as evidenced by the media's response, it is a love that captivates the world.

Jesus and Muhammad led very different lives and were exemplars for their people in very different ways. The message of Islam is that Muhammad is the best man who ever lived on earth, but I think this world needs an example that is beyond this earth. It needs a heavenly solution, something that makes no sense from a natural perspective and yet leaves all who witness it with a deep sense of awe that this is the answer.

Ronnie's death was the voice of a martyr testifying to the love of Christ, and Anita's letter was his megaphone. This love can change the world.

PART 4

THE QURAN OR THE BIBLE?

TWO DIFFERENT SCRIPTURES

CHAPTER 13

THE BURNING OF SCRIPTURE

In 2011, on the first day of April, twenty thousand demonstrators gathered before the gates of a United Nations compound in Mazar-e-Sharif, a city long believed to be one of Afghanistan's safest. Hastily scrawled signs carried by the throng bore clichéd reproaches: "Down with America" and "Death to Obama." They were accorded little time to prepare novel slogans, as it was earlier that very day when worshipers had gathered at the local mosques for Friday prayers, that three imams sparked and stoked a flame among the crowds with one singular intent: Bring Americans to justice.

The people responded en masse, choosing the UN compound to demonstrate their unrest. Very quickly the demonstration became a protest, and the protest became a mob. Afghan National Police did not control the crowd, refusing assistance from a NATO-led security force. The task of defending the compound fell to the UN guards. As the crowds swelled and their confidence in numbers grew, some of the more zealous protesters began rioting and stoning the UN building. The guards proved powerless, and the situation rapidly devolved: Rioters overran the guard towers, toppling them to the ground. Wresting guns from the guards, they first began to beat the guards, then started shooting them. After killing four, they set fire to the compound and began hunting foreigners. The riot did not disperse until Westerners lay beheaded.

Among the slain were two Scandinavians: the first female pilot in Norwegian military history and a Swedish human rights scholar who had arrived in Afghanistan scarcely a month earlier. Additional casualties included the four guards, all of whom were Nepalese Gurkhas; a Romanian specialist in political affairs; and five Afghan rioters.

The loss of twelve lives is tragic, especially when we consider that the UN is a humanitarian organization and that those who join it often do so for the sake of aiding in foreign crises. But what takes this event beyond tragedy is just how nonsensical the violence was. The mob demanded justice from Americans, but instead they slaughtered innocent Europeans and Asians. What happened? Why did they attack the UN?

The year before, an obscure political activist and pastor from Florida announced his plans to burn the Quran "for its crimes against humanity" on the ninth anniversary of September 11. He became an international pariah overnight. Many in the media and government urged him to reconsider, as burning the Quran could lead to American casualties abroad. Under pressure from the White House, the activist asserted that, though he was not convinced, he was considering their words and planned to dialogue with key imams. September 11 thus came and went, and he did not burn the Quran. The media spotlight left him, the situation dissipated, and all went silent.

But off camera, the dialogues failed. Six months later, when virtually no one was watching, he moved forward with his plans. He held a mock trial, condemned the Quran on charges of violence and oppression, and executed judgment by burning it. The video would have remained in obscurity, like dozens of other Quran burning videos before it, except that media outlets broadcasted the video globally. Government officials, in turn, widely publicized their condemnations. As one news source reports, it was through Hamid Karzai's denouncement of the burning that most Afghans learned about it. In response to the news from the Afghan president, the firebrand mullahs of Mazar-e-Sharif incited rampage and slaughter.

The series of events is so tragic that it is easy to overlook the absurdity of it all. In response to the activist's claim that Islam causes oppression and violence, Afghan imams demanded he be silenced and precipitated the slaughter of innocents. The media, reveling in their denouncement of the activist's life-risking behavior, put the limelight on him, thereby themselves catalyzing the murderous reaction from the East. The rioters of Mazar-e-Sharif, unable to discern between Westerners, took the lives of innocent Europeans. They stereotypically proclaimed death to

Obama, the American president who has been most vocal in his support of Islam, having said, "I consider it part of my responsibility as President of the United States to fight against negative stereotypes of Islam wherever they appear." Of course, even having to comment on the relation of Gurkhas to this debacle leaves us shaking our heads.

But let us now take note of the principal matter: Throughout the series of events, no one doubted that burning the Quran would lead to riot and murder. This was such a firm fact that no one even suggested otherwise. Not the activist, not the media, not the government, and not even Muslim leaders. Everyone knew that the offense of burning the Quran would lead to violence.

We ought to contrast this to a similar event, close in both time and proximity. In 2009, at Bagram Airfield in Afghanistan, the US government announced that it burned dozens of Bibles. A military official provided the illuminating reason: The Bibles were trash, and the military burns its trash.

This bears repeating. The US government officially announced that the Bibles were trash, and accordingly they were burned. I do not repeat this to evoke sentiment, but to provide contrast: In this instance, there was not the remotest concern that any Christians would go into a murderous rampage because the government burned Bibles.

To further clarify the matter, let's consider how the Bible burning came to light. The Christian soldier from whom the Bibles were confiscated did not publicly complain, nor did the church that sent them stir an outcry, even though the military ought to have simply sent the Bibles back to the church instead of burning them.

The announcement from the military was yet another attempt to appease Afghan Muslims. A news outlet had recently aired a video that showed soldiers at a Christian chapel service, and military officials feared that this would cause local Muslims to think that the military was there to evangelize. To quell their anger, imagined though that anger might have been, the military announced that they had been burning Bibles. They emphasized that they were so committed to not offending Muslims that they chose to burn Bibles rather than return them, on the off chance that the church would try to send them again.

Let us take note again of the principal matter: Throughout all the reports and government decisions, no one believed that burning the Bibles would lead to riot or murder. This was such a firm fact that no one suggested otherwise. Not the soldier, not the media, not the government, and not even church leaders. Everyone knew that the offense of burning the Bible would not lead to violence.

THE DIFFERENCES BETWEEN THE QURAN AND THE BIBLE

Why? Why is it so obvious that burning a Quran in Florida will endanger lives halfway around the world, even if perpetrated by an obscure activist? Why is it so obvious that burning dozens of Bibles and calling them "trash" will not provoke any reaction of the sort, even if perpetrated by a government?

I am not arguing that Afghan Muslims are uneducated and temperamental, easily provoked to mindless rage; nor am I suggesting that Christians are either too indifferent or too docile to be passionate about their Holy Scripture. These are both caricatures that miss valuable insight.

I believe the answer lies, at least partly, in the fact that the Quran has a different place in the hearts and minds of Muslims than the Bible does in the hearts and minds of Christians. Both scriptures are considered holy to their people, certainly, but their uses are different, their histories are different, and indeed, their very natures are understood differently.

CHAPTER 14

COMPARING THE QURAN AND THE BIBLE

When the Quran burning controversy was at full bore, my ministry partner and I decided to publish our official position on the matter: We certainly endorsed free speech, but we resolved that burning the Quran was a poor idea. Apart from being unnecessarily inflammatory, we felt it would be a more productive use of free speech to discuss the teachings of the Quran rather than to burn its pages.

But I had an additional reason for not endorsing the action: The place the Quran holds in the heart of Muslims is beyond the estimation of most Westerners, and so is the offense of burning it. There is nothing flammable on earth that Christians revere as much as Muslims revere the Quran. That is not to say that Christians do not highly revere the Bible, because they certainly do. But the traditional Muslim reverence for the Quran is almost inestimable. To understand this, we have to remember a point from the previous two chapters: The Quran is, to Muslims, the eternal Word of Allah himself. It is the closest thing to God incarnate. To Christians, the eternal Word of Yahweh is Jesus. The Quran holds in Islam the place that Jesus holds in the Christian faith. So let's put it together: To comprehend the insult of burning a Quran, a Christian would have to imagine someone burning Jesus.[1]

Truly, burning a Bible is offensive, but not that offensive. Christians simply do not see the Bible as an eternal expression of the triune God. Christians believe that God inspired men to write exactly what he wanted them to write at specific times in history. Thus Christians believe that the Bible is inspired by God but not eternal. Once we begin to understand this fundamental difference, we will begin to understand much more.

Since Muslims believe the Quran is an eternal expression of Allah, they do not think that the Quran was written by men in any sense. It is the very speech of Allah, inscribed on a heavenly tablet, from which it was read by Gabriel and dictated to Muhammad. It is not inspired in the Christian sense of inspiration, but rather it is revealed: Allah revealed it piecemeal to Muhammad, dictating it through the angel Gabriel. Muhammad had nothing to do with shaping the text; he only relayed it.

This is why, as a young American Muslim child who spoke Urdu with his Pakistani parents at home and English with his friends at school, I was taught that Arabic was literally the language of heaven and the best of all languages. So adamant was my mother about teaching me to recite Arabic that I had recited the entire Quran in Arabic by the age of five, before I had learned to read English or Urdu. My mother was serious about the traditional Islamic insight: If the eternal speech of Allah was written in Arabic, then Arabic had to be Allah's preferred language.

This reverence for Arabic underlies many Muslim practices. It is why Muslims recite prayers in Arabic, even if they have yet to learn the meaning of the words they recite; it is why Muslims are hesitant to call non-Arabic versions of the Quran "translations," believing that there is mystical value and hidden meaning in the Arabic that cannot be translated; it is why some Muslims look for mathematical patterns in the Quran as proof of divine authorship; it is also why Muslims are confident that the Quran is inimitable in its literary excellence, as Allah himself generated it in the language of heaven.

Christians, on the other hand, are more than willing to translate the Bible from its ancient Hebrew, Aramaic, and Greek into modern languages. Of course, it is always best to read something in its original language, because the original language may carry subtleties that do not translate easily, especially when translating from more nuanced languages like ancient Greek into less precise tongues like English or the Semitic languages. This is why scholars and students of the Bible prefer to read it in its original languages. But if someone reads a translation,

Christians do not assume that some deep mystical value is lost, only exegetical implications that can be explained through study Bibles and commentaries.

By grasping the different natures of the books in the eyes of Muslims and Christians, we begin to understand the differences between the Quran and the Bible: The Islamic view of the eternality of the Quran affects the place it holds in Muslims' hearts, something that finds a Christian analogue not in the Bible but in Jesus himself.

THE COMPOSITION OF SCRIPTURE

Each religion's view of the nature of its scripture is closely connected to the history of its composition.

Since the Quran is eternal, it was not composed at a specific time. Rather, it was revealed piecemeal to mankind over twenty-three years through Muhammad. It is reported that when someone asked a question of Muhammad, or when he faced certain problems, he would start perspiring and a recitation would come to him. The Syriac word for "recitation" is *quran*, and Muhammad would pass this quran on to his followers, usually in small packets of verses. Muslims would then recite these passages in their prayers, committing them to memory. All these recitations were ultimately collected in a book and arranged in 114 *suras*. A sura can contain verses next to one another that were revealed two decades apart. There may be any number of reasons for its present arrangement, but from what is obviously discernible, the Quran can be described as having its longer suras toward the beginning and shorter suras toward the end. In addition, Muslim scholars have made attempts to discern which suras of the Quran reflect revelations given to Muhammad during the first portion of his prophethood, called Meccan passages, and those given during the latter portion of his prophethood, called Medinan passages.

By contrast, Christians have traditionally taught that God inspired specific men in history to write his words, using their experiences and their language to convey his message. God masterfully used the speech of chosen men to convey exactly what he desired and has preserved that message through the millennia. The result is the Bible, a collection of sixty-six books written by about forty people over fifteen hundred years. The first thirty-nine books are called the Old Testament, and the final twenty-seven are called the New Testament. *Testament* is roughly a synonym for *covenant*, so the Old Testament was written during the time of God's covenant with Moses, whereas the New Testament was written after God came to earth, upon the advent of the new covenant initiated by Jesus and prophesied in Jeremiah 31:31–33.

THE CONTENTS OF SCRIPTURE

Since Muslims believe the Quran was revealed via dictation to one person, it makes sense that it contains essentially only one genre and one perspective: Allah speaking to Muhammad. Although there are significant exceptions, such as the first chapter, which is the speech of men, the Quran more or less reads in the same manner throughout its text.

On the other hand, since the Bible was written by so many people over so many years, it makes sense that there are many genres and perspectives. The Old Testament is often divided into three sections: the Law (Hebrew: *Torah*), the Prophets (*Navi'im*), and the Writings (*Ketuvim*). The Jews refer to the text using an acronym for these three Hebrew words: *Tanakh*, asserting the diversity of the Scriptures. As examples, long sections of ceremonial law can be found in the Torah, whole books of history are found in the Prophets, and Hebrew poetry is found in the Writings. When we look to the New Testament, we see that it is divided into five historical books, twenty-one letters, and a book of apocalyptic prophecy. Unlike the Quran, the Bible is very diverse in its literary genres and perspectives.

Seeing the New Testament as an addition to the Tanakh might help Christians understand how Muslims see the Quran. It is the final revelation confirming that which was before it—"the Newest Testament," in a sense. The Quran asserts that the Torah is actually inspired scripture, as is the gospel (5.68), but that the Quran has now come as the final scripture to guide mankind.

THE ORAL OR WRITTEN MODALITIES OF SCRIPTURE

It is also important to note the difference between written texts and oral texts. To understand this, consider the difference between writing a letter and having a transcript of a telephone conversation. Although it might be the same person communicating the same ideas, the mode in which he would write is very different from the mode in which he would speak, primarily because people have more time to consider what to say when writing and more time to consider what has been said when reading. For these reasons, written communication is more thorough and less repetitive than oral communication, along with a host of attendant corollary characteristics.

Since Muslims teach that the Quran was dictated from Allah through Gabriel to Muhammad, and that Muhammad then relayed it orally to his scribes, it makes sense that the Quran is primarily an oral text. Not only is it mostly used in an oral manner, recited aloud in prayer for people to hear and memorize, but also it reads like a transcript of spoken communication. For example, instead of sharing full stories, Allah usually says, "Remember the time when . . ." and begins in the middle of a story, assuming the hearer has already heard the story elsewhere. Otherwise he will start at the beginning and stop in the middle of a story. This is why devout Muslims are often able to refer to names of prophets but not to full life stories. Because of its oral modality, there are almost no full stories in the Quran, with the notable exception of the story of Joseph.

The Bible, on the other hand, is composed of mostly written texts.[2] Stories and records are linear and complete. This is why devout Christians are able to share birth-to-death accounts of not just Joseph but dozens of people: Jacob, Moses, David, Solomon, John the Baptist, and Jesus, among many others.

ABROGATION AND THE FINAL FORM OF SCRIPTURE

Grasping the orality of the Quran helps with understanding the controversial phenomenon of abrogation. While Muhammad was still alive, he would give recitations that cancelled previous ones. In other words, he would tell his followers that certain portions of the Quran he had relayed before were no longer to be recited as part of the Quran. This was met with resistance, as people asked him how the Word of God could be cancelled. The response is recorded in 2.106 of the Quran, which asserts that Allah can substitute verses in his divine scripture because "he has power over all things."[3]

People accustomed to written texts might balk at the concept of abrogation; how can God command removing portions of his eternal word? But Quranic abrogation makes much more sense when we recall that the Quran was primarily oral. People were not expected to tear out pages from their Qurans or take a red pen to certain verses and strike them out. Rather, they were expected to simply stop reciting those passages in prayer, and thereby to forget them.

Although Muhammad's revelations were considered inspired texts as he relayed them, which was well before the Quran's final form, the Bible's books were finalized before the church recognized them as scripture. At that point, there was no room for abrogating portions. Therefore, having a different modality and different history, the Bible never underwent any abrogation.

THE SUFFICIENCY OF SCRIPTURE

Not all abrogated verses were left out of the text of the Quran, though. Muslim scholars have classically taught that there are multiple types of abrogation, including abrogation of text-not-law and abrogation of law-not-text. In other words, they teach that Allah intended certain verses to be recited but not practiced, and other verses to be practiced but not recited. For these reasons, Muslims scholars turn to the records of Muhammad's life, the hadith, for clarification. In addition, as we have already seen, most Islamic practices actually come from hadith and not from the Quran.

This is why Muslims do not believe the Quran is sufficient for Islamic practice, but it requires authoritative hadith. Very few Muslims believe in the sufficiency of the Quran, and these "Quran only" Muslims are often deemed heretical by mainstream Muslims.

The Bible, on the other hand, requires no complementary texts to decipher its teachings or provide supplementary Christian practices. It is sufficient and serves as the sole authority for Christian doctrine.[4]

THE EXEGESIS OF SCRIPTURE

The abrogation of the Quran, its piecemeal nature, and its heavy reliance upon hadith have traditionally been part of the reason why the average Muslim does not engage in Quranic exegesis. What if the verse they are reading has been abrogated and no longer applies? What if the context of a verse is not clear, since the verses before it or after it could be from completely different occasions? Besides, the Quran is in classical Arabic, a language no one speaks natively any longer. For these reasons and others, Muslims generally defer to scholars and imams for the explanation of verses and texts. That is why the vast majority of Muslims do not directly use the Quran themselves for anything but liturgy: memorization and recitation for prayers.

The Bible, on account of its written modality, sufficiency, and translatability, is accessible enough for the average literate Christian to read it directly and learn from it. One does not need to be a scholar to interpret what the Bible says. Of course, knowing more context is helpful, and the insights of scholars and theologians are valuable, but the nature of the biblical text allows devout Christians to go to it directly and learn from it, and so they do.

THE EPISTEMIC PURPOSE OF SCRIPTURE

Muslims believe that the Quran primarily serves as a guidance for mankind, of course, but since they do not usually exegete it themselves it is fair to classify this as an indirect purpose for the average Muslim. Rather, it is the mystical value of the Quran that serves as its primary purpose. This is illustrated by devout Muslims' average encounter with the Quran: its recitation in Arabic, even if the Muslim does not speak Arabic. In this case, it is not guidance but blessings that Muslims seek.

So great is the traditional Muslim's confidence in the mystical value of the Quran that it serves as the primary proof of Islam's veracity; Muslims are confident Islam is true because the Quran is so perfect. This epistemic use of the Quran traditionally goes back to Muhammad himself, who pointed to the Quran as the validation for his claim to prophethood. "How could any man produce such a perfect book? It must be from God." So the primary use of the Quran is to serve as the basis of *why* Muslims believe in Islam.

On the other hand, as we have seen, the Bible is intelligible to the average Christian who can access it in one's own language and exegete it for oneself. Of course, there are some who use the Bible for mystical purposes, but that is not its traditional or primary use. Similarly, there are some who believe in the Christian message because of the Bible, but it is usually not the reason why people are Christian. Unlike the Quran, the primary use of the Bible is to serve as the basis of *what* Christians believe, not *why* they believe.

And so, in discussing the differences between the Quran and the Bible, we have come full circle. The primary purpose of each scripture is related to its nature: The Quran is valuable in its mystical transcendence, while the Bible is valuable in its translatable and accessible guidance. There are many other ways in which the Quran and the Bible differ from one another, but the ones we have just covered will give us the needed insight into common disagreements and misunderstandings between Muslims and Christians over scripture.

CHAPTER 15

QUESTIONING TEXTS

At the end of the twentieth century, one name dominated Muslim-Christian dialogue: Ahmed Deedat. Born in India in 1918, Deedat immigrated to South Africa at a young age and started his adult life making ends meet as a furniture salesman. In that multicultural environment, Deedat encountered evangelists who challenged him to consider the gospel, and he started studying Islamic apologetics in response. By his midtwenties he was teaching apologetic lectures of his own, and for the next forty years he devoted his life to promoting Islam, printing booklets, and even establishing an Islamic seminary. Despite the support of his friends and some significant donations, most of his early work was unsuccessful.

But everything changed for Deedat in the 1980s when he started debating well-known Christians like Josh McDowell and Jimmy Swaggart. He presented challenges from a nuanced Islamic perspective that were uncommon to those accustomed to dialogue with skeptics and the irreligious. The novelty of his arguments combined with his sharp rhetoric often made it appear he had bested his opponents. His fame skyrocketed virtually overnight, and he was received with honor by presidents of Muslim nations and received rewards for his service to Islam.

Along with Deedat's fame grew his inflammatory rhetoric. As a response to the pope's positive stance toward interfaith dialogue, Deedat challenged John Paul II to a debate. When the pope refused, Deedat published a pamphlet titled "His Holiness Plays Hide and Seek with Muslims." He also famously began to argue that the Bible was pornographic. Further inflammatory speech during a Good Friday lecture

113

in Sydney earned him the castigation of the Australian government, and he was even banned from entry into Singapore.

In 1996, at the height of his career, Deedat suffered a severe stroke. Among other neurological deficiencies, Deedat was no longer able to speak, and he remained bedridden until his passing in 2005. Some suggested that God had punished him for his words, and other rumors spread that Deedat had repudiated Islam just before his passing. Within the Islamic world, though, both these suggestions are resolutely dismissed. Deedat's fame continues to grow, even after his death, into legendary status. His rhetorically charged style of argumentation has been picked up by the present face of Islamic apologetics, Zakir Naik, who has a following of millions of Muslims around the world.

The technique that Naik employs, the one that Deedat mastered and that many Muslims use on account of him today, is to challenge the Bible while proclaiming that the Quran is unassailable. Most commonly, they charge the Bible to be full of contradictions, whereas they assert that the Quran has none.

SCRIPTURE AND CONTRADICTIONS

There is much to be said about this challenge. In essence, Christians agree that inerrant, inspired scripture will not contradict itself. But now that we have discussed the differences between the Quran and the Bible, it might be more clear why this is such a staple of Muslim-Christian dialogue.

First, the Quran is written in one uniform style, whereas the Bible is written in many genres. When someone accustomed to only one mode of speaking comes across texts like "God is love" in 1 John and "God hated Esau" in the Psalms, they often forget to consider the genres.

Ranging from history to law to poetry and even a record of the loving relationship of Solomon and his bride, the Bible is a collection of very diverse books, and we ought not read all the books in the same way. The genre of a book affects the way we interpret it. For example, one should not read the book of Psalms in the same way as the book of Romans; the former is a book of poetry and should be read as a sanctified expression of the heart, whereas the latter is an epistle that explores Christian doctrine and should be among the first foundations of a systematic theology. Another example of poor exegesis would be reading the gospel of John in the same manner as the book of Revelation. Even though they are written by the same author, their genres are very different: The gospel of John is historical and biographic, whereas the book of Revelation is a book of apocalypse, and intends to be understood in prophetic terms. So although we can be quite confident that Jesus literally walked in Galilee (e.g., John 1:43), it is poor exegesis to read about a dragon sweeping away the stars in the same literal way (Rev. 12:4)! Understanding genre is an essential part of interpreting Scripture, yet Muslim apologists often raise the challenge of contradiction without taking genre into account.

Second, the Quran serves as the basis for Muslim confidence in their religion; it is the "why" of Islamic faith. Muslims understand that the Quran is the keystone of Islam's truth, and they assume the same for the Bible. But the Bible is not the "why" of Christian faith; it is the "what." The "why" of the Christian faith is the life, death, and resurrection of Jesus. So Muslim apologists direct much dialogue toward Christian Scripture, assuming it ought to have the same impact as a challenge to the Quran would, though that is not the case.

I was guilty of this mistake myself when I was a Muslim. In 2002, I sent an email to my friend David with dozens of alleged Bible contradictions, and he responded. We went back and forth for months. What I ultimately realized then, and am more confident of now, is that allegations of contradictions often reflect more about a reader than the text.

There are two ends to the spectrum of interpreting apparent inconsistencies in a text. On the one hand, a reader can deem every inconsistency a contradiction; on the other, a reader can attempt to harmonize the differences and try to make exceptions for the apparent inconsistencies. If a reader is friendly toward a text, he or she will give it the benefit of the doubt and harmonize it, whereas if a reader is antagonistic, he or she will discredit the text as contradictory. This is almost always what happens when Muslims and Christians lodge accusations of contradictions against one another.

On that note, Christians often do accuse the Quran of having contradictions. One website, for example, charges the Quran with containing over 120 contradictions.[1] Some examples: 6.163 says Muhammad was the first believer, 7.143 says Moses was the first, and 26.40 says that Pharaoh's magicians were; 88.6 teaches that the only food in hell will be thorns, whereas 69.36 says it will be pus, and 37.66 says it will be devil-like fruit; 7.54, 10.3, 11.7, and 25.29 teach that Allah created the world in six days, whereas 41.9–12 gives a total of eight days; 2.29 says Allah created the earth before the heavens, and 79.30 says he created the heavens before the earth; 96.2 says Allah created man from blood, 25.54 says from water, 15.26 says from clay, and 30.20 says from dust; 109.1–6 says non-Muslims worship different gods, whereas 2.139 says Jews and Christians worship the same God as Muslims; 4.48 says Allah does not forgive idolatry, and 4.153 shows him forgiving idolatry; 4.78 says all blessings and afflictions are from Allah, whereas 4.79, the very next verse, says blessings are from Allah and afflictions are brought on by those who suffer them. These are but a few of hundreds of alleged Quran contradictions.

Even though Quran contradictions are far more devastating to the case for Islam than Bible contradictions are to the case for Christianity, I find these arguments about contradictions to be unproductive and bordering on fatuous. I prefer the constructive dialogue of giving each text the benefit of the doubt and discussing the merits of what they are asserting, rather than reading the texts inimically and accusing them of contradictions wherever possible.

HOW DO YOU HANDLE THIS VERSE?

Along the same lines of genre and exegesis, Christians often approach their Muslim friends and ask them how they interpret certain passages of the Quran. For example, Muslims in the West often say that Islam is a religion of peace, to which Christians ask how they handle verses like 9.111, which says: "Allah has bought your life and your property for this, that you may slay and be slain." Muslims will often respond at this point that they are not sure how to handle it, but that does not change their minds about Islam being a religion of peace.

Christians may be frustrated by pointing to the apparent meaning of a verse to no effect, but they should remember that Muslims do not generally exegete the Quran themselves; and by asking for an interpretation of a verse, they may very well be asking a Muslim to do something they have never done before. Muslims receive such guidance and interpretations from their imams, and a Christian should not be surprised to hear the retort, "Don't ask me, I'm not a scholar!"

What might be more helpful for a Christian who wants to point out such verses in the Quran to a Muslim friend is to find a scholar in that Muslim's line of authority, and see if that scholar's interpretation says the same thing. If it does, present the verse along with the scholar's judgment and continue the conversation from there.

THE BIBLE HAS BEEN CORRUPTED

Finally, we turn to the most common Muslim accusation against the Bible: that its text has been changed over time. It should also be clear now why Muslims accuse the Bible of having been altered: because the Quran says it teaches the same thing as the Bible, confirming the Torah and the gospel, yet the teachings of the Bible are clearly different. In the same vein, the Quran teaches that Muhammad was prophesied in the Bible, but there appears to be no such prophecy.[2]

Interpreting what the Quran says about the Bible is controversial business. There are a few texts in the Quran that Muslims take to teach that the Bible has been changed, but closer investigation seems to reveal that these verses actually teach that Christians and Jews abandon their teachings for falsehood—not that the words of their Scriptures have themselves been corrupted. The overall meaning of the Quran seems straightforward: Jews and Christians still had their holy texts at the time of Muhammad, and they could follow the straight path by reading them. Regardless, Muslims very commonly accuse the Bible of significant alteration.

When lodging this criticism, a small minority of Muslims are envisioning insignificant biblical alterations that they perceive to be significant. To understand this, we again have to see through an Islamic lens. Muslims believe the Quran has to be perfectly preserved right down to the very letter because of the Quran's mystical nature. But an altered letter is not a problem for Christians, because Christians are concerned with the preservation of the meaning of the Bible, and the same thing can be said in multiple ways in Greek without changing the meaning. For example, the words "Jesus loves Peter" can be written sixteen ways in Greek. The letters could be altered in sixteen different ways without affecting the meaning whatsoever. So this kind of accusation might be true, but it is insignificant from the Christian perspective.

What most Muslims envision when they say the Bible has been corrupted, though, are wholesale omissions or insertions of New Testament teachings, intentional alterations by ruling powers. This sort of corruption of the biblical text simply never happened, nor could it have happened.

As an example, let us consider the book of the Bible called 1 Peter. When the disciple Peter wrote this letter, he sent it to its recipients. They made copies of it and sent the copies to other churches in other cities. Those churches made copies of it and sent them out to yet other churches. Now let's imagine that the church to which Peter sent it made five copies, and each church they sent a copy to made five more copies. Even at this early stage in the life of the letter, there are thirty-one extant copies. If someone wanted to effectively alter the text, they would have to recall all thirty-one copies. But nobody had the ability to do that. Nobody had ruling power over all of Christendom until the fourth century, three hundred years after Jesus. By that time, there were thousands of copies of the biblical texts, and even someone with authority over them would not have the practical ability to collect them all.

Even if someone had the capacity to recall all the texts and edit them, there would certainly have been some record of such a massive recall. It is virtually impossible to envision every Christian calmly handing over sacred texts to be altered without some trace of resistance or complaint.

So the only way the Bible could have been corrupted on such a grand scale is if someone early in Christian history had the authority and the power to recall all the texts, destroy them, and issue official copies, resulting in complaints and resistance. Yet no such person or record of events has ever existed. Interestingly, such a person and such a record do exist in the early history of the Quran.

CHAPTER 16

THE FIRST BURNING
OF THE QURAN

Muhammad's third successor, the Caliph Uthman, had authority over the entire Muslim *ummah* from approximately AD
644–655. Already by his time, variant recitations of the Quran were
causing dissension among Muslims, and Uthman decided he had to do
something before the hostilities spread.

Within about twenty years after Muhammad's death, the leader of
the Islamic Empire recalled all Quranic manuscripts, destroyed them
by fire, and issued official, standardized copies. When this happened,
devout companions of Muhammad strongly resisted the recall of their
texts, and the records of their dissent remain with us today.

So the Bible could not have been altered because there was no central
control over it in early Christian history, and as such it was never recalled
or edited. But there certainly was such control over the Quran in early
Muslim history, and there was an exact time when it was recalled and
edited. Islamic history makes no attempt to hide the official burning
of all Qurans and the propagation of its officially standardized version.

Apart from ignorance or bias, I am not sure how anyone can continue to accuse the Bible of corruption when the Quran would stand
condemned under consistent scrutiny. Indeed, the history of the Quran
was one of the factors that stopped me from accusing the Bible of corruption when I was a Muslim. On account of Uthman's control over
the Quran, there simply is no basis to accuse the Bible of large-scale
corruption without condemning the Quran.

THE DIVERSITY OF SCRIPTURE

In addition to its more pristine textual history, the diversity of the Bible is a strength. It reflects God's love for diversity. One language is not superior, one people are not superior, one mode of writing is not superior. Rather, God intends for humans to learn from history books, from law, from poetry, from proverbs, from apocalyptic literature, and more. He can teach through a fisherman like Peter, through a theologian like Paul, through a statesman like Moses, through a queen like Esther, and through his own incarnation. There is beauty and power in diversity, and the Bible reflects that.

More to the point of trustworthiness, in order to accept the Quran, one has to first accept Muhammad, as he is the only one who received Quranic revelations from Gabriel. On the other hand, whole communities testified to the inspiration of the biblical Scriptures, and they did not come from the mouth of one person.[1]

THE BIBLE SPEAKS TO THE HEART OF MAN

As a Muslim, even though I had plenty of evidence to trust the Bible and had learned about Uthman's recension of the Quran, the ultimate tipping point for me came when I asked God himself to lead me. At the end of my rope, completely distraught and emptied of tears, I asked God, whether Allah or Jesus, to guide me through his Scripture. I needed his comfort, and I was turning to him.

I started by opening the Quran. This was my first time opening the Quran for personal guidance instead of simply reciting memorized portions of it or asking an imam for help. As I looked through its pages, I realized there was not a single verse in it designed to comfort me while I was hurting. Although there were certainly verses that promised Allah would reward me for doing the right thing, there was nothing that said Allah loves me for who I am or that sought to comfort me despite my failures.

The Bible, on the other hand, was overflowing with the comfort of God and his love for me. God spoke to me through Matthew 5:4, which says, "Blessed are those who mourn, for they will be comforted" (NIV). Here there is no condition, no requirement of performance; God comforts those who are mourning. Verse 6 amplified this: "Blessed are those who hunger and thirst for righteousness, for they will be filled" (NIV). Not blessed are the righteous, but blessed are those who hunger and thirst for righteousness. As if written for someone like me, someone hurting and just reaching out to God, the Bible spoke to me of God's love.

It spoke to *me*. Not to Muhammad, not to seventh-century speakers of Arabic, but to me. And that is the power of God's Word—it traverses the ages and resonates with all his people. There is no word like the Word of God.

PART 5

JIHAD OR THE CRUSADES?

TWO DIFFERENT HOLY WARS

CHAPTER 17

THE FIRST CRUSADE

In Clermont, France, on November 27, AD 1095, Pope Urban II issued the First Crusade. He goaded Christians into traveling from Western Europe to the Middle East, where Muslims had lived for over 450 years, in order to fight against the "infidels" and "barbarians," "an accursed race wholly alienated from God." He urged not only knights but even mercenaries and robbers to "obtain the eternal reward" by joining in the effort "to destroy that vile race from the lands."[1] Many were moved by the pope's call to arms, and Europeans soon departed to carry the cross eastward into battle.

In the spring of 1096, an army of crusaders advanced through the Rhineland led by Count Emicho, where it was believed that Jewish moneylenders kept hoards of wealth. Emicho's army went from city to city slaughtering innocent Jews as "enemies of Christ," plundering their wealth to finance the Crusade. His army killed thousands of Jews and forced others to convert or face the same fate.

As the crusaders continued toward the Holy Land, their attacks against various cities delayed their arrival to Jerusalem until June 1099. After a few days' siege, the crusaders were finally able to overcome the city's defenses and fulfill their quest. A contemporary account, *The Deeds of the Franks*, chronicles the massacre from a soldier's perspective. As soon as one of the knights scaled the fortifications,

> all the defenders of the city quickly fled along the walls and through the city. Our men followed and pursued them, killing and hacking, as far as the temple of Solomon, and there was such a slaughter that our men were up to their ankles in the enemy's blood . . . Entering

the city, our pilgrims pursued and killed the Saracens up to the temple of Solomon. There the Saracens assembled and resisted fiercely all day, so that the whole temple flowed with their blood. At last the pagans were overcome and our men seized many men and women in the temple, killing them or keeping them alive as they saw fit . . . Then the crusaders scattered throughout the city, seizing gold and silver, horses and mules, and houses full of all sorts of goods. Afterwards our men went rejoicing and weeping for joy to adore the sepulchre of our Saviour Jesus and there discharged their debt to Him.[2]

Shortly after this bloody conquest, the crusader lords wrote a letter to the pope, chronicling their journey and culminating in a description of how the Muslims suffered at their hands. "If you desire to know what was done with the enemy who were found there, know that in Solomon's Porch and in his temple our men rode in the blood of the Saracens up to the knees of their horses."[3]

These are the records of history, and the nine hundred intervening years do nothing to blur the vivid images of the First Crusade in the collective memory of modern Muslims.

AMERICAN MUSLIMS, THE CRUSADES, AND JIHAD

I cannot speak for all American Muslims, but my family is very patriotic. My father served the US Navy faithfully for twenty-four years, starting as a seaman and retiring as a lieutenant commander in 2000. It was he who taught me, while I was visiting his naval base in Groton, Connecticut, to put my hand over my heart while reciting the national anthem. My mother, among other matters, impressed on me the importance of voting. On the day of a presidential election, I discovered that my parents were voting for opposing candidates. When I suggested to my mother that they should both just stay home that night since their votes would cancel out, she responded, "Son, it is our duty to vote."

In those years, we traveled often to New York City for vacation since it was a short two-hour drive from our home. My sister, a cosmopolitan at heart, developed a great love for the city. Her eyes always grew large when staring up at the skyscrapers, and she never left Manhattan willingly. Throughout her teen years, the most prominent decoration in her room was a large, framed image of the New York City skyline on her wall. It was still there on September 11, 2001, when our world crashed around us.

I am convinced that the attack on the World Trade Center hit patriotic American Muslims harder than the average citizen. We reeled with the rest of the nation at the deaths of fellow Americans, but we were simultaneously hit with an identity crisis. The terrorists had killed our countrymen in the name of our God. As we were trying to come to grips with these opposing realities, most Americans had no dilemma because they could simply denounce Islam. We were forced to somehow stand up for our faith while also standing up for our country, all in light of the potential that people would demonize not just Islam but us Muslims as well.

Thankfully, prominent Americans stood up to defend Muslims, not the least of whom was former president Bill Clinton. In a speech in Washington, DC, less than two months after the attack, Clinton said, "In the first Crusade, when the Christian soldiers took Jerusalem, they . . . proceeded to kill every woman and child who was Muslim on the temple mound. The contemporaneous descriptions of the event describe soldiers walking on the temple mound, a holy place to Christians, with blood running up to their knees. I can tell you that that story is still being told today in the Middle East and we are still paying for it."[4]

President Clinton, who had always been popular with our Muslim community, was impressing upon his audience that Christians had been guilty of wanton violence in the name of their God. This sentiment resonated with Muslims more than Clinton may have realized, because it accorded with the narrative that we had inherited in the Islamic community: Islam had spread peacefully after the advent of Muhammad only to be opposed by violent crusaders in the East and the Spanish inquisition in the West. Christians were the aggressors, and Muslims were the victims. Jihad, so we had learned, was either a spiritual or a defensive enterprise.

Along with Clinton's admission, it seemed that others were coming to agree with this perspective. Most Americans I knew looked at the Crusades with shame. A scholar at Georgetown University, John Esposito, described the Crusades as the beginning of hostilities between Muslims and Christians: "Five centuries of peaceful coexistence elapsed before political events and an imperial-papal power play led to a centuries-long series of so-called holy wars that pitted Christendom against Islam and left an enduring legacy of misunderstanding and distrust." Sharing a similar understanding, Ridley Scott released a movie in 2005 called *The Kingdom of Heaven*, which depicted Christians as the aggressors against civil Muslims who simply desired peaceful coexistence. At that time, it seemed to me that jihad had been vindicated even in the eyes of the West and that no one could point a finger at Islam, given the atrocities of the Crusades.

Still, I was convinced that no one should judge a religion by its followers. That's why, as I was considering the truth of Christianity and Islam, I would not allow *mujahideen*—those who enact jihad—to impact my view of Islam, and I would not allow crusaders to impact my view of Christianity. In my mind, there were only two people whose behavior mattered: Muhammad and Jesus. I was convinced that neither crusaders nor *mujahideen* had anything to do with the original teachings of their religions.

But that, as I found out, was a step too far.

THE CRUSADES IN CONTEXT

Many years after leaving Islam, while conversing with colleagues, I expressed my dismay at Christians who take the name of Christ but do not try to live according to his principles. When I used the Crusades as an example of such hypocrisy, a good friend challenged me with a very straightforward question: "Nabeel, have you ever investigated the history of the Crusades?" To my shame, I had to admit that I had not. I just assumed that everyone agreed the Crusades were an abomination and an inexcusable blight upon Christian history. Without condoning the atrocities, my colleague suggested I take a fresh look at the Crusades so I could have a well-rounded understanding.

When I started investigating, it immediately became clear that neither party in these wars had clean hands. In 1268, Sultan Baybars I, a Muslim notoriously known as the Lion of Egypt, taunted a Christian ruler whose city had just been conquered in the latter's absence. Baybars vividly describes what Count Bohemond VI would have seen had he been present in Antioch:

> Death . . . came among the besieged from all sides and by all roads: we killed all whom you appointed to guard the city or defend its entrances. If you had seen your knights trampled under the feet of horses, your provinces given up to pillage, your riches distributed by full measures, the wives of your subjects placed on the market for sale; if you had seen the altars and crosses overturned, the leaves of the Gospel torn and cast to the winds, and the sepulchers of your ancestors profaned; if you had seen your enemies, the Muslims, trampling upon the tabernacle and burning alive monks, priests, and deacons in the sanctuary; in short, if you had seen your palaces given up to the flames, the dead devoured by the fire of this world, the Church of St. Paul and that of St. Peter completely and entirely destroyed, certainly you would have cried out, "By Heaven, I wish that I had become dust!"[5]

According to the records, Baybars torched Antioch and emptied the city of its inhabitants. Fourteen thousand Christians were killed, and a hundred thousand were taken into slavery. This is an atrocity on par with the First Crusade's massacre in Jerusalem. I was not expecting this, as the narrative I had always heard was that the crusaders were the only ones perpetrating atrocities, not Muslims. It occurred to me that the only way to vindicate my inherited narrative was if this massacre was belated retribution for what the crusaders had done in 1099, so I started studying the context of the battles, including the First Crusade. It was then that I discovered that the narrative I had inherited was lamentably misinformed.

Just a few years before Pope Urban II called the First Crusade, the Seljuq Turks had conquered Nicaea, the same city where, 750 years prior,

Constantine had convened the church's First Ecumenical Council. The Seljuq Turks were Sunni Muslims, and they had taken Nicaea from the Byzantine emperor, a Christian. It was he, the Byzantine emperor, who asked Pope Urban II for help defending his lands at the Council of Piacenza in 1095. In other words, Muslims were actively attacking and conquering Christians, and the First Crusade was a defensive effort.

But what I learned next was even more shocking: The Seljuq army contained warriors called *mamluks*, slave children who were trained to ultimately become young professional fighters. These slave warriors were first used by Muslim caliphs in the ninth century, and for the next thousand years they were ubiquitous in Islamic lands. According to one scholar, sixteen of the seventeen preeminent Muslim dynasties in history systematically used slave warriors.[6] These slave boys were often captured from places like Egypt, where Christian territories had been conquered by Muslims. This means Muslim rulers were capturing Christian boys and turning them into slave warriors to fight against other Christians.[7]

The records indicate that Muslims had been conquering Egyptian Christians and taking their children since the early days of Islam. Amr ibn al-As, one of Muhammad's companions, brutally swept through Northern Egypt in AD 640, just eight years after Muhammad's death. John of Nikiu, a bishop in the Nile delta, records one such conquest: "[W]hen with great toil and exertion they had cast down the walls of the city, they forthwith made themselves masters of it, and put to the sword thousands of its inhabitants and soldiers, and they gained an enormous booty, and took the women and children captive and divided them amongst themselves, and they made that city a desolation."[8]

Reading through John's chronicles, I found that this was one of Amr's more merciful conquests. He records the capture of Nakius, a city left defenseless when its soldiers fled the oncoming Muslim army. John tells us how Amr treated the undefended Christians: "Amr and the Muslim army . . . made their entry into Nakius and took possession. Finding no soldiers, they proceeded to put to the sword all whom they found in the streets and in the churches, men, women, and infants. They showed mercy to none. After they had captured this city, they marched against other localities and sacked them and put all they found

to the sword . . . Let us now cease, for it is impossible to recount the iniquities perpetrated by the Muslims after their capture of the island of Nakius."[9]

This was just one of many massacres the bishop records of Amr ibn al-As, the friend of Muhammad. History records similar Muslim attacks on Christian lands from the mid-600s through the year 1095 and well beyond. By the time the Byzantine emperor asked for the pope's help, *two-thirds of the Christian world had been captured by Muslims.*

This is why Crusade scholar Thomas Madden says, "The crusades were in every way a *defensive war*. They were the West's belated response to the Muslim conquest of fully two-thirds of the Christian world."[10] When we read the full context of Pope Urban II's plea to European Christians for the First Crusade, this becomes abundantly clear:

> Your brethren who live in the east are in urgent need of your help, and you must hasten to give them the aid which has often been promised them. For, as most of you have heard, the Turks and Arabs have attacked them . . . and have overcome them in seven battles. They have killed and captured many, and have destroyed the churches and devastated the empire. If you permit them to continue thus for awhile with impunity, the faithful of God will be much more widely attacked by them. On this account I, or rather the Lord, beseech you as Christ's heralds to publish this everywhere and to persuade all people of whatever rank, foot-soldiers and knights, poor and rich, to carry aid promptly to those Christians and to destroy that vile race from the lands of our friends.[11]

Further context is also enlightening. The pope ordered no slaughter of Jews, and as some crusaders were massacring Jews in the Rhineland, other Christians were protesting and doing all they could to protect them. The Archbishop Ruthard of Mainz tried to shelter Jews at his personal residence until he was overcome by Count Emicho. The bishops of Speyer and Worms similarly tried to protect the Jews as best they could. The crusaders who were killing Jews were defying their Christian leaders and brothers, and their actions ought not be imputed to all of Christendom.

REVISITING THE NARRATIVE OF THE CRUSADES

This is at least one reason why not all Christians in the First Crusade should be painted with the same brush. Historical understanding requires a more careful approach, and when we start analyzing the Crusades from a nuanced perspective, even more becomes clear. For example, we ought not see the Crusades as simply "Christians versus Muslims" or vice versa. Christians and Muslims were far too divided for such a monolithic view. Christians were not united among themselves, which is why it ultimately took hundreds of years for the Western Christians to come to the aid of the Byzantine Christians.

Muslims were even less united, which is the primary reason the crusaders were able to conquer Jerusalem in 1099. The Seljuq sultan had just died in 1092, and multiple family members were vying for power. The Fatimid dynasty, a Shia caliphate based in Egypt, took advantage of this internal division to wrest control of Jerusalem from the Seljuq Empire in 1098, just one year before the Crusade. The Fatimids themselves had just come out of a civil war, and they were still in turmoil from the deaths of their caliph and his grand vizier in 1094. Their inveterate enemies, the Abbasid Muslims, had just lost their caliph in 1094 as well, and these factors all combined to leave the terribly divided Muslim lands prone to attack. This is why Crusade scholar Jonathan Riley-Smith says, "Although none of the crusaders knew it, they were marching toward a door that had swung wide open."[12]

Clearly, there were many competing interests vying for power in the region. Medieval historian Christopher Tyerman tells us, "The appearance of the western armies of the First Crusade in 1097–8 merely added one more foreign military presence to an area already crowded with competing rules from outside the region."[13] The crusaders were just one interest among many. In fact, they were among the less relevant ones, since they were essentially defeated when Saladin retook Jerusalem in 1187.

Perhaps that is why Muslims more or less forgot the Crusades until the end of the nineteenth century. According to Riley-Smith, "The Muslims looked back on the Crusades with indifference and complacency. In their eyes, they had been the outright winners . . . The first history of the Crusades in Arabic, which had appeared in 1865, had been a Christian one." Christians had to invent an Arabic word for the Crusades, as Muslims apparently did not give much thought to them until the turn of the twentieth century.[14]

Considering the historical realities, the common Muslim perspective of the Crusades—the perspective I inherited—is a modern invention. The narrative of an offensive Crusade against peaceful Muslims, along with the overtones of Ridley Scott's *The Kingdom of Heaven* and John Esposito's "five centuries of peaceful coexistence," turn out to be fanciful slants based on motivations other than history. The reality is that the Crusades were launched in defense of the Byzantine Empire after two-thirds of the Christian world had been conquered by centuries of Muslim attacks. Muslims understood this and held no grudge against crusaders until modern times, when postcolonial narratives came into vogue.

LEARNING FROM JIHAD AND THE CRUSADES

Given the facts, did crusaders commit inexcusable atrocities? Absolutely. Did *mujahideen* commit inexcusable atrocities? Absolutely. In no way do I intend to excuse those who committed these crimes. All the same, I do not think a religion ought to be judged on the basis of some of its followers. The actions of some Christians do not necessarily say anything about Christianity, and the actions of some Muslims do not necessarily say anything about Islam. As I concluded while still a Muslim, what matters are the teachings of Jesus and the teachings of Muhammad.

But it is a step too far to say that neither crusaders nor *mujahideen* have anything to do with their religions. As it turns out, both Jesus and Muhammad had a lot to say about violence, and the crusaders and the *mujahideen* were listening.

CHAPTER 18

COMPARING THE TRADITIONS
OF THE FOUNDERS

In 2009, David Wood and I received invitations to the Islamic Society of North America's annual convention, themed "Life, Liberty, and the Pursuit of Happiness" and held over the Fourth of July weekend in Washington, DC. We registered to attend, eager to hear the messages and mingle with the Muslim attendees. We watched lectures on the history of the Quran and the status of women in Islam, we met with acclaimed Muslim scholars, and we even interviewed one of the conference organizers. Although we thought there was a great deal of misinformation, there is no doubt that the organizers and speakers were very hospitable and sincere about their messages.

Many of my Muslim childhood friends and acquaintances were at the conference, and I made awkward attempts at reconnecting with them. Two such friends, both former members of the Ahmadiyya sect who had become Sunni Muslims, were willing to join David and me for dinner after the conference. Talking over halal Chinese food, the four of us discussed a full range of topics, but what sticks out in my mind is our conversation about apostasy.

"What do you think," I asked one of my friends, "about the punishment for leaving Islam?" I was curious because my friend, a former Ahmadi, had come from the most peaceful sect of Islam, whereas the Sunni Muslim punishment for apostasy is a violent death.

"There's no question here," he began. "The Prophet (SAW) made it abundantly clear that apostates must be killed for leaving Islam."[1] His serious tone gave no hint of ambivalence.

"I agree that he did," David piped in, "but come on! You can't really think that people should be killed for their beliefs? I mean, this is the twenty-first century. People believe in freedom of worship."

My friend did not budge. "Leaving other religions is fine, but people should be killed for leaving Islam. Yes, there is freedom of worship here in America. Since it is illegal to kill apostates, American Muslims are bound by the law of the land and cannot kill former Muslims. But in Muslim countries, apostates can and should be killed."

I could not believe what my friend was saying. I had to challenge him just a little more to see how serious he was. "So if we were in a Muslim country right now, would you kill me?"

Matter-of-factly, without malice or sarcasm, he responded, "Yes, I would kill you right now. It is the command of the Prophet (SAW)."

There was pin-drop silence at the table as everyone waited for me to respond. "Well then," I laughed, "I praise God we're not in a Muslim country! God bless America!" The blunt attempt at humor moved the conversation along, but his words remain emblazoned in my mind.

PEACEFUL MUSLIMS, APOSTASY, AND THE EXAMPLE OF MUHAMMAD

The contrast between my friend's view and the conference's theme was jarring. All weekend long, the conference was trying to prove that Islam is compatible with American values and Western freedoms, but here was a fervent young Muslim who was saying that American law was the only thing keeping him from killing me for my beliefs. How can we understand the disparity?

My friend did what Muslims have traditionally done: He turned to the example of Muhammad for *sharia*. The hadith are full of references to Muhammad's killing apostates and ordering them to be killed.[2] Therefore, there is little question for the Muslim who follows Muhammad as his exemplar: Apostates ought to be killed. The evidence is so solid that all major schools of Sunni Islam and Shia Islam teach the law of apostasy, disagreeing only about the details and circumstances.

Of course, killing people for their beliefs is an assault on the sensibilities of Western morality, including the sensibilities of many Muslims in the West. So in adapting their understanding of Islam to fit Western notions of morality, they often argue that Islam could never teach such a thing. Unfortunately, quite the opposite is true: Islam always has. From a historical perspective, denying the punishment of apostasy is a modern phenomenon, as is insistence on a predominantly peaceful Islam.[3]

Some Muslims point out that the Quran does not command the killing of the apostates, and arguably they are correct. But Islam is not a *sola scriptura* faith; it has always used hadith to supplement the Quran. Anyone who prays the five daily prayers would have to admit this, because not only are the words for the prayers not given in the Quran, even the number of daily prayers is not mentioned. The Quran mentions only three daily prayers, and it does not delineate the words or postures for any of them. Although there are legitimate "Quran-only" Muslims, they have always been an extreme minority in Islam. Most Muslims who argue against the law of apostasy using a Quran-only approach are using reasoning that would radically alter their Islamic practice if applied consistently.

Along similar lines, some peaceful Muslims argue against the law of apostasy based on Quranic verses such as 2.256, which says, "There is no compulsion in religion." In order to say this, though, they are also disavowing Muhammad's example. Muhammad did not interpret that verse in that manner, as his actions in hadith repeatedly show. That is why, classically, Muslim theologians have listed 2.256 among the abrogated verses we discussed in the previous chapter.[4] Ibn Kathir, for example, says 2.256 was abrogated by 9.29, which tells Muslims to fight Jews and Christians.[5] Popular Muslim scholars have vociferously defended these traditional interpretations throughout the twentieth century.

Of course, I hope peaceful Muslims gain the majority voice in the international Islamic community and sway Islamic practice in their favor. Far from being insincere, most Muslims who advocate a peaceful practice of Islam truly believe it is a religion of peace. At my mosque, that is exactly what we were taught and what we repeated to others. But in order to follow a peaceful Islam, one has to ignore or reject vast swaths of traditions from Muhammad's life as well as virtually the entire history of Islamic jurisprudence.

My friend in DC used to be a part of the same peaceful mosque my family attended, and he was taught by the same peaceful imams. Ultimately, he left that version of Islam and embraced a more violent one in the name of following Muhammad's true teachings. Muslims who most consistently follow the records of Muhammad's life believe in an Islam that would not satisfy Western notions of peace. These are the majority of Muslims throughout history.

MUHAMMAD AND JIHAD

The *Economist* published an article titled "The Persistence of History" on August 22, 2015. The first image of the article is chilling: dozens of burka-clad Nigerian teenage girls kidnapped from their school in Chibok by Boko Haram. The article goes on to speak of thousands of Yazidi women captured by ISIS, the Islamic State. In *Dabiq*, ISIS's professionally produced magazine, ISIS argues that these women are spoils of war and that sex slavery is a practice sanctioned by the Quran.

Does Islam allow sex slavery? We must do as my friend in Washington, DC, did, and as Muslims have always done, to answer questions like this: turn to the hadith. When we turn to the example of Muhammad's life, we find multiple accounts of Muhammad not just allowing sex slavery but also encouraging Muslims who were hesitant to use their newly captured women for sexual intercourse.[6] Whether they were hesitant because they were afraid the women would become pregnant or because their husbands were still alive, according to the hadith, Muhammad encouraged them. The hadith say that this is the very reason why 4.24 of the Quran was revealed, so that men would not be hesitant to have sex with female captives whose husbands were still alive. These accounts of Muhammad's life influenced Muslims throughout the classical age of Islam and delineated their rules of war. These are the accounts to which ISIS appeals now.

Of course, many Muslims disagree with ISIS's practice, but their reasons are enlightening. An open letter sent by 140 Muslim scholars to

ISIS reads, "After a century of Muslim consensus on the prohibition of slavery, you have violated this; you have taken women as concubines."[7] They argue that Muhammad looked favorably on releasing slaves, which may very well be true, but they do not go so far as to say that Muhammad did not allow sex slavery. That is simply not what the records show, and ISIS knows it. Unfortunately for these 140 Muslim scholars and for the rest of the world, ISIS is interested not in the consensus of Muslim scholars one hundred years ago but in the example of Muhammad in the seventh century.

ISIS takes not only females captive but also boys. The world was recently horrified by accounts of captured boys being made to remove their clothing and facing execution if they were found to have pubic hair. But once again, this practice was based on Muhammad's treatment of the Qurayza Jews. Muhammad had commanded that, except in night raids, children could not be killed in war. So when a group of people were taken captive, such as the Qurayza Jews, the boys were separated from men by the growth of pubic hair, and the men were executed.[8] ISIS was simply lifting this account from Muhammad's life and applying it to their own circumstances.

Of course, this allowance of Muhammad also explains why the Seljuq Turks and virtually all other Muslim dynasties had no qualms about capturing boys and making them slave warriors. Muhammad himself enslaved Jewish boys, perhaps a merciful act in light of the fact that their fathers were all beheaded that day.

So jihad, in its classical practice and in those manifestations considered "Islamist" or "radical" today, is often an attempt to simply follow Muhammad. Those who argue for more peaceful practices of Islam have to do one of three things: deny the example of Muhammad's life altogether, like the Quran-only Muslims; proclaim Muhammad's teachings defunct, like the 140 Muslim scholars; or disavow select portions of Muhammad's life as recorded in history, like the average Muslim.

JESUS AND THE CRUSADES

Following Jesus results in a very different notion of warfare. Jesus never led an army; far from it, he never even sanctioned violence. When it comes to Jesus' clearest dictum on fighting, there is no missing his message: "Put your sword back in its place . . . for all who draw the sword will die by the sword" (Matt. 26:52 NIV). Even in matters of self-defense, his teaching is so utterly peaceful that it seems to come from another world: "I tell you, do not resist an evil person. If anyone slaps you on the right cheek, turn to them the other cheek also. And if anyone wants to sue you and take your shirt, hand over your coat as well. If anyone forces you to go one mile, go with them two miles" (Matt. 5:39–41 NIV). This works in tandem with the otherworldly way Jesus tells his followers to treat their enemies: "Love your enemies and pray for those who persecute you" (Matt. 5:44 NIV).

Jesus' teachings were so peaceful that they posed a problem for early Christians who felt obligated to defend the oppressed with violence. Because Jesus made no clear allowance for war, such Christians developed an elaborate notion of "just war" starting with Augustine at the turn of the fifth century. Delineating stringent conditions of war, Augustine argued that fighting could be within the will of God, but it remained a necessary evil and something that required penance.

When launching the Crusades, Christians relied on the arguments of Augustine and other similar perspectives to vindicate their defense of the Byzantines, and they initially did treat their wars as a necessary evil to combat a greater evil. It was during the Crusades, though, that holy war started to be seen positively, itself a means of gaining forgiveness. In this, they were going far further than Augustine.

This idea gained popularity, as a contemporary historian wrote, "God has instituted *in our time* holy wars, so that the order of knights and the crowd running in their wake . . . might find *a new way* of gaining salvation."[9] So it was not until the Crusades, over a thousand years after Jesus, that Christians saw holy war as a positive endeavor that, instead of being a sin requiring penance, would actually forgive crusaders of their sins.

COMPARING MUHAMMAD AND JESUS ON VIOLENCE

By contrast, it was Muhammad himself who taught that fighting in jihad was holy and good. According to hadith, Muhammad taught Muslims that invading the Christian city of Constantinople would purge *mujahideen* of their sins: "The first army amongst my followers who will invade Caesar's city will be forgiven their sins."[10] Fighting in jihad was so good in Muhammad's eyes that there is nothing equal to it in this world.[11] When a man asked him if there was any deed in this world equal to jihad, Muhammad responded, "I know of no such deed."[12]

Recapping the chronology: Jesus' clear words against violence led to over three hundred years of nonresistance among Christians, and then Augustine's arguments led to six hundred years of war as a justifiable evil. It was not until Christians were a thousand years removed from Jesus that they believed holy war could purge sin, whereas Muhammad himself taught Muslims that fighting in jihad can forgive sin, and indeed is the best thing in the world.

There is much more to be said about jihad and the Crusades,[13] but one matter is beyond dispute: The historical Jesus never sanctioned violence and endorsed absolutely nothing like the Crusades, whereas the historical Muhammad engaged in jihad as the greatest deed a Muslim can perform. Violent jihad is a result of strict adherence to the life and teachings of the historical Muhammad, whereas strict adherence to the life and teachings of the historical Jesus results in pacifism and sacrificial love for one's enemies.

CHAPTER 19

QUESTIONING CHRISTIAN PEACEFULNESS

A week after David Wood and I went to ISNA's 2009 national convention, we traveled to London to engage Muslims in public dialogue and debate. Of the twenty or so public debates in which I have participated, my favorite was the one that David and I did together, dialoguing with two former Christians who had converted to Islam. The topic was "Is Islam a Religion of Peace?" and in addition to the interesting subject matter, the two-on-two nature of the debate kept the interaction fast-paced and gripping. An audience member after the debate commented that it was "more exciting than football," and I would agree, because I assume he meant soccer.

During the course of the debate, it became clear that the two Muslim debaters were in part arguing that Islam was peaceful when juxtaposed with a certain view of Christian teachings. Focusing on words of Jesus such as, "Do not suppose that I have come to bring peace to the earth. I did not come to bring peace, but a sword" (Matt. 10:34 NIV), they argued that Christianity allowed for violence in certain instances, and so does Islam. If Christianity is peaceful though violence is allowed, Islam can be peaceful as well.

To be fair, Augustine and Christians after him provided justification for war in part by asking questions about passages like these. But my response to Augustine would be the same as our response was to the Muslim debaters: "What is Jesus actually saying in this verse? We should read the context." In context, it is incontrovertibly clear that Jesus is talking not about war but about division among families: "I did not come to bring peace, but a sword. For I have come to turn 'a man against his father, a daughter against her mother, a daughter-in-law against her mother-in-law—a man's enemies will be the members of his own household'" (vv. 34–36 NIV). There is nothing here about war.

This is a common misunderstanding I have encountered among the Muslims I converse with: They challenge the peaceful teachings of Jesus by taking his words out of context. As we saw in part 4, this makes sense given Quranic exegesis and its relative lack of emphasis on context. But in biblical exegesis, the context of a passage is an essential element in determining its meaning. When Jesus says he has come to bring a sword, he tells us exactly what he means by that statement: His advent will divide families.

An even closer study of Jesus' words reveals that the "sword" to which Jesus refers is not a *rhomphaia*, the kind of sword used only for war.[1] The sword that Jesus brings is a *machaira*. Like a machete, a *machaira* is a long knife or a short sword designed as a multipurpose tool, such as cutting meat or cleaning fish. Also like a machete, a *machaira* can be used for fighting, but it is not its only or primary purpose. Its primary purpose is to divide, and here Jesus says his coming is as a *machaira* to divide families.

This clarification helps us understand another commonly misunderstood passage. In Luke 22:35–38, Jesus tells his disciples to take swords, *machaira*, with them on their journey.[2] Ancient Christians in favor of Just War asked the same question many modern Muslims ask today: "Why would Jesus have told his disciples to bring a sword if not to fight, or at least defend?" Now that we know what a *machaira* is, the answer is simple: He was telling them to be prepared for a long journey and to take along the appropriate tools. Context is helpful again: Jesus gives them a list of traveling accessories to take with them (money belt, bag, and sandals), and the sword appears in that list. As if to clarify this, Jesus told his disciples that two swords would be enough. If he envisioned a battle, two swords would never have been enough among that many; but they are plenty if envisioned as traveling tools.

Another verse that can cause confusion if context is ignored is Luke 19:27, in which Jesus says, "But those enemies of mine who did not want

me to be king over them—bring them here and kill them in front of me"
(NIV). Reading the whole passage makes the statement clear. Jesus is
telling a parable, sharing a teaching about a hypothetical king. He is not
actually demanding that his enemies be brought before him and killed.
Throughout the gospel of Luke, Jesus tells many parables, including
ones about an evil judge who ignores a woman (Luke 18), a farmer who
sows seeds (Luke 8), a vineyard owner who orders a tree to be cut down
(Luke 13), and a woman who searches for a lost coin (Luke 15). These
parables are not meant to imply that Jesus himself is an evil judge who
ignores women, that he is a farmer who sows seeds, that he is a vineyard
owner who orders trees to be cut down, or that he is a woman looking for
a coin. Similarly, his parable in Luke 19:27 is not meant to imply that he
is a king who wishes to kill people. Rather, Jesus uses stories to provide
memorable illustrations, and his parable in Luke 19:27 prefigures the
outcome of those who have rejected God on the final day of judgment.

One last matter to consider regarding these verses is a basic axiom
of hermeneutics: Always interpret unclear verses in light of clear ones.
Jesus' clear words and teachings remain "love your enemies" and "put
away your sword." Never in the Gospels do we find Jesus carrying a
sword, and the only physical altercation in the Gospels results in Jesus
castigating his disciple for fighting.[3] This, in addition to the context
of the verses in question, helps the reader see the consistency of Jesus'
peaceful teachings.

VIOLENCE IN THE OLD TESTAMENT

Another common objection from the Islamic perspective, one which the
two debaters raised during the very first minute of our public dialogue
in England, pertains to violence in the Old Testament. Although there
are many ways to formulate the objection, its primary thrust is that God
commands violence in the Bible, therefore Christianity is not peaceful.
As we saw in part 4, this objection fails because Christians are under
a new covenant, not the covenant made with Moses and the Hebrews.
The commands that God gave the Jews are not the commands given
to Christians.

Yet there are related, more nuanced objections that deserve attention. God does command violence in the Old Testament. For this reason, as a Christian I do believe God can command violence. As a corollary, I cannot object to Islam simply based on its use of violence.

All the same, the nature of the violence is significantly different in the Old Testament versus in Islam. What we see in the Old Testament is judgment commissioned by God in a very specific time and place, a judgment deferred for four hundred years. In Genesis 15:13–21, God promises Abraham that his descendants will inherit the land of Canaan. Abraham himself, though, will not receive this land because "the sin of the Amorites has not yet reached its full measure" (Gen. 15:16 NIV). God foretells the violent battles of the Hebrews against the Canaanites, but the Canaanites would be given four hundred years to repent. This is the violence we see in the Old Testament: judgment directed toward specific peoples on account of specific sins, and deferred for as long as possible.

The violence taught by Muhammad, on the other hand, extends to all non-Muslims in Islamic lands unless they fulfill certain conditions. According to the Quran, polytheists are given three options: convert to Islam, depart from the land, or be killed (e.g., Quran 9.3–11). These options are not limited to place or person but apply to all who do not believe in Islam in lands claimed by Muslims. Looking again at the text, 9.5 says, "Kill the *polytheists* wherever you find them, and seize them, and besiege them, and wait for them at every place of ambush. *But if they repent and establish salaat and give zakaat*, then leave their way." In other words, the Quran commands Muslims to kill people for being polytheists, but if they become Muslim, then leave them be. The next verse offers an additional option of exile.

Jews and Christians are allowed a further option in the Quran: pay a ransom tax in submission (e.g., Quran 9.29). In this case, it is even more clear that the violence is based on their beliefs. The Quran literally says, "Fight those who do not believe in Allah . . . nor acknowledge the true religion, from those who were given the scripture [i.e., Jews and Christians]." In other words, fight Jews and Christians who do not acknowledge Islam or believe in Allah. The next verse makes the reasoning clear: "The Jews said Ezra is the Son of God and the Christians said the Messiah is the Son of God . . . May Allah destroy them." Their doom is merited on account of their beliefs. This was the verse that justified an offensive attack against the Romans in the ill-fated Battle of Tabuk, even though the Romans had never attacked Muslims.[4]

Given these teachings, it should be no surprise that the records of Muhammad's life in Sahih Muslim show him saying, "I will expel the Jews and Christians from the Arabian Peninsula and will not leave any but Muslim."[5] The violence he espouses in the hadith and sirah do not appear to be limited to specific people or a specific time.

Before moving on from this point, it is worth mentioning chronology. These verses promoting violence against Jews, Christians, and polytheists are all found in chapter 9 of the Quran, and according to the Islamic records, this was the last major chapter of the Quran revealed to Muhammad.[6] *The Quran's last words and marching orders, as it were, are the most violent teachings found in its pages.* This is especially important given the traditional Islamic notion of abrogation, which teaches that earlier verses can be cancelled by later ones.

The violence in the Old Testament, on the other hand, was part of God's campaign of making his sovereignty known early in Jewish history; it is nowhere near the last word of the Bible. For Christians in particular, the final marching orders are the Great Commission: to spread the good news of God's love and mercy throughout the world by multiplying disciples of Jesus.

Whereas the culmination of Quranic teaching is the most violent chapter of the Quran, the culmination of biblical teaching is grace, love, mercy, and self-sacrifice. When we approach the violence of the Old Testament carefully, we see it has very little bearing on Christian praxis.

This conclusion reinforces our basic assertion: One must divert attention from Jesus to justify violence in Christianity. A strict adherence to Jesus' teachings simply allows no basis for violence. By contrast, one must divert attention from Muhammad to argue that Islam is a religion of peace, since he says that a Muslim who does not fight in jihad or at least express a desire to fight is a hypocrite.[7]

CHAPTER 20

JESUS VERSUS JIHAD

Before leaving London in July 2009, David and I made a stop at Speakers' Corner in Hyde Park. For a few hours every Sunday, Britons gather for a rousing display of free speech in the park, taking to ladders to proclaim their messages amid throngs of listeners. From politics to protests to proselytization, orators are never short of subjects or passion at Speakers Corner, and hundreds gather to hear. Although many are present simply to heckle the speakers or otherwise observe such spectacles, some in the audience are truly interested in dialogue.

David and I, each being over six feet tall, forsook ladders and proclaimed the gospel where we stood. We were almost immediately surrounded by Muslims who loudly challenged our views in return. Responding to them over the din of the crowd was more difficult than I had anticipated, and after about thirty minutes of dialogue and repartee, my voice grew too hoarse to continue. I abandoned my efforts and joined the various discussions that had sprung up around us.

I spotted two impassioned interlocutors and decided to join their conversation. A young Mennonite woman was dialoguing with a Muslim man on the issue of women's rights. When the young woman referred to 4.34 of the Quran, which allows men to hit their disobedient wives, he responded that 1 Corinthians 14:34 goes further in denying women their rights. Up until this point, the dialogue was productive and I had simply observed the discussion, but what happened next has been etched in my mind for years.

The young woman opened a Bible she had in her hand, intending to clarify the context of 1 Corinthians 14. While she was turning the pages, the man forcefully pushed her hand down, saying, "I don't trust your Bible. Don't bother!"

Without thinking, I grabbed him by his lapel and shoved him back, saying, "Don't you dare touch her!"

He was stunned, a genuine look of shock across his face. "Nabeel," he said, "you're a Christian! I thought Christians were pacifists!"

Still a little hot under the collar, I retorted, "I'm no pacifist, and if you touch her again you'll really find out!" Perhaps he realized his mistake, or perhaps he wanted to avoid finding out how not-pacifist I was, but he apologized to the young woman and they continued their dialogue.

Years later, I cannot help but recall his stunned expression. He was utterly convinced that Christians must be pacifist, and as I consider Jesus' words more carefully, I have to wonder whether he was right. My actions in Hyde Park that day illustrate, in a very microcosmic sense, that defending victims with violence is a natural reflex. But throughout the Gospels, Jesus teaches us to forsake our natural inclinations for his otherworldly teachings.

Could it be that, even when it comes to defending victims, Jesus does not want Christians to fight? Honestly, I am not sure. I find such a teaching hard to believe, but if I were pressed on the matter, I think I might have to default to Jesus' words in Scripture and forsake violence altogether, even defensive violence.

Although this is a dilemma for me as a Christian, being caught between pacifism and defending the oppressed, I think it is an excellent place to be theologically. It means that Christians who want to engage in defensive violence must do so while reckoning it as a moral abomination. No adherent of Jesus' teachings can entertain the notion of violence as inherently good, even defensive violence. This would have been very different if Jesus had sanctioned some sort of violence. Such an allowance would invariably have opened the door for those predisposed to shedding blood.

This is what we see occurring throughout Islamic history—with ISIS today and with other inevitable Islamists in the future. Even Muslims who believe that Islam is a religion of peace generally concede that Muhammad allowed fighting under some circumstances, and it is the life of Muhammad to which Islamists appeal in order to justify their terrorism.

If Muhammad, after gaining an army, commissioned or participated in eighty-six battles over the course of nine years, one would consider such activity among his followers to be inevitable. By contrast, it is beautiful that Jesus Christ, the exemplar for Christians, is never once reported to have even carried a sword. That leaves his followers somewhere between an otherworldly reliance upon God in pacifism and a reluctant use of violence for the defense of the oppressed. There is absolutely no room for exulting in violence for the follower of Jesus.

CAN WE KNOW WHETHER ISLAM OR CHRISTIANITY IS TRUE?

A decade of experiences as a Christian contrasted with my first twenty-two years of life as a Muslim leaves me no alternative conclusion: Christianity is very different from Islam. The message it preaches is pure grace, the God that it proclaims is objective love, its founder on earth was none other than the incarnate God, its scriptures are communal and diverse, and it leaves no room for exulting in violence. Islam, as traditionally understood, differs significantly at every turn.

Virtually no one with a conservative, devout upbringing in Islam would be under the illusion that Christianity is the same as Islam, especially not someone with as much to lose as Fatima. After growing up Muslim and passionately defending her faith, she became disillusioned with Islam and left her religion. It was in full awareness of Islam's teachings that she found Jesus' message compelling. So not only did Fatima realize that the two are different, but the fact that she was willing to accept Christianity after leaving Islam testifies that the differences make a difference, and it was worth whatever risk.

I journeyed from Islam to Christianity as well, but my path was not quite the same as Fatima's. I did not first become disillusioned with Islam, nor did I see the beauty of the gospel. As compelling as I find the Christian message now, I did not find it compelling at all as a Muslim. I believed that Allah was loving, that Muhammad was peaceful, that the Quran was beautiful, that *tawhid* was the perfect doctrine, and that truly following sharia made one righteous before Allah. I did not feel any need for the gospel, and I certainly did not see it as a superior message.

But despite my preference for Islam, I had met people from a plethora of religious backgrounds, and there was an undeniable trend: Christians preferred Christianity, Jews preferred Judaism, Hindus preferred Hinduism, and so on for all people from all backgrounds. Was that why I, as a Muslim, preferred Islam?

Recognizing that people tend to be more than comfortable with their given worldview, I did not want to base my faith in Islam simply because it was compelling to me. Rather, I was a confident Muslim because I believed Islam was the truth.

THE PURSUIT OF TRUTH

As a passionate young Muslim, I used to proclaim Islam's teachings to whoever would hear me. In my mind, there was not the least shred of potential that Christianity was true, so I regularly engaged in dialogue, advancing the claims of Islam against the claims of Christianity.

In this, Christianity and Islam are different from many other religions. While worldviews often provide subjective reasons to believe, Christianity and Islam both make claims about the past that can be tested against the records of history. When it comes to the person of Jesus, their truth claims are contradictory, and both cannot be true.

For example, a foundational Christian teaching is that Jesus died by crucifixion in the first century (Mark 15:37; Matt. 27:50; Luke 23:46; John 19:33; Acts 10:39; 1 Cor. 15:3). By contrast, the Quran teaches the exact opposite: Jesus was not killed, nor was he crucified (4.157). Neither religion treats these accounts of Jesus as a myth, so we cannot resolve these contrary positions in some metaphorical sense. He either died by crucifixion or he did not. Either Islam or Christianity has to be wrong.

Being absolutely convinced that Islam was correct on all such matters, I was more than ready to challenge Christianity's truth claims in order to call people to Islam. That was the reason why I started investigating, to convert people to Islam, particularly my friend David. David challenged me, though, to apply equal standards of investigation to both Christianity and Islam. Of course, being convinced of the truth of Islam, I agreed and attempted to study the religions as objectively as I could.

Examining the claims of Islam and Christianity over four years, I went from utter conviction in Islam to reluctantly embracing the gospel. The evidence in favor of Christianity was so strong I had no choice.

What I discovered during my journey is what I will be sharing in the next five parts of this book.

THE CASE FOR CHRISTIANITY

When David and I started discussing our faiths, we began somewhat haphazardly. Just a few weeks after having met, while on the road for a university event, we ended up rooming together. As the evening was drawing to a close, David pulled out his Bible from his backpack and started reading. Having been trained as a young Muslim to dispute Christianity, I challenged him, charging the New Testament with textual corruption. That encounter opened the door to a wide range of conversations, from the inspiration of Scripture to inerrancy to Jesus' deity and the Trinity and much more. It was an organic flow from one topic to the next, covering issues as they arose in the course of our friendship.

There certainly was value in discussing these matters in the contexts of our real lives, but after a year of such discussions, I realized that my knowledge of Christianity was more shallow than I originally thought. It was not that I realized I was wrong; rather, I simply noticed I was not able to defeat David's arguments. For the sake of being more careful and thorough, I wanted to start investigating these matters more systematically. It was then that we tried to distill Christianity and Islam to their cores.

At minimum, what would need to be true in order for the Christian message to be true? Conversely, what would need to be true for the Islamic message to be true? We wanted to cut through all the fluff and distraction, and these questions allowed us to get past all the less relevant matters and denominational disputes. There are many branches of both religions that have different doctrines, but neither David nor I was interested in sect-specific teachings or peripheral issues. What defines Christianity at its core, and what defines Islam?

For Christianity, we found the answer in Romans 10:9: "If you declare with your mouth, 'Jesus is Lord,' and believe in your heart that God raised him from the dead, you will be saved" (NIV). Here we found the entire gospel message formulated as the minimum requirement for saving faith. It has three components: (1) that Jesus died, (2) that he rose from the dead, and (3) that he is God.[1]

Thankfully, each of these three components can be tested from a historical angle. Did Jesus die on the cross or not? As we just saw, this is a fundamental teaching of Christianity that would have happened in history, so we can open the pages of our historical records to see if they support or rebut Jesus' death. The same is true for his resurrection. Although it would be a supernatural event, it would still have happened in history, so we can investigate the historical records to see if they corroborate the truth claim that Jesus rose from the dead. Lastly, do the historical records indicate that Jesus claimed to be God or not?

If all three are true, we have good reason to accept the Christian message, as these three components together form a compelling case. To illustrate, we should remember that many people claim to have supernatural authority and be divine. Usually such claims are pathological delusions of grandeur, and we are more than justified in dismissing them as madness. But if someone were to demonstrate their supernatural authority to validate their claim, then that would give us good reason to believe them.

In other words, if someone were to say, "I am God," we would think them crazy; but if they were to then say, "I will prove my claim by rising from the dead," and then they actually were to rise from the dead, we would have good reason to believe them. This is exactly what Jesus says the resurrection is for.[2] When people who were skeptical of Jesus' claims asked him for a sign, he said that the one sign he would show them is his resurrection.

Therefore, if history testifies that Jesus claimed to be God and rose from the dead, we have good reason to accept the Christian message.

One very important matter to note about the core of the Christian faith is that Islam rejects all three components. The Quran explicitly denies that Jesus ever claimed to be God (5.116), and it also explicitly denies that he died by crucifixion (4.157), thereby implicitly denying that he rose from the dead.

To understand my journey, and to understand the fundamental

incompatibility between Islam and Christianity, it is absolutely critical to internalize this point: *The central claims of Christianity are explicitly rejected by Islam. Islamic doctrine is antithetical to the core message of Christianity.* Evincing the case for Christianity disproves Islam, and vice versa.

As we have already explored, there are many points of agreement between Islam and Christianity, even regarding the life of Jesus, such as his virgin birth and ability to work miracles. But none of those points of agreement are the central proclamation of the gospel; the Scriptures do not say, "If you believe in the virgin birth, you will be saved." It does say we need to believe Jesus is God, that he died, and that he rose from the dead. Islam categorically denies these beliefs.

THE CASE FOR ISLAM

When David and I considered how to distill Islam down to its essence, we found the answer clearly in the *shahada*: "There is no God but Allah, and Muhammad is his messenger." At minimum, one must believe that Allah is God and that Muhammad is his appointed messenger in order to be a Muslim.

But is Allah, the God of Islam, the one true God?[3] And is Muhammad truly a messenger of God? To investigate these, one must turn to the Quran and the records of Muhammad's life. The Quran, being Allah's self-revelation and the "why" of Muslim belief, must be carefully scrutinized. Similarly Muhammad, being the only direct recipient of the Quran and a presence in the *shahada*, must be critically examined to determine whether he actually is a messenger of God.

If we can determine that the Quran is the Word of God, or if we can determine that Muhammad is a messenger of God, then we have good reason to accept Islam. Unlike the Christian case, where all components need to be true to build the case, defending the prophethood of Muhammad vindicates the inspiration of the Quran and vice versa. The case for Islam should therefore, in concept, be easier to establish, as only one point needs to be well defended: either the prophethood of Muhammad or the inspiration of the Quran.

So, after careful consideration, David and I chose to study these five points:

1. Jesus' death by crucifixion
2. Jesus' resurrection from the dead
3. Jesus' claim to be God
4. The prophetic authority of Muhammad
5. The divine inspiration of the Quran

Together, these five points constitute the case for Christianity and the case for Islam.

THE INSPIRATION OF THE BIBLE AND THE CASE FOR CHRISTIANITY

Missing from this list, perhaps conspicuously, is the divine inspiration of the Bible. Although David and I had investigated the Bible, and its inspiration was very important for Christian doctrine, we both realized that it constituted the "what" of the Christian faith, not the "why." Wanting to focus on the minimal requirements for Christianity, we had to exclude many matters that were very important but not central to the case, and the inspiration of the Bible was one such matter. Theoretically, even if the Bible had never been written, Jesus could still have died on the cross for our sins and risen from the dead, making the Christian message true. The inspiration of the Bible is not central to the case for Christianity.

Unlike the Bible, the Quran is the "why" of Muslim belief. When skeptics challenged Muhammad to provide evidence for his claims, the primary proof he provided was the inspiration of the Quran.[4] Repeatedly, at least five times, he offered the divine origin of the Quran as the reason why people should trust Islam. By contrast, when the early Christians proclaimed the gospel, the primary proof that they pointed to was the resurrection of Jesus, not the text of the Bible.[5]

For these reasons, the Quran forms a central pillar in the case for Islam, whereas Jesus forms the pillar in the case for Christianity. This accords with what we have already learned about Islam and Christianity: The Quran and Jesus are the analogues in the two faiths, not the Quran and the Bible.

That said, let us be careful not to conflate divine inspiration and historical reliability. We will be considering what various books of the Bible say about Jesus' death, resurrection, and deity, so it behooves us to consider whether their records on these matters are historically reliable. But of course, assessing the accuracy of specific claims found in books of the Bible is very different from determining whether or not the whole Bible is the inspired Word of God.

No early Christian ever argued the latter as a defense of the gospel, so we will not consider that argument here, though we will be considering the historical reliability of the Bible as far as it affects our case for Christianity. By contrast, on account of being the primary proof offered by Muhammad and early Muslims, we will be considering the inspiration of the Quran.

OBJECTIVITY: DEFENDING THE FAITH VERSUS ASSESSING THE FAITH

Before diving into this investigation, I want to share something that took me years to really grasp: It is virtually impossible to study these matters objectively. Not only do we all have a vested interest in defending the faiths we and our social circles have believed for years, but our beliefs also color the way we receive information. The same data will be interpreted differently by people from disparate worldviews. When we investigate Islam and Christianity as devout believers in one faith or the other, our Christian or Muslim presuppositions affect the way we interpret the evidence, and we often see what we want to see.

When I started investigating the data, I came to the table with the presupposition that Islam was true, and I interpreted the data accordingly. No matter what facts David provided, I either made them fit my Islamic paradigm or I found some way to dismiss them. It is not difficult to defend what you already believe, and anyone who sets their mind to it will be able to do so, whether Muslim, Christian, or anything else.

What is difficult is pursuing the truth about your faith and assessing it honestly. This feat requires one to be introspective and self-critical at frequent intervals. Although we can never completely overcome our biases, the most important step we can take is to pursue fair-mindedness with intentionality. While considering the data, we need to repeatedly ask ourselves the question: "Would an objective observer find the arguments compelling?"

In the next five parts of this book, I will regularly raise this question while assessing the cases for Christianity and Islam. After examining the first three points, which impact the case for both Islam and Christianity, there will be a midway summary to solidify the findings to that point before examining the case for Islam.

While still a Muslim, I decided that the best question to start investigating would be the one that is a fulcrum of disagreement yet is easy to investigate historically, allowing the least room for subjectivity: Did Jesus die on the cross?

PART 6

DID JESUS DIE ON THE CROSS?

CHAPTER 21

THE POSITIVE CASE

UNANIMOUS RECORDS

In 2002, David and I arranged a friendly interfaith dialogue with my father and two of David's friends, Mike Licona and Gary Habermas. Mike was a martial arts instructor and insurance salesman who had started pursuing graduate studies in religion, and Gary was one of his professors. Gary had participated in many interfaith dialogues, Mike regularly hosted people from different religious backgrounds at his home, and my father was always enthusiastic about proclaiming Islam, so everyone felt comfortable gathering together and discussing deeply held beliefs.

Part of the reason I felt comfortable, though, was because I had chosen a topic that we had heard discussed dozens of times by Muslim leaders and scholars: Did Jesus die by crucifixion? In addition to our relative familiarity with the topic, the Quran took a bold stance on the matter, and I was confident in the word of Allah.

The Quran explicitly denies Jesus' death by crucifixion. In 4.157, it states, "And their [sic] saying, 'indeed we killed the Messiah, Jesus son of Mary, messenger of Allah.' *But they did not kill him, nor did they crucify him, but it was made to appear so to them.* And those who disagree about it are in doubt about it. There is not anything of knowledge in this for them except the pursuit of conjecture. They did not kill him, for certain" (emphasis mine).

Muslims interpret this verse in multiple ways. The view that my father and I were defending that day was the view that Muslim debaters like Ahmed Deedat and Shabir Ally espoused: Jesus did not actually die on the cross but rather just appeared to die. Although this is the position of notable Muslim intellectuals, it is the minority among Muslims at large. The majority of Muslims, going back to the earliest commentaries in Islam, believe that Jesus' visage was placed on another person who was crucified in his place.

My father presented our view for the first part of the evening, and Mike and Gary then interacted with us, explaining their reasons for believing that Jesus did actually die on the cross.

SCHOLARLY UNANIMITY

The most salient point of the evening for me, the one that mattered most to a mind accustomed to thinking in terms of authority, is that virtually no non-Muslim scholar agrees with the Islamic position. For all intents and purposes, there is a unanimous opinion within academia that Jesus died by crucifixion. Although scholarly unanimity is not evidence per se, it was a jarring perspective check.

Of course, I was not in the least surprised that Christian scholars were unanimous on this point. What surprised me was the insistence from non-Christian scholars that this matter was so firmly established that it was beyond dispute.

Gerd Lüdemann is a German scholar who so doubted the Bible that he infamously said, "The person of Jesus himself becomes insufficient as a foundation of faith."[1] Yet even he did not mince words when it came to Jesus' death. In his book, *What Really Happened to Jesus*, Lüdemann critically reexamines the life of Jesus from many angles, often dismissing the traditional Christian position outright. But in his section titled "The death of Jesus," he spares only two sentences: "The fact of the death of Jesus as a consequence of crucifixion is indisputable, despite hypotheses of a pseudo-death or a deception which are sometimes put forward. It need not be discussed further here."[2] He then moves on, as if lingering on the matter were pointless.

Paula Fredriksen, another well-known scholar who frequently challenges Christian beliefs, also concludes similarly to Lüdemann, positing, "The single most solid fact about Jesus' life is his death: he was executed by the Roman prefect Pilate, on or around Passover, in the manner Rome reserved particularly for political insurrectionists, namely, crucifixion."[3]

The matter was stated most succinctly by perhaps one of traditional Christianity's most evocative critics, John Dominic Crossan, who says, "There is not the slightest doubt about the fact of Jesus' crucifixion under Pontius Pilate."[4] As if that were not emphatic enough, he elsewhere states, "That he was crucified is as sure as anything historical can ever be."[5]

Having been a graduate student of historical studies for the past decade, I have learned that scholars disagree on almost every historical point they discuss, and it is almost impossible to find scholarly unanimity, yet virtually all New Testament scholars today agree that Jesus died on the cross. Even those scholars who have no hesitation in dismissing traditional Christian beliefs, as we have seen, say that Jesus' death by crucifixion is "indisputable," "the most solid fact about Jesus' life," and "as sure as anything historical can ever be."

I am not here arguing that Jesus must have died by crucifixion because virtually all non-Muslim scholars believe it. That would be an appeal to authority, a logically fallacious contention. I am simply recounting what Mike and Gary pointed out to me that night, which caused me to consider just how much of an uphill battle we were fighting if we thought Jesus did not die on the cross. The evidence for Jesus' death by crucifixion is so strong that virtually every scholar who studies Jesus' life believes it.

In fact, the evidence is so strong that at least one Muslim scholar agrees.[6] In the flurry of media attention that followed the release of his book *Zealot*, Reza Aslan made it abundantly clear that Jesus "was most definitely crucified."[7] Aslan is one of the most well-known Muslim scholars in the West, and on account of the historical evidence, he also believes that Jesus died on the cross, despite what the Quran teaches. He believes so strongly in Jesus' death by crucifixion that he uses it as the foundation for his entire theory of Jesus' life.

What is the evidence that so convinces all these scholars—Christian, non-Christian, and even Muslim?

THE RECORD OF THE CROSS

As I was taught by my professors at Oxford, the foundation for any good historical argument should always be the primary sources: What do the historical records themselves indicate?

By all standards of ancient history, the reports of Jesus are very early and very diverse. Starting just a few years after Jesus' crucifixion, Christians, Jews, and Romans report that Jesus died by crucifixion. The testimony is unanimous for over one hundred years.

Perhaps the earliest reports are found in a letter written to the Corinthian church. According to many New Testament scholars, Christian and non-Christian alike, 1 Corinthians 15 contains a creed that was formulated within five years of Jesus' crucifixion, and it testifies that Jesus died and was buried: "For what I received I passed on to you as of first importance: that Christ died for our sins according to the Scriptures, that he was buried . . ." (1 Cor. 15:3–4 NIV).[8]

It is critical to understand the import of this data: Before the New Testament was even written, Christians were passing down to one another the core doctrines of their faith, and the death of Jesus was among their first concerns. Not only was the teaching present in the very earliest days of Christianity, but also it was a central component of their doctrine. That we have a record of such tradition that comes within five years of Jesus' death is almost unheard of in ancient history; in comparison with most historical records, it is lightning fast.

Another such creedal formulation, one which many scholars believe also predates the New Testament, is found in the letter to the Philippians. Here again, we find Jesus' death not just present, but highlighted: "[Christ Jesus] humbled himself by becoming obedient to death—even death on a cross!" (Phil. 2:8 NIV).

The earliest biographers of Jesus' life all testify that Jesus died by crucifixion: Mark, Matthew, Luke, and John. In addition, many other New Testament authors and books lend their weight in agreement.

Without having carefully considered the implications, some might argue that these sources are from the Bible, and therefore are biased and ought not serve as evidence. There are at least two problems with this view. First, all historical sources are biased, and although we ought to weigh biases as we investigate, the sheer presence of bias is not reason enough to discredit reports. We would have to throw out all of history, indeed all news reports and personal stories from friends, if that were the case. Second, these sources are written by people of various backgrounds, and generally speaking, they did not start their lives as Christians. Though originally non-Christians, they found the Christian message convincing enough to convert, often at great cost. Therefore, if anything, their testimony may be granted an extra measure of credibility.[9]

Regardless, the testimony of the early Christians is corroborated by non-Christian reports: Josephus, the failed Jewish general who befriended the Roman emperor, also reports in the first century that Jesus died by crucifixion. He is joined shortly after by Tacitus, a Roman historian who also reports Jesus' death.

In the first one hundred years after Jesus, we have Christian, Jewish, and Roman reports that Jesus died by crucifixion, and not a single report that he may not have died by crucifixion.

This last fact is more compelling when we consider the report that some people were trying to explain why Jesus' tomb was empty.[10] Instead of arguing that Jesus did not die on the cross, they argued that his body was stolen. So even though there was a perfect opportunity to suggest that Jesus did not die by crucifixion, it appears that this argument did not occur to anyone.

And there is a good reason for this: People were all too familiar with the terror of the cross.

THE TERROR OF THE CROSS

Simply put, the cross was one of the most vicious, torturous, and effective methods of execution that human depravity has ever devised. The torment of the cross was so extreme that a word was invented to describe it: *excruciating*, which translates from Latin to describe a pain "from the cross."

Cicero, the ancient roman orator, describes crucifixion as "that most cruel and disgusting penalty" and "the worst extremes of torture." According to him, even thinking about "the terror of the cross" was too horrible for Roman citizens: "The very word 'cross' should be far removed not only from the person of a Roman citizen but from his thoughts, his eyes and his ears."[11]

Seneca the Younger penned this paragraph, describing the despair of the crucified: "Can anyone be found who would prefer wasting away in pain, dying limb by limb, or letting out his life drop by drop, rather than expiring once for all? Can any man be found willing to be fastened to the accursed tree, long sickly, already deformed, swelling with ugly tumours on chest and shoulders, and draw the breath of life amid long-drawn-out agony? I think he would have many excuses for dying even before mounting the cross!"[12]

Crucifixion was an execution reserved by Rome when they wanted to make a statement.

There was no standard procedure for the crucifixion, as executioners were often given license to express profligate brutality. Victims were at times fixed to the cross in awkward poses, at times nailed through their groins, at times forced to watch the violation of their wives, at times made to witness the slaughter of their whole families, and at times having their slain sons hung around their necks.[13] Crucifixion was not just another means of execution, as there are much more efficient ways to kill. The cross was intended for brutality, and victims were not treated gently.

The cross often came after a flogging, as in the case of Jesus, which was itself a horrendous torture. The whip was designed to rip into skin and turn muscle to pulp, making a victim's "blood flow in streams."[14] Josephus tells us that victims were "whipped to the bone" and that their intestines were at times exposed by the flogging.[15] This is why Seneca describes a victim, by the time he is on the cross, as a "battered and ineffective carcass."[16]

The ultimate end of crucifixion was execution, and it was easy to determine whether victims of the cross were alive or dead: Simply observe whether they were still moving. If they were not, they were dead, because it meant they were not breathing. On account of the way crucifixion victims were made to hang, their rib cages were fully expanded and their lungs could not generate the pressure necessary to exhale. In order to breathe out, they had to push up against the nail in their feet, and they could inhale as they sank back down. Once they had reached the limit of sheer exhaustion or blood loss, their bodies would sink down, they would no longer be able to breathe out, and they would die of asphyxiation.

That is why one method of expediting or ensuring the death of victims was to break their knees, as is reported to have occurred to the bandits on either side of Jesus. Once their knees were broken, they could no longer breathe out and they would soon expire.

Yet the Romans had other means of ensuring death. Among other methods, they were known to light peoples' bodies on fire, to feed the bodies to wild animals, or, in the case of Jesus, to pierce the heart.

This is a highly condensed and abbreviated description of the terror of the cross. It was an execution reserved for what Rome deemed the most worthless or heinous of criminals. Perhaps now it is understandable why the word *cross* was used as a rank curse word among the lower class in ancient Rome: "Get crucified!"[17] It should come as no surprise that never in recorded history has anyone survived a full Roman crucifixion.[18]

What should come as a surprise, though, is that a religious movement could ever be started with the ridiculous proclamation that their Savior was crucified.

THE FOLLY OF THE CROSS

Given the insuperable stigma of crucifixion, it should be a shock that Christians propagated their message by saying that their Savior died on the cross. How could Jesus save anyone if he died such a horrendous death?

That is why people ridiculed Christians for this belief. The earliest known pictorial representation of Jesus on the cross is a drawing intended to mock a Christian named Alexamenos. It depicts Jesus on the cross as having the head of a donkey, and the scrawled caption reads, "Alexamenos worships his god!" To be crucified was exceedingly shameful; to worship such a one, even more so.

This is the focus of an anti-Christian polemic written by Minucius

Felix, who says, "To say that their ceremonies center on a man put to death for his crime and on the fatal wood of the cross is to assign these abandoned wretches sanctuaries which are appropriate to them and the kind of worship they deserve."[19] In other words, if Christians are so degenerate that they worship a crucified man, they deserve to worship a crucified man.

Not just Romans but also Jews saw the cross as a tremendous stigma. Deuteronomy 21:23 teaches that "the curse of God is on the one who is hanged on a stake (for capital punishment)." By and large, Jews were not expecting a suffering Messiah, let alone one upon whom rested the curse of God.

This is why the Corinthian church had to be assured that, despite all appearances, the cross of Jesus was still good news: "For the message of the cross is foolishness to those who are perishing, but to us who are being saved it is the power of God" (1 Cor. 1:18 NIV). Once we recognize the common understanding of the cross, it makes complete sense why it would appear to be "foolishness." Undoubtedly, the message of a "crucified messiah (is) a stumbling block to Jews and foolishness to Gentiles" (1 Cor. 1:23 NIV).

To Jews and non-Jews, the message of a crucified Savior was abhorrent and ridiculous. In other words, everyone who heard the message of the cross would have been repulsed by it, at least at first. It was certainly not an attractive proclamation.

The question that we must consider, given that the cross would elicit such derision and aversion, is, Why would Christians preach such a message? Why not preach an alternative, more attractive message, like Jesus' survival of the cross, or that, despite appearances, Jesus was never placed on the cross to begin with? Better yet, why not leave the cross out of Christian preaching entirely, teaching that he died by some other means or perhaps never died at all but was raised directly to heaven? All of these would have made the Christian message much more appealing to everyone who heard it.

There is only one probable answer: Jesus actually did die by crucifixion, and the disciples were preaching what they had to preach if they wanted to proclaim the truth.

SUMMARIZING THE POSITIVE CASE

A whole book can be dedicated to Jesus' death, as indeed dozens have, but we may summarize the positive case before considering the Islamic response.

The basis of any historical case must be the primary sources, and in this case, the sources are unanimous, diverse, early, and plentiful: Jesus died by crucifixion. Starting almost immediately after Jesus' death, *over a dozen authors and traditions* recorded the death of Jesus by crucifixion, including Christian, Jewish, and Roman sources, and their testimony was unanimous. For more than one hundred years, no record even suggests that Jesus survived death on the cross or otherwise circumvented his execution. This coheres well with what we know of crucifixion practices, in that there is no person in recorded history who ever survived a full Roman crucifixion. Positing that Jesus did not die on the cross would have served the agenda of the early Christians and those opposed to their message, but such a suggestion appears inconceivable.

For those who study Jesus' life in academia, the idea that Jesus did not die by crucifixion remains, to this day, outside the realm of possibility.

CHAPTER 22

THE ISLAMIC RESPONSE

IT WAS MADE TO APPEAR SO

After hearing the position of Gary and Mike, it was clear that on this topic, my father and I would be fighting an uphill battle. Regardless, we argued the positions we had been taught in the mosque, and there was much to say. Here I will recount the bulk of what we argued, as well as present the more common Muslim argument against Jesus' death.

The Islamic responses to the argument above can be categorized according to the two main interpretations of 4.157. Recall the central portion of the verse: "They did not kill him, nor did they crucify him, but it was made to appear so to them." The two most common interpretations place relative emphasis on different parts of this verse. The view that Muslim debaters often hold, that Jesus survived the cross, focuses on the first part—"They did not kill him"—whereas the majority view focuses on the latter part: "but it was made to appear so to them."

THEY DID NOT KILL HIM

My father and I argued the position that Jesus was placed on the cross but he was not killed. Jesus miraculously survived the cross, was taken down alive, placed in a tomb to heal, and then escaped the clutches of the Romans.

This is not the same theory that Christian apologists dubbed the Swoon Theory, which met its demise hundreds of years prior under the critical atheist scholar David Strauss. A naturalistic view, the Swoon

Theory argued that Jesus *somehow* survived crucifixion. Strauss's critique was powerful: Even if Jesus had somehow managed to survive the crucifixion, his body would have been broken and mutilated, and he would have required desperate medical attention. The disciples may have been relieved that he survived, but that does not explain the inception or the preaching of the early church. According to the historical record, the disciples preached Jesus as the Lord of life risen in glory, and that belief propelled them to spurn death to such a degree that they were more than willing to die. According to Strauss, that would not have happened had Jesus just survived the cross.

The Christian apologists who had responded to the Swoon Theory focused on a different, more visceral point: If Jesus had somehow survived the cross, his feet would still have been broken, his hands paralyzed, his sides pierced, his body mutilated and otherwise incapacitated. They argued that it would have taken a miracle for Jesus to even walk out of the tomb!

But as Muslims, we recognized that it would have taken a miracle, and that's what we argued. This was what I called the Theistic Swoon Theory, and we argued that God miraculously preserved Jesus' life on the cross. We presented the argument in a pithy package: "If God can perform the grand miracle of raising Jesus from the dead, why can he not perform a lesser miracle of preserving him from death in the first place?" In effect, it circumvented the inevitability of Jesus' death. No matter how brutal the cross, God's ability to preserve Jesus is greater.

We also argued that there were subtle traces of this divine design still present in the Gospels: Pilate did not want to kill Jesus on account of a dream God had given his wife; his attempt to release Jesus failed when the crowd demanded Barabbas; Pilate may have resorted to colluding with the executing centurion to ensure Jesus' body was neither killed nor hung on the cross for the usual length of time; Joseph of Arimathea may have also conspired with Pilate, as evidenced by his request to have the body of Jesus; the women who came to the tomb must have brought aloes and myrrh for medicinal purposes; Jesus was disguised as a gardener in order to escape the guards; the holes in Jesus' hands indicated he had not been raised from the dead, etc.

We also argued that Jesus himself did not want to die, as demonstrated by his prayer in the garden of Gethsemane. Jesus was so anxious about the cross that he was sweating drops of blood. The best explanation of this, we argued, is that he was imploring God to save him from the cross. We coupled this contention with the verse from the epistle to the Hebrews, which reads: "During the days of Jesus' life on earth, he offered up prayers and petitions with fervent cries and tears to the one who could save him from death, and he was heard because of his reverent submission" (Heb. 5:7 NIV).[1] Allah, being a God of mercy who protected his prophets, heard Jesus' prayers and miraculously saved him from death on the cross.

Given that Allah is more than able to save Jesus, and that the biblical records still contained evidence in favor of this theory, we argued that Jesus did not die by crucifixion.

BUT IT WAS MADE TO APPEAR SO

The more common position among Muslims on Jesus' death, however, is often called the Substitution Theory. It is the belief that Jesus' face was placed on someone else. Most often, Muslims argue that this was either Simon of Cyrene, who literally switched places with Jesus as he was carrying the cross to the site of crucifixion, or Judas Iscariot, who justly deserved the punishment for betraying his prophet.

This is a position that cannot be easily defended with historical argumentation, but it is often supplemented with such arguments, primarily criticisms of the biblical report. For example, a common charge is that the Gospels disagree as to what happened when the women went to the tomb on the third day. Mark's gospel depicts a youth dressed in white, Matthew tells of an angel who rolled back the stone, Luke describes two men who appeared next to the women, and John says two angels were sitting where Jesus had been. The disagreement among the Gospels reflects the confusion in each of their reports; the writers did not know what actually happened.

Those Muslims who argue the Theistic Swoon Theory also use these points to supplement their case, and the words of the Quran, "It was made to appear so," also apply to their theory, but in a lesser sense. Allah performed the miracle of preserving Jesus' life, and ultimately it appeared as if Jesus had died, whereas he did not. In the Substitution Theory, the words "it was made to appear so" have a much more active sense. The very miracle that Allah performs is making it appear as if Jesus had died, whereas he actually did not.

CONCLUDING THE MUSLIM RESPONSE

Ultimately, Muslims respond that, despite how it may have appeared, Allah saved Jesus from the cross. He may have done this either by miraculously preserving Jesus' body, as is subtly implied in the Gospels, or he may have done it by substituting Jesus with somebody else. On the whole, the biblical records are not reliable, and therefore there is no good reason to trust their account.

CHAPTER 23

ASSESSING THE ISLAMIC RESPONSE

THE QURAN AND THE HISTORICAL JESUS

Both major Islamic theories regarding Jesus' death on the cross deserve a careful treatment. Let us consider each closely while digging more deeply into the majority belief of the Substitution Theory by considering the context for some of the Quran's teachings about Jesus.

RESPONDING TO THE THEISTIC SWOON THEORY

Before responding to the argument proper, it is worth noting what the verse of the Quran actually says: "And they did not kill him, *nor did they crucify him.*" The verse appears to say he was never even affixed to the cross, but we and other Muslims who argued the Theistic Swoon Theory took the latter clause to mean, "he was not killed by crucifixion." So essentially, we interpreted the verse in this way: "They did not kill him in any way, and they did not kill him by crucifixion." It was a strained interpretation, but pointing out problematic Quranic exegesis does not respond to the argument.

To test the theory, we should isolate its main point: Although Jesus might have died on the cross under natural circumstances, he did not die because God miraculously preserved him. This, of course, is an explanation that requires a miracle, but we have to frequently remind ourselves that we are trying our best to investigate as objective observers. Should an objective observer conclude that such a miracle occurred?[1]

I would argue that an objective observer should not conclude that a miracle has occurred unless there is no other probable explanation, and even then only in special circumstances.[2] In this case, there is another explanation, and it is extremely probable: Jesus died on the cross. For an objective observer to conclude that a miracle occurred in this case, one must believe that Jesus' death on the cross is not even probable. But of course, it is more than probable; it is the obvious explanation.

Regarding the biblical verses cited as subtle traces of God's divine plan, it needs to be pointed out that these verses occur in the context of four Gospels that repeatedly proclaim Jesus prophesied his death and that he did die. To extract verses from their context and say they assert the exact opposite of their context is a poor handling of texts, unless there is good reason to do so.

In this case, not only is there no good reason to do so, but also there is a good reason not to: The verses prophesying and proclaiming Jesus' death are abundant and clear, whereas these "subtle traces" are often solitary and require an unlikely interpretation. One of the basic rules of proper hermeneutics, whether Quranic or biblical or secular, is to interpret unclear statements in light of clear ones, not the other way around. To ignore the clear statements of Jesus' death, and to point to these verses as hints that God saved him, is a poor method of investigation.

Some might point to the Gospels' varying accounts, such as the scene at the empty tomb, as reason to discard the testimony of the Gospels, but that does not logically follow. A conservative Christian might respond that these verses can all be harmonized: In reality, there were two angels at the scene who appeared as young men. All four Gospel accounts are compatible with this understanding, though none of them say it explicitly. But even less conservative investigators who might agree that the accounts of the empty tomb are incompatible do not need to conclude that this somehow negates the uniform testimony of Jesus' death on the cross. That does not logically follow.

In addition, the Theistic Swoon Theory does not cohere with important historical realities. For example, it casts Pilate in a God-fearing light, willing to collude with Jews to save an innocent man. Historically speaking, the opposite appears to be true. Pilate was ruthless and did not hesitate to kill Jews if it meant preserving order and Roman rule. This is true in history, as Josephus records Pilate's willingness to kill innocent Samaritans[3] as well as steal from the temple treasury and beat to death those who protested.[4] And it is true in the Gospels as well, for even though he did not consider Jesus guilty, he ordered him crucified when faced with the threat of treason.

Finally, and very problematic for the careful historian, the Theistic Swoon Theory gives no account for the inception of the Christian church. What was it that drove the early Christians to preach Jesus crucified and resurrected if they had themselves colluded in saving him? Were they liars, or must we discard additional reams of evidence and argue that they did not preach a crucified and resurrected Messiah? Ultimately, this theory requires the investigator to disregard not only all the evidence about Jesus' death but also our entire understanding of early Christianity, though it is formed from dozens of sources. This is an important matter to which we will return in the midway summary after part 8.

RESPONDING TO THE SUBSTITUTION THEORY: THE QURAN AS A SOURCE ON JESUS' LIFE

The Substitution Theory is even less of a historical argument than the Theistic Swoon Theory, and it must be remembered that no objective observer should conclude God conducted a miracle when an obvious explanation is available. Why would anyone argue that Jesus did not die and that God instead transposed Jesus' image onto someone else? In this case, there really is little room for doubt: The basis for this Islamic belief is simply that the Quran asserts this.

To be fair, though, we should assess the potential that the Quran is correct. Do we have good reason to believe the Quran might know something about Jesus that the New Testament missed? Of course, we have to remind ourselves that we are investigating as objective observers, and we cannot start off with the assumption that the Quran is inspired by God.

Unless we can trace the Quran's teachings about Jesus to an earlier time, we have to conclude that it is testimony six hundred years late and over six hundred miles removed, and it is therefore unlikely to tell us anything more accurately than the Gospels, whose accounts come from the lifetime of Jesus' eyewitnesses and from the vicinity of his very community.

But the Quran's teachings about Jesus *can* be traced to an earlier time. Much of what the Quran teaches was taught before. For example, let us consider 5.110: "When Allah says, 'O Jesus, Son of Mary, remember My provision upon you and upon your mother; when I strengthened you with the Holy Spirit and *you spoke to the people while in the cradle* and in maturity; and when I taught you writing and wisdom and the Torah and the Gospel; *and when you made the likeness of a bird from clay, with My permission, then you breathed into it, and it became a bird with My permission*; and you healed the blind and the leper with My permission; and when you brought forth the dead with My permission; and when I restrained the Children of Israel from you . . .'"

We will focus on the two teachings in italics, starting with the latter: the Quran teaches that Jesus miraculously gave life to clay birds. We find no narrative context for this miracle; it is simply provided in a list of Allah's provisions for Jesus.[5] But for those familiar with apocryphal gospels, they will already know the context of this story, because it is famous.

In the middle of the second century, people began to produce stories about Jesus, "fan fiction," if you will, often situating their stories in his mysterious childhood years and focusing on his ability to do miracles. These fictitious gospels are called the infancy gospels. One of the more entertaining examples is the Infancy Gospel of Thomas.

In this infancy gospel, Jesus is five years old and particularly mischievous, often bullying other boys with his supernatural powers. While Jesus was by a mountain stream making puddles, another boy came and released the puddles, so Jesus cursed him and straightaway the boy withered. Later, another boy happened to run past Jesus and bump into his shoulder, so young Jesus cursed the boy, who died immediately. The parents of these boys came to Joseph and told him to control Jesus, at which Jesus struck them blind. When Jesus' tutor tries to teach him respect for elders, five-year-old Jesus rebukes him and begins to teach the teacher instead! Everyone was amazed at what kind of child Jesus was.

It is not until his teacher exclaims in frustration that Jesus must be an angel or God himself that Jesus laughs in approval and heals all the people he cursed. So the story continues, with boy Jesus using his miraculous abilities to curse some people, to cure others, to carry water inside his clothes, or even to fix furniture. His mischief relented whenever people exclaimed that he must be God or an angel of God. In order to give the story an air of reality, the author concludes by tying this story into the gospel of Luke, in which Jesus is twelve years old and in the temple, where the elders were amazed at his knowledge, just as they were in the Infancy Gospel of Thomas.

It is this entertaining fiction that gives us the context for the Quranic teaching that Jesus gave life to clay birds. Early in the story, when a certain Jew saw Jesus making clay birds on the Sabbath, he went to Joseph to accuse Jesus of doing what was unlawful on the sacred day. Knowing that fashioning clay birds on the Sabbath is unlawful, but playing with live birds is not, mischievous little Jesus blew life into the birds so he could get away with his indiscretion. Without providing the context, the Quran refers to this famous account in 5.110, assuming it to be historical truth.

The same verse of the Quran also says that Jesus spoke to people while in the cradle. Sura 19 of the Quran, the chapter named after Mary, gives more details. Verse 23 shows Mary in the throes of childbirth, driven to lean against a palm tree. In her pain, she says, "O, I wish I had died before this!" In response, Jesus, to whom she is giving birth, says, "Do not worry, your Lord has given you a stream beneath you." Shortly thereafter, when her people asked her if she'd had impious relations, she gestured to Jesus implying they should ask him themselves. They respond, "How can we speak to a child in the cradle?" Baby Jesus responds, "Indeed, I am a slave of Allah. He gave me the scripture and made me a prophet."

This account has striking parallels with another infancy gospel, the Arabic Gospel of the Infancy of the Savior, otherwise known as the Arabic Infancy Gospel. In its introduction, after a few historical blunders regarding Joseph and Caiaphas, it says, "Jesus spoke, and, indeed, when He was lying in His cradle said to Mary His mother: I am Jesus, the Son of God, the Logos, whom thou hast brought forth, as the Angel Gabriel announced to thee; and my Father has sent me for the salvation of the world."[6] Baby Jesus' proclamation in the Quran sounds very much like an Islamic version of baby Jesus' proclamation in the Arabic Infancy Gospel.

RESPONDING TO THE SUBSTITUTION THEORY: THE GNOSTIC INFLUENCE ON 4.157

Many other Quranic teachings can be traced to earlier fictional accounts, but the important one for now is the message of 4.157: "He was not killed, nor was he crucified, but so it was made to appear." Is there reason to believe that this teaching predates the Quran, and perhaps is more reliable than the gospel accounts?

As it turns out, another well-known second century source taught exactly this. It is the Gospel according to Basilides,[7] a Gnostic teacher whose school of thought lasted for centuries after his death. The word *Gnostic* refers to secret knowledge, as the Gnostics believed that people needed secret knowledge to be freed from the material world, which is inherently evil.

Irenaeus records what Basilides taught about the death of Jesus on the cross: "He [Christ] did not himself suffer death, but Simon, a certain man of Cyrene, being compelled, bore the cross in his stead; so that this latter being transfigured by him, that he might be thought to be Jesus, was crucified, through ignorance and error, while Jesus himself received the form of Simon, and, standing by, laughed at them."[8]

So Jesus was neither killed nor crucified, but it was made to appear so because he switched faces with Simon of Cyrene. This correlates exactly with the Substitution Theory, the majority interpretation of the Quran. But why did Basilides teach this? Was it because Basilides had access to some historical truth? If so, perhaps the Quran knows something the New Testament does not.

Gnostics had a wide range of beliefs, but one of the most common was that there are many gods that have emanated from the Father, the unborn god. Basilides subscribes to this belief, teaching that the first emanation of the Father is the *nous*, or mind of the Father. That is Jesus, the firstborn god. After other emanations producing lower gods, it was the lowest god who created the material world. According to Basilides, that is the God of the Jews, along with his angels. The Father sent Jesus to deliver Gnostics from the God of the Jews, the creator of this evil world.

Since the material world is evil, Basilides teaches Jesus must not have had a material body, and therefore he could not have been crucified. We find this stated in the passage that immediately follows:

> For since he was an incorporeal power, and the Nous of the unborn father, he transfigured himself as he pleased, and thus ascended to him who had sent him, deriding them, inasmuch as he could not be laid hold of, and was invisible to all. Those, then, who know these things have been freed from the principalities who formed the world; so that it is not incumbent on us to confess him who was crucified, but *him who came in the form of a man, and was thought to be crucified,* and was called Jesus, and was sent by the father, that by this dispensation he might destroy the works of the makers of the world.[9]

So the Quranic teaching about Jesus that "they did not kill him, nor did they crucify him, but so it was made to appear" seems to trace back to a second-century Gnostic source. This late, fictitious gospel is propagating "secret knowledge" to support its polytheistic worldview, not providing historical information about Jesus' life. We can be confident that the account in 4.157 is not the kind that an objective investigator would consider reliable as historical evidence, and therefore we must reject the Substitution Theory.

RESPONDING TO THE SUBSTITUTION THEORY: A FINAL WORD ON CONTEXT

A Muslim investigator, such as I was, might be tempted to respond that the Quranic verses are from Allah, not from these fictitious sources, and that they are historically sound regardless. But as before, I needed to frequently remind myself that I was investigating as an objective observer and could not conclude this without assuming the Quran was inspired. The chronological priority of the fictitious gospels is obvious, as is the fact that their accounts are not historically sound.

But there is an even more powerful reason to challenge that notion. The information in these three passages makes excellent contextual sense in the fictitious gospels but little or no sense in the Quran. In the Infancy Gospel of Thomas, Jesus blew life into clay birds as a miraculous mischief-maker, which fits the context perfectly; in the Arabic Infancy Gospel, he spoke words at birth because he was the eternal Word of God; in the Gospel according to Basilides, he was neither killed nor crucified because he was divine and did not have a material body.

But in the Quran, why does Jesus give life to clay birds? No reason or context is provided; the Quran simply refers to a well-known account. Why can baby Jesus speak at birth? Again, no reason is provided; he just can. Why was Jesus not crucified, and why was someone else made to appear like him? The Quran does not suggest a reason; it simply asserts this secret knowledge as true.

These three accounts fit much better in the context of the fictitious gospels, and given that the Quran is a later source than all of them, we ought to conclude that the Quran's ideas about Jesus come from these late, fictitious sources that are historically unreliable and theologically opposed to Islam.

CHAPTER 24

CONCLUSION

JESUS DIED ON THE CROSS

Leaving Mike's house that evening, I did not change my mind about Jesus' death. One can rarely overturn a lifelong belief overnight. But one thing was becoming clear to me: My belief that Jesus did not die on the cross was based on faith in Islam, not facts of history. Historically speaking, the evidence regarding Jesus' death was categorically in favor of Christianity and against Islam.

Of course, Islam could still be true. If there were other good arguments to believe the Quran, such as the common Muslim arguments for the inspiration of the Quran, and if those arguments outweighed the historical evidence of Jesus' death, then I would be justified in maintaining my faith in the Quran and in Islam. For that reason, as far as my personal beliefs were concerned, I did not falter in my Islamic faith. In my heart I believed that the Quran would be vindicated soon enough.

But, as far as my investigation on this issue was concerned, I recalled my commitment to objectivity and had to be honest with myself. Would an objective observer conclude that Jesus died by crucifixion? Of course, the atheist and agnostic scholars answered that question for us with a resounding voice: Yes, one certainly would. The reasons were overwhelming: The record of Jesus' death appears at lightning speed, it is asserted dozens of times within a hundred years, and the chorus of reports is composed of Christian, Jewish, and Roman voices. No one had ever survived a full Roman crucifixion, and had Jesus done so, that would have been a much more appealing message for the early church to proclaim than was the stumbling block of a crucified Savior.[1]

Islam's responses, the Theistic Swoon Theory and the Substitution Theory, are not plausible, both because they suggest miracles in the face of much more obvious, probable explanations and because they would require a total overhaul of the historical realities of early Christianity, as we will explore further shortly. In addition, as a historical source about Jesus' life, there is very little reason to trust the Quran because it was composed six hundred years after Jesus and more than six hundred miles away from where he lived. Although there are accounts in the Quran that come from an earlier period, those are from late, fictitious gospels that are historically unreliable.

In conclusion, we have to agree with Gerd Lüdemann: "The fact of the death of Jesus as a consequence of crucifixion is indisputable."

PART 7

DID JESUS RISE FROM THE DEAD?

CHAPTER 25

THE POSITIVE CASE

THE BEST EXPLANATION OF THE FACTS

Jesus' death on the cross is not the end of the Christian message. The gospel is that Jesus then rose from the dead. Whereas every other life ended in death, Jesus' death ended in life, and his resurrection is the basis of all Christian confidence. Death is nothing to be feared. Jesus has conquered it, and we are in him.

His resurrection has been the locus of Christian confidence from the inception of the church. In the book of Acts, Luke records the first Christian sermon, in which Peter concludes by proclaiming the resurrection: "God has raised this Jesus to life, and we are all witnesses of it" (Acts 2:32 NIV). In his next recorded sermon, Peter says, "You killed the originator of life, but God raised him from the dead. We are witnesses of this" (Acts 3:15).[1] No fewer than eleven passages in the book of Acts record the early church proclaiming Jesus' resurrection. This was the message that established the early church: Jesus rose from the dead.

But the importance of the resurrection is perhaps stated most clearly by Paul, who says in 1 Corinthians 15:14, "And if Christ has not been raised, our preaching is useless and so is your faith" (NIV). Christian preaching and Christian faith are useless if Jesus remains dead and was not raised. If he did not overcome death, neither will we.

Did Jesus rise from the dead? Do we have good reason to believe in Christ's resurrection? If so, it is a solid foundation for Christian faith. If not, Christians are the most pitiful people of all.[2]

That was what Mike argued about a year after my father and I sat in his living room, but this time, seven hundred other people were listening.

In 2004, Mike Licona debated Shabir Ally, the famous Muslim debater, on the question: "Did Jesus rise from the dead?"[3]

THE MINIMAL FACTS APPROACH

That night, Mike was advancing an argument pioneered by his friend Gary, called the Minimal Facts Approach. The advantages to the argument are that it is powerful, easy to understand, and so simple that it can be stated in one sentence: There are historical facts surrounding Jesus' crucifixion that virtually all historians agree upon, and by far the best explanation of those facts is that Jesus rose from the dead.

To provide some background, Gary had spent thirty years cataloguing the positions of historical Jesus scholars, whether agnostic, atheist, Jewish, Christian, or any other worldview. He read everything published about the historical Jesus in scholarly journals and monographs written in French, English, or German. He noticed that, on some matters, well over 90 percent of scholars were unanimous.[4] While considering those facts, he realized that they were best explained by Jesus' resurrection. By far. Every other explanation either ignored or strained the historical facts surrounding Jesus' death.

Truly, when we consider the task of the historian, it is to do exactly that: provide a narrative model that makes the best sense of the historical records. In this case, the only model that really fits the facts is that Jesus rose from the dead.

Taking the list of facts from Gary, Mike has since whittled it down to three, which we will briefly explore now:

1. Jesus died by crucifixion
2. Jesus' followers truly believed the risen Jesus had appeared to them
3. People who were not followers of Jesus truly believed the risen Jesus had appeared to them

Fact 1: Jesus died by crucifixion. The previous chapter explored Jesus' death by crucifixion in detail. More than any other matter concerning Jesus, historians remain convinced that Jesus' death is a fact of history.

Fact 2: Jesus' followers truly believed the risen Jesus appeared to them.
Historians are also convinced that Jesus' followers came to believe that
they had seen the risen Jesus. Their reasons are manifold.

First, the proclamation appears extremely early in church history.
First Corinthians 15:3–7, the "news flash" Christian creed that reported
Jesus' death within a few years of his crucifixion, also contains a formulation of the people to whom he appeared. It reports "that Christ died
for our sins according to the Scriptures, he was buried, he was raised on
the third day according to the Scriptures, and that *he appeared to Peter,
then to the Twelve, then he appeared to more than five hundred brothers at
the same time, of whom most remain until now, though some have fallen
asleep. Then he appeared to James, then to all the apostles."*

According to the acclaimed and respected scholar James Dunn, "This
tradition, we can be entirely confident, was formulated as tradition within
months of Jesus' death."[5] The teachings that the very first Christians
chose to formulate into creeds and pass on to one another included a list
of people to whom the risen Jesus appeared. Not only is Peter first in this
list, essentially hanging the proclamation on his authority, but also the list
says that Jesus appeared to five hundred people at once.

Second, the proclamation of Jesus' resurrection invites verification
from eyewitnesses. For example, while reporting the above creed about
twenty years after Jesus' death, Paul says that most of the five hundred
eyewitnesses are still alive, as if to say, "If you want to talk to the eyewitnesses of the risen Jesus, there are over 250 to choose from!"

This follows the pattern we find reported in Acts 10:40–41, where
Peter emphasizes they were eyewitnesses: "God raised him from the
dead on the third day and caused him to be seen. He was not seen by
all the people, but by witnesses whom God had already chosen—by us
who ate and drank with him after he rose from the dead" (NIV).[6] Of
course, Luke reports other accounts which emphasize that there were
eyewitnesses of the risen Jesus, such as the very first proclamation of the
gospel found in Acts 2:32, to which we have already referred: "God has
raised this Jesus to life, *and we are all witnesses of it*" (NIV). To Paul,
Peter, and Luke, we can add John's emphasis of being a witness to the
risen Jesus as recorded in John 21:24.

Third, the disciples were willing to die for their belief that the risen Jesus had appeared to them. Of course, being willing to die for a belief does not make that belief true, but it almost always ensures sincerity. People do not often give up their lives for what they know is wrong. In this case, the disciples were willing to die for something that they claimed to have personally seen: the risen Jesus. The martyrdoms of various eyewitnesses are found in recorded history, starting with Stephen's martyrdom (Acts 7:60) and including such high-profile disciples as James the brother of John (Acts 12:2) and Peter himself (1 Clement 5:2–7). Having seen Jesus conquer death, they no longer feared death as they had in the garden of Gethsemane. They truly believed Jesus was risen.

For these three reasons and more, the vast majority of scholars are convinced that Jesus' followers truly believed he had risen from the dead. Accordingly, A. J. M. Wedderburn has said, "It is an indubitable historical datum that sometime, somehow the disciples came to believe that they had seen the risen Jesus."[7]

Fact 3: People who were not Jesus' followers truly believed the risen Jesus appeared to them. Finally, there were some who were not following Jesus that truly believed Jesus had appeared to them after rising from the dead. The first and foremost of these is Saul of Tarsus, also known as Paul. During Jesus' lifetime, Paul was a student of Rabban Gamaliel who was one of the *tannaim*, the most influential teachers of the oral Torah in history. According to tradition, Gamaliel was the grandson of the great Jewish teacher Hillel, the eponymous founder of the school of Jewish thought known as the House of Hillel. With such a noble Jewish pedigree, Paul began persecuting Christians, having the authority and zeal to arrest them and even preside over their executions.

Yet something happened to Paul which led him to join those he persecuted, even giving up his high Jewish rank and position. According to Paul, the risen Jesus appeared to him. In the book of Acts, Luke records Paul sharing his testimony three times, where he makes it clear that he converted on account of having seen the risen Jesus. Paul testifies of this reason himself in 1 Corinthians 15. For his proclamation that Jesus had risen from the dead, he was flogged with lashes five times, beaten with rods three times, stoned until assumed dead, and ultimately beheaded.[8] Paul had many chances to change his mind or repent, but he gave up everything, including his life, testifying that he had personally seen the risen Jesus.

Another key figure that denied Jesus during his life but followed him after the crucifixion is James the brother of Jesus. In Mark's gospel we find Jesus' brothers coming to collect Jesus because they thought he was "out of his mind" (3:21, 31 NIV), and in John's gospel, Jesus' brothers taunt him such that the gospel says "not even his brothers believed him" (7:3–5 NIV). Even as Jesus was being crucified, his brothers did not come to support him, such that their mother Mary had to be entrusted to John's care (John 19:26–27). But then, *after* Jesus' crucifixion, we see his brothers counted among the believers (Acts 1:14). The creed in 1 Corinthians 15 tells us why: The risen Jesus appeared to James (v. 7), who then became a leader of the church in Jerusalem (Gal. 1:19) before being executed by Ananus ben Ananus. Four ancient sources report the execution of James the brother of Jesus, including the Jewish historian Josephus.[9]

So in addition to the disciples, Paul and James—men who were not following Jesus during his lifetime—gave their lives on account of having seen the risen Jesus.[10] The self-described "liberal, modern, secularized"[11] scholar E. P. Sanders says, "That Jesus' followers, and later Paul, had resurrection experiences is, in my judgment, *a fact*."[12] David Catchpole, emeritus professor at the University of Exeter, adds, "The appearance to James was . . . not one that could work from an already existing sympathy or commitment. In that respect it was not dissimilar to what happened later to Paul."[13] To this, scholars Shanks and Witherington add, "It appears that James, like Paul, was a convert to the Jesus movement because at some juncture he saw the risen Jesus, for nothing prior to Easter can explain his having become such a follower of Jesus, much less a leader of Jesus' followers."[14]

FROM FACTS TO ARGUMENT

Let us now summarize the minimal facts. When considering the life of Jesus, we can be very confident of these three conclusions: Jesus died by crucifixion; Jesus' followers truly believed the risen Jesus appeared to them; and people who were not Jesus' followers truly believed the risen Jesus appeared to them.

Given that the task of a historian is to provide a narrative model that makes the best sense of the historical records, what is the best historical conclusion regarding Jesus' life? According to the Minimal Facts Approach, the best explanation of the facts, by far, is that Jesus actually rose from the dead. Every other explanation ignores or strains the facts too much to be plausible.

For example, one of the more common alternative hypotheses is that the disciples hallucinated Jesus' resurrection. It is a well-known medical phenomenon that people recently bereaved of loved ones may hallucinate their presence. Could it be that the disciples, having spent years following Jesus and trusting deeply that he would be their Messiah, were so desperate to see Jesus again that they hallucinated his return?

Jesus' death by crucifixion (fact 1) certainly can fit in this theory, but does the fact that Jesus' followers truly believed they had seen the risen Jesus (fact 2) fit? When we consider that he appeared first to Peter, then to the twelve, and then to five hundred people at once, followed by James, it seems hard to account for all these appearances as bereavement hallucinations. There certainly is no medical parallel for five hundred people having the same bereavement hallucination at the same time. For that reason alone, this hypothesis is highly unlikely. Even if there were an unprecedented five hundred people who had bereavement hallucinations, it seems unlikely that every one of them would be convinced they saw Jesus himself instead of a passing dream.

But for the sake of the argument, let us assume that the hallucination hypothesis accounts for fact 2: his disciples truly believed they had seen him risen, but what they actually saw was a hallucination. Even giving that hypothesis the benefit of the doubt, it simply does not account for fact 3: People who did not follow Jesus truly believed he had appeared to them. Paul does not fit the psychological profile of one who would hallucinate the return of Jesus. He had no emotional attachment to Jesus and no hopes vested in him, and Paul had everything to lose. Why would Paul have hallucinated the risen Jesus? It simply does not fit.

Thus the hallucination hypothesis strains fact 2 and does not fit fact 3. It is not a likely hypothesis.

Another theory is that Jesus' body was stolen by the disciples, and that they promulgated the message of a resurrected Jesus to vindicate their maligned Messiah, though it was a hoax. Fact 1, Jesus' death, fits into this hypothesis, but fact 2 does not: The disciples truly did believe they had seen the risen Jesus. It is not likely that Peter and James and Stephen and others would have died for a known lie, and certainly not so willingly. Of course, the same can be said of fact 3. Paul and James, men who had not followed Jesus during his life, would have no reason to perpetrate this hoax.

The stolen body hypothesis fits neither fact 2 nor fact 3. It is not a likely hypothesis.

The common Muslim response, as we saw in the previous chapter, is that Jesus did not die on the cross. That theory accounts for facts 2 and 3, but it is a direct contradiction of fact 1: that Jesus died by crucifixion. To posit this hypothesis is, again, to go against the facts.

The Swoon Theory does not fit fact 1. It is not a likely hypothesis.

The hypothesis that fits all the facts, and fits them very well, is exactly what the disciples were proclaiming, along with others who were not disciples: Jesus rose from the dead. It is the only explanation that fits the puzzle pieces together.

The resurrection hypothesis accounts for facts 1, 2, and 3. Since it is the one and only hypothesis that explains the historical facts without straining or ignoring them, an objective observer ought to conclude that Jesus' resurrection is by far the best explanation of the data.

MIRACLES AND THE OBJECTIVE OBSERVER

At this point, most non-Christian scholars of the historical Jesus follow Sanders in saying, "What the reality was that gave rise to the experiences

I do not know."[15] Since there is no probable naturalistic explanation, they do not suggest one. That is responsible enough, except that it imposes a naturalist bias—that we cannot conclude a miracle has happened. I would argue that an objective investigator should not have such a bias. We must be open to the idea but be very cautious, not readily jumping to the explanation of a miracle.

It is important to note that in the previous chapter I said, "An objective observer should not conclude that a miracle has occurred unless there is no other probable explanation, and even then only in special circumstances." In the case of the resurrection of Jesus, unlike the Substitution Theory or the Theistic Swoon Theory, there is no other probable explanation. All other conclusions strain credulity. Even though that is the case, it is *still* not enough for an objective observer to conclude a miracle has happened. We need special circumstances; specifically, we need a context charged with supernatural expectation.

For example, let us imagine that a blind man who is rummaging through a cupboard above his head accidentally knocks over a bottle, spilling its contents. Oil pours over his head. As he wipes it away, he finds that he can see again. Should he conclude that a miracle has occurred? I would argue that he should not. Although something extraordinary and inexplicable has happened, one should not automatically conclude that all extraordinary and inexplicable occurrences are miracles.

Now imagine that the same blind man has prayed faithfully for years that his sight be restored. While praying one day, he is convinced that God is leading him to go to a stranger's home. After arguing with himself aloud because he has never heard God speak before, he decides he has nothing to lose, and he makes his way to that home and knocks on the door. The owner of the home comes to the door, and as the man fumbles with words to explain who he is, the owner says, "You don't have to tell us who you are. Just now my family and I were praying together, and we had a strong intuition that God was sending a blind man to us for healing, and that we were to pray for his sight to be restored and to anoint his head with oil." The blind man is seated, and as the family prays for his sight to be restored, they anoint him for healing. Oil pours over his head. As he wipes it away, he finds that he can see again.

In this latter scenario, should the blind man conclude that a miracle has occurred? I would argue that, in the latter case, he is justified in concluding that a miracle has occurred. Even though the physical act is the same in both scenarios—oil pouring over his head—the latter scenario is charged with supernatural expectation. On account of the context, it is not unreasonable to conclude he has experienced a miracle.

Furthermore, if the circumstances can be verified by an investigator, the investigator also ought to conclude that a miracle has occurred. Let us imagine that the man's praying and arguing with God were caught on surveillance video, as were the family's prayer session and anointing with oil, with the result that the blind man can now see. Not only can an objective investigator responsibly conclude that a miracle has happened, *it is his duty to do so*. Otherwise, he is not being objective but is importing a naturalist bias.

In the same way, if something extraordinary and inexplicable has happened in history, and that extraordinary event is charged with supernatural expectation, and there are solid historical facts surrounding the event that have no other probable explanation, a historian can reasonably conclude that a miracle has indeed happened.

CONCLUSION

As a Muslim observing Mike's debate, I had to agree that if Jesus really did die on the cross, there was excellent reason to believe he rose from the dead. Historically speaking, the three facts are indisputable: Jesus died by crucifixion, his disciples truly believed they had seen him risen, and even men who were not his disciples truly believed they had seen him risen. Nothing accounts for these facts without strain apart from the resurrection hypothesis, and even as objective observers, the spiritually charged context allows us to conclude that a miracle has happened. Along with the early church, history testifies that Jesus rose from the dead.

But despite what history indicated, I was not yet convinced Jesus actually died on the cross. There was one other matter that I and the Muslim world around me found not just problematic but highly offensive.

CHAPTER 26

THE ISLAMIC RESPONSE

ALL PAUL'S FAULT

After Mike presented the minimal facts for Jesus' resurrection, Shabir Ally took the stage to defend the Islamic stance. He responded primarily by challenging fact 1, asserting that we cannot be sure Jesus died by crucifixion. Not only was this an understandable response on account of 4.157 of the Quran, but it was actually the expected response. Muslims are normally less concerned with the supernatural implications of the resurrection than with the physical death of Jesus in the first place.

Part of the reason why is because, along with Christians, most Muslims believe in Jesus' ascension. Immediately after denying Jesus' death on the cross, the Quran says in 4.158, "Rather, Allah raised him toward himself." On account of this belief, the average Muslim does not immediately conceive of the resurrection as a problem, usually assuming it to be a corollary of the Christian misunderstanding that Jesus died on the cross. According to the average Muslim, yes, Jesus was raised to heaven, but no, he did not first die on the cross. It was not a resurrection but an ascension.

For these reasons, of the hundreds of Muslim-Christian dialogues I have seen and taken part in, first as a Muslim and then as a Christian, Muslims make a robust effort to challenge Jesus' death but generally leave the rest of the case for the resurrection untouched. Apart from what was discussed in chapter 22, there is no common response to the arguments for the resurrection, with one significant exception.

MUSLIMS AND PAUL

Since the Quran teaches that Jesus was a prophet and that his followers were righteous men, we regarded Jesus' disciples with high esteem.
According to 3.52, the disciples answered Jesus' call to righteously follow Allah, and in 3.55, Allah promises to exalt Jesus' followers, making
them superior to others until the Day of Resurrection.[1]

That said, Muslims today recognize that Christian teachings are
diametrically opposed to Islamic doctrine. Christianity teaches that
God became a man and died on the cross for our sins—doctrines that
Muslims consider inconceivable and blasphemous. So, from our perspective as a Muslim community, Christian teachings had been corrupted.

But when were they corrupted? When we trace these beliefs back,
we find that they were the beliefs of the *earliest* church. Therefore,
Muslims have to believe that somehow, during the time of the disciples
themselves, the early church was infiltrated and its message corrupted.
This had to be the work of someone powerful, someone other than the
disciples.

There is only one obvious figure who fits that description: Paul.

It is for this reason that Paul's motives, character, and authority are
called into question. It was Paul who took the religion taught by Jesus
and turned it into the religion about Jesus. In the debate with Mike,
Shabir Ally described mainstream Christianity as a Pauline invention.
"Later Christianity would follow the line of Paul," argues Ally. "There
was tension between Paul and the original disciples of Jesus and the
family of Jesus, so Paul was celebrated and the family and disciples of
Jesus were denigrated." Ally implies that the disagreements Paul had
with Peter and James are evidence of a schism in early Christianity
wherein the Pauline version ultimately won.

A second common and important argument is that Jesus told his
disciples to follow the Law, whereas Paul said the Law has been abolished. The evidence for this position is found by highlighting Matthew
5:17, in which Jesus says, "Do not think that I have come to abolish
the Law or the Prophets; I have not come to abolish them but to fulfill
them" (NIV). This verse seems to imply that Jesus has come to uphold

198 Did Jesus Rise from the Dead?

the Law, but Paul says in Romans 3:28, "For we maintain that a person is justified by faith apart from the works of the law" (NIV). Therefore, Muslims say Paul contradicts Jesus.

There are many other common challenges to Paul that Muslims suggest, but the third and final one we will cover here is one of the most significant. Muslims often argue that Paul never saw Jesus, and that he rarely comments on the historical Jesus in his letters. Therefore, Paul must not have been concerned about who Jesus actually was, but rather was interested in turning Jesus into the Son of God, even God himself.

This has been but a quick foray into the reasons why Muslims distrust Paul and consider him to be the corrupter of true Christianity and the founder of the blasphemous religion that worships a man and ignores God's law—that is, today's mainstream Christianity. This view is espoused by Muslim apologists and imams worldwide, and it filters down unabated to the average Muslim, as it did to me. In truth, almost every single Muslim-Christian conversation about early Christianity I have heard comes to a gridlock on the person of Paul. It is hard to exaggerate how much Muslims distrust Paul and how much they hold him accountable for the shape of Christianity today.

CONCLUSION OF THE ISLAMIC RESPONSE TO THE RESURRECTION

Not only do Muslims disagree that Jesus actually died on the cross, they consider the entire foundation of Christianity to be questionable because a man who was not a disciple and who never even saw Jesus successfully infiltrated the ranks and hijacked the early church. The religion taught by Jesus became the religion about Jesus, and what was a religion about following God's law and worshiping God alone became a religion that ignored the law and worshiped a man alongside God. Though Christianity originally looked much more like Islam, it has been lost forever because of Paul.

CHAPTER 27

ASSESSING THE ISLAMIC RESPONSE

PAUL AND THE DISCIPLES IN PROPER PERSPECTIVE

To be fair, the Muslim challenge to Paul is not entirely unwarranted. He is a very surprising character in the early church with an equally surprising degree of influence. Can we really trust Paul? If Paul never met Jesus before the crucifixion, how could he accurately relay the religion taught by Jesus? Might today's Christianity be a Pauline product?

This question became a popular one in academic circles during the 1980s, and a few Western scholars even answered it affirmatively. Perhaps the most notable such response was by the Jewish scholar and dramatist Hyam Maccoby in his 1986 book, *The Mythmaker: Paul and the Invention of Christianity*. Maccoby goes as far as saying it was Paul who founded Christianity.[1] Arguments similar to his were popularized by the equally idiosyncratic Karen Armstrong, a favorite of many Muslim apologists, who said, "Paul has not only been an important influence on Christianity, but . . . in a very real sense he was its founder. He could be called the first Christian."[2]

On account of efforts such as theirs, this view became a hot topic of discussion in university forums, but the dust settled quickly and the victory was decisive: Paul remained a follower of Christ, not the founder of Christianity. The scholarly consensus has remained firm ever since.[3]

With all this in mind, it goes without saying that this is a good question that deserves much more space to cover than we have here, so we will answer the question of Paul broadly and briefly. After that we will consider the particular problem that this challenge to Paul causes for the Islamic view of Jesus's disciples before finally recentering this discussion on Jesus' resurrection.

EXAMINING PAUL

Part of the reason why almost no scholar today agrees with the common Muslim characterization of Paul is that it depicts him as a usurping deceiver. I recall an imam at our mosque teaching us that Paul saw a power vacuum among the disciples after Jesus died, so he infiltrated the church and climbed the ranks to take over the reins. The problem with this portrayal is obvious to those who know Paul's background: He was far more secure in his power as a student of Gamaliel, in the line of Hillel, than he would have been in the persecuted church. He already had the authority to arrest heretics and preside over executions, and his power would only have grown. Instead he chose the meek life of a persecuted man who labored for his wages (Acts 18:3).

That Islamic portrayal of Paul as a deceiver is also doubtful because Paul was sincere enough to die for his faith. The record of his martyrdom comes within a few years of his beheading, and scholars do not doubt it.[4] As we explored before, people willing to go to their deaths for their beliefs may very well be mistaken, but they are almost certainly sincere. According to the records, Paul was lashed five times, beaten with rods three times, and even stoned until assumed dead before he was ultimately executed (2 Cor. 11:24–25). If he were simply deceiving people, he had ten opportunities to repent before receiving life-threatening punishments. Would he not have given up the charade? What was there to gain by deceiving everyone if he was about to lose his life? In truth, Paul gave up power, prestige, personal safety, and even his life. He did not receive any material gain by following Jesus.

Paul, the Jewish Law, and the Authority of the Disciples

It is true that Paul had an argument with Peter, as recorded in Galatians 2:11–14, but it is important to read the context. Paul informs us that shortly after his conversion, he went to Peter and stayed with him for fifteen days. After sitting under Peter and at times James the brother of Jesus, Paul went from city to city proclaiming the gospel for fourteen years. Then, to make sure he was still preaching according to the disciples' teaching, he traveled back to Jerusalem and *submitted his preaching to the disciples*. After hearing him, *Peter, James, and John gave him their approval* and sent him on his way back to Antioch saying that he should preach to the Gentiles while they preached to the Jews in Jerusalem. All the while, Paul refers to the disciples as "pillars" of the church and those of "high esteem" (Gal. 2:6, 9 NIV).

The argument only occurs when Peter was placed in a new situation and, so as not to offend some people, he acted with double standards. Leaving Jerusalem, where he was a preacher to the Jews and the church was full of believers from Jewish backgrounds, Peter traveled to Antioch in Syria, "the headquarters of Gentile Christianity."[5] Although the law of the Jews forbade them from eating with Gentiles, Peter was willing to eat with the Gentiles because he no longer considered the law binding (Gal. 2:12; cf. Acts 10; 15:10–11). But when believers from a Jewish background came to Antioch from Jerusalem,[6] Peter did not want to offend them, so he stopped eating with the Gentiles. This, understandably, caused problems in Antioch, and Paul corrected Peter for his double standard.[7]

Virtually none of this account fits with the common Muslim characterization of Paul. It was Paul who first went to Peter and stayed with him and James. Later, Paul submitted what he was teaching to the disciples and continued preaching only when he received their approval. These are not the actions of someone who is trying to subvert the church, but rather those of a man who is submitting himself to the authority of the disciples.

When it comes to the Jewish law, it was Peter who gave his approval for Paul to be a minister to the Gentiles, and it was Peter who did not consider Christians to be under the law, such that he ate with the Gentiles. The only measure that Paul used to argue with Peter was Peter himself: Peter had been willing to eat with the Gentiles at one time but refused to do so at another. Paul never attempted to invoke any authority over Peter but questioned Peter by his own standards: "If you, being a Jew, live like Gentiles and not like Jews, how can you compel the Gentiles to live like Jews?" (Gal. 2:14).

According to the book of Acts, it was Peter himself who inaugurated the preaching of the gospel to the Gentiles. The tenth chapter of Acts shares the story of Peter's receiving a vision to preach to the Gentiles and then being led by God to Caesarea to do exactly that. While preaching to Cornelius and those with him, Peter says, "You are well aware that it is against our law for a Jew to associate with or visit a Gentile. But God has shown me that I should not call anyone impure or unclean" (Acts 10:28 NIV). It was this encounter that Peter invoked in Acts 15:7–11 when Peter himself suggested that Gentiles not be bound by the law.[8]

So Paul does not rebel against Peter and James. Rather, he submits to their authority. When there is need to correct Peter, Paul does not dare invoke his own authority but reminds Peter of his own standards. Finally, Paul is not the one who absolves Gentiles of following the law; that is Peter, the very disciple who ushered in the era of evangelizing the Gentiles.

Jesus Came to Fulfill the Law

So if Peter and Paul are in agreement that people are not bound by the law, what should we make of Jesus' words in Matthew 5:17 when he says, "Do not think that I have come to abolish the Law or the Prophets; I have not come to abolish them but to fulfill them" (NIV)? Does this mean that Jesus has come to follow the Law and expects his followers to do the same?

The first thing to note is Jesus says he has come to "fulfill" the Law and the Prophets. Not "follow" but "fulfill." The Greek word here, *pleroo*, has the senses of *fullness* and *bringing to an end*, just as the word *fulfill* does in English. When someone fulfills something, it is finished and one is no longer bound to it. For example, if we take a loan, we are bound to make regular payments, but once we have fulfilled our loan, having paid it in full, our payments are brought to an end. In the same sense, Jesus is saying, "I am not cancelling the Law and the Prophets; I am their fulfillment, bringing them to their completion and finishing them." To say that "fulfilling" the Law and the Prophets means to "follow" the Jewish law is to misunderstand the verbiage of Matthew 5:17 and to miss its meaning.

Secondly, when Jews referred to the Law and the Prophets in this way, they were referring to the books of the Old Testament, not the commandments of the Jewish law. Remember, the Hebrew Bible is composed of the Law and the Prophets and the Writings. So Jesus is here saying he has come to fulfill the Old Testament, not to follow commandments.

Drawing these insights together, we can understand the verse more correctly: Jesus is saying that the Old Testament finds its completion in him. He is not abolishing it but completing it. The Old Testament is being fulfilled because Jesus has come.

There is more to say about these rich verses, especially since the verses immediately following Matthew 5:17 are sometimes thought to enforce the notion that Jesus expected people to follow the Jewish law. A careful reading shows that is not the case.[9] It should also be noted that in the Sermon on the Mount, Jesus teaches some ethics that go directly against Jewish law, such as not taking oaths.[10] Elsewhere in Matthew, Jesus says a few times that he has come to bring something new, not to simply follow the old (Matt. 9:16–17; 13:52).

So Peter's teaching that people are not bound by the law are teachings that Paul consistently applied to the Gentiles, and they are entirely compatible with Jesus' message.

Paul and the Historical Jesus

The last challenge concerning Paul that we will cover is the assertion that Paul, never having seen Jesus, was less concerned with the historical Jesus than he was in turning Jesus into the Son of God, even God himself.

Although commonly assumed, it is not certain that Paul never saw Jesus during Jesus' earthly ministry, because this is a conclusion mostly based on silence.[11] It is true that Paul does not often talk about the historical Jesus in the New Testament. But this does not mean he was unconcerned with the life of Jesus. After seeing the risen Jesus, Paul went to visit Peter for fifteen days (Gal. 1:18). What are we to assume Paul and Peter did during those two weeks? As the scholar C. H. Dodd famously put it, "We may presume they did not spend all the time talking about the weather."[12] Paul learned about the historical Jesus while sitting under the authority of Peter. In fact, the word Paul uses for his meeting with Peter is *historeo*, the very Greek word from which the English word *history* derives. He was keenly interested in the historical Jesus.

So why do we not see Paul talking more about Jesus' life in his letters? In fact, he does talk about the historical Jesus, most notably in the book of 1 Corinthians where he paraphrases Jesus' words or discusses Jesus' life a total of six times.[13] In addition, some of the accounts Paul relays about Jesus' life indicate that he knew much more that he did not say in his letters, such as the words "on the night he was betrayed" (1 Cor. 11:23 NIV). One could hardly imagine that Paul would say these words without knowing what actually did happen on the night Jesus was betrayed. Yet Paul never actually talks about the details in his letters.

Which leads to the second, more important point: Letters are not meant to be comprehensive, especially letters between close relations. I have written fewer than a dozen letters to my wife, and if people were to read those letters assuming they contained everything I ever wanted to tell her, they would be sorely disappointed. I have a strong relationship with my wife, and we talk with each other for hours every day. What has been said in person will go unsaid in written communication, and usually only emergent matters are stated in letters, while the most established matters have already been stated in person. In the same way, Paul personally knew those to whom he wrote his letters, and he spent weeks, at times years, in their company. To expect something different of Paul's letters is to burden them with unrealistic expectations.[14]

So we can conclude Paul was very much interested in the actual life of Jesus, not just the theological Jesus. The question of whether Paul turned Jesus into the Son of God, or perhaps even God himself, will be explored more fully in the next chapter.

Summarizing Paul

There is little reason to doubt Paul's sincerity. He received his teaching from Peter, and he submitted to Peter's authority. He followed Peter in teaching that the Gentiles did not need to follow the law, a corollary of Jesus' teaching implicit in Matthew 5:17. Even though Paul did not know Jesus during Jesus' ministry, we can be confident that Paul learned about the historical Jesus from Peter and knew much that he did not mention in his letters. The common Muslim assertion that Paul hijacked Christianity, imposed his own teachings, and corrupted the true religion not only goes against the biblical records but also is unwarranted from a historical point of view and enjoys very little scholarly support.

But beyond this, there is a theological problem for Muslims who would argue that Paul corrupted Christianity.

THE PROBLEM WITH THE ISLAMIC VIEW OF PAUL

The common Muslim view of Paul has significant problems even when considered from an Islamic perspective. First, what happened to the disciples? How were they so easily overcome by Paul that either they were convinced by his trickery and followed him, or their voices were completely drowned out and there is no record of their dissent? Was this outsider that much more powerful than Jesus that he was able to undo all of Jesus' work and teachings? As a Muslim, I never provided a model as to how this might have occurred, and I have never heard one after leaving Islam.

The problem becomes sharper when we revisit one of the Quranic verses that makes a promise to Jesus: "Indeed, I will cleanse you (Jesus) from those who disbelieve, and I will make those who follow you superior to those who disbelieve, until the day of resurrection" (3.55).[15] Allah promises to make the disciples superior to disbelievers, and Jesus would be made free from such disbelievers. The Muslim view of Paul, that he overcame the disciples and hijacked Jesus' message, seems to ignore the Quran's promise to the disciples.

It would be helpful if the Quran had something to say about Paul, but it says absolutely nothing, never so much as mentioning his name. Given the pivotal role Muslims often think Paul had in corrupting Christianity, the silence is deafening. Why does the Quran not mention him? Is it on account of the Quran's omission that Muslims in the early and classical periods of Islam, such as Tabari and Qurtubi, saw Paul as a follower of Jesus?[16]

In US criminal law, as in other places around the world, three aspects of a crime must be established before a suspect can be found guilty: a means, a motive, and an opportunity. The Islamic view that Paul hijacked Christianity fails to secure any of these three. Paul could not have had the means because Allah promised to make the disciples insuperable; there is no viable motive for Paul to deceive the church as his efforts earned him only persecution and a death sentence; and there is no model suggested that clarifies how Paul might have had an opportunity to overcome all the disciples and hijack the church. Of course, not only should Paul be considered innocent until proven guilty, but as far as this investigation is concerned, there simply is no evidence to convict him. Case closed.

RECENTERING ON THE RESURRECTION

Finally, let us return to the original question: Did Jesus rise from the dead? The truth is, even if we disregard Paul entirely, we still have good reason to think Jesus rose from the dead. The disciples preached Jesus' resurrection many times in the book of Acts, and their conviction that Jesus rose from the dead is the best explanation for their transformation from fearful followers in the garden of Gethsemane to bold martyrs at the hands of the Romans and others. They no longer feared death because Jesus had defeated death. The same is true for James, Jesus' unbelieving brother, who was willing to pay the ultimate price after seeing the risen Jesus. These records are found in the Gospels, the book of Acts, the Johannine epistles, 1 Peter, Hebrews, 1 Clement, Josephus, and elsewhere. In order to effectively argue against the resurrection from an Islamic perspective, one would have to do more than just discredit the Pauline accounts.

Jesus' resurrection encompassed the disciples. It was their initial catalyst, their core message, their driving conviction, and their ultimate hope. To deny this through an Islamic perspective, one which respects Jesus and the disciples as men of God, is to overlook everything we know about the inception of the church.

CHAPTER 28

CONCLUSION

JESUS ROSE FROM THE DEAD

At the end of the debate, my friend David and I discussed what we thought of the Christian defense of the resurrection and the Islamic critique. We ended up sitting in his car for a few hours in the parking lot, processing thoughts and mulling over the arguments. There was no question in my mind that Shabir Ally was the more polished speaker and the better debater, and that he did an excellent job of winning over the crowd.

But when I considered the arguments carefully, even as a Muslim, I had to conclude that Mike's Minimal Facts Approach was more compelling than Shabir's critique. History certainly seemed to testify that Jesus died by crucifixion, that his followers then honestly believed they had seen him risen, and that even some who were not his followers honestly believed they had seen him risen. Mike suggested that the best explanation for these historical facts was that Jesus rose from the dead.

Shabir did not suggest a better alternative. Rather, Shabir tried to discard data that did not fit the Islamic perspective: Jesus' death and Paul's reliability. When we consider the arguments that Muslims commonly use to discredit Paul's testimony, we find that they are very problematic. There is no reason to think that Paul was insincere; the evidence indicates that he submitted to the authority of the disciples, that Peter was the one who suggested new Christians not be bound to the Law; and it was indeed Peter, James, and John who extended their hand to Paul in his ministry to the Gentiles. The common Islamic characterization of Paul as the one who hijacked Christianity not only ignores Allah's promises in the Quran but also fails to provide a motive or a means for Paul's corruption of the church, and it requires a wholesale disregard for the records of the early church's history.

So when answering the question I had set out for myself, "Would an objective observer conclude that Jesus rose from the dead?" I had to admit that Jesus' resurrection was indeed the best explanation of the historical facts. Mike's explanation of the evidence was much more convincing than Shabir's selective rejection of the evidence.

But just as when I had investigated Jesus' death, my conclusion did not compel me to leave Islam. I believed that my Islamic faith would be vindicated by other means, and that the Christian faith still had at least one fatal flaw: Jesus never claimed to be God.

This, for me, was the critical point. As far as I was concerned, Jesus' death and resurrection were important matters to investigate, but whether Jesus claimed to be God was the real game changer. I was ready to pull out all the stops to defend my faith and prove that he did not.

PART 8

DID JESUS CLAIM TO BE GOD?

CHAPTER 29

THE POSITIVE CASE

JESUS WAS ALWAYS GOD

At no point is the schism between Christian and Islamic theologies broader than on the person of Jesus. For Muslims, the doctrine of a divine Christ is anathema, and the Quran teaches that he who subscribes to it will make his home in the flames of hell (5:72). For the Christian, belief in the lordship of Christ is necessary for salvation (Rom. 10:9). What wider divergence could there be?

As a Muslim in the West, I very proudly saw myself as a real monotheist who respected Jesus appropriately. By contrast the Christians around me were, whether wittingly or unwittingly, blaspheming the one true God and insulting Jesus by deifying him. All other differences between Muslims and Christians were secondary to me, far less important than this most significant matter. In fact, I even boldly told Christians that Islam was superior to Christianity simply on account of this issue. "Islam is the true monotheism," was the motto we heard at mosques.

The Quran informs Muslims that Jesus never claimed to be divine. Rather, people began to believe this after Jesus left the earth (5.116–117). So we believed that later Christians were responsible for corrupting the true Christianity. Learned men at our mosque told me that Roman paganism influenced Christian thought, as Roman gods often had sons who were demigods. Other Muslims argued that the Council of Nicaea was responsible for Jesus' apotheosis, while yet others accused Paul of this blasphemy. Regardless of the exact model, most of us believed that the Bible did not even depict Jesus as God, and certainly Jesus never claimed to be God himself.

But did he? If we put aside our Islamic beliefs and ask the question as objective observers, will we conclude that Jesus claimed to be God? Based on my own experience, the answer is an arresting, revolutionizing yes. More than anything else, investigating this question has changed my life forever.

My greatest opponent in discovering the answer was my own will. I did not want to see Jesus' claim to deity in the pages of history, so I kept retreating and altering my position to avoid what was becoming more and more obvious. While I cannot trace all the points of this internal fencing competition, I will provide the conclusion of each major bout.

DOES THE NEW TESTAMENT TEACH THAT JESUS IS GOD?

At the outset, I was unsure whether the New Testament said anywhere that Jesus is God. I remember watching a Muslim speaker, Hamza Abdul Malik, challenge Christians by saying the teaching is not found anywhere in the Bible. But then I watched a debate between him and the Christian debater James White, and the matter was thoroughly settled: Apart from anything that could potentially be obscured, 2 Peter 1:1 (NIV) calls Jesus "God and Savior," as does Titus 2:13.[1]

DO THE GOSPELS TEACH THAT JESUS IS GOD?— JOHN'S GOSPEL

Of course, Muslims owe no allegiance to the Bible as a whole, nor even the New Testament. The Quran says that the *Injil* was revealed as the Word of God, the gospel. I quickly staked my claim that, regardless of what the other books of the Bible said, Jesus is not God in the Gospels. It was then that my friend David pointed me to the gospel of John.

There can be no doubt that Jesus is presented as divine in this Gospel. From the outset, John emphatically declares that Jesus is God, that he has always existed, and that he is the very means of all creation (1:1–3). Thus the first three verses of John's gospel introduce Jesus as "God, the Eternal One through whom the universe was created." John's prologue concludes by calling Jesus "the only begotten God" (1:18).

As John's gospel progresses, the Christology is unpacked and elaborated. Jesus is worthy of the honor due to God (5:23); he asks people to have faith in him as they have faith in God (14:1); he claims to be the enabler of salvation (5:21) and the earthly manifestation of God (14:8); he is the king of another world (18:36–37); he assumes dominion over all things (3:35); and he claims to be able to do whatever people ask in his name after he is gone, more or less implying that he has omniscience, omnipotence, and omnipresence (14:13). In addition, he admonishes his opponents that his identity is central to salvation (8:24) and that he perpetually preexists Abraham (8:58), in both of these cases using the divine name of Yahweh from the Old Testament, the "I Am."[2] In what some consider the climax of the gospel, a disciple realizes who he is and exclaims in affirmation, "My Lord and my God!"[3] to which Jesus responds, "Because you have seen me, you have believed; blessed are those who have not seen and yet have believed" (20:28–29 NIV). The height of John's gospel is a disciple proclaiming that Jesus is God, and Jesus' commending his affirmation. From the first to the last, John's gospel identifies Jesus as divine.[4]

This discovery was a jolt to my Islamic confidence. If Jesus actually claimed to be God, then the Quran was wrong about Jesus, which in turn meant that Islam was false. I could not concede this point, so I had to find a way out.

DO THE GOSPELS TEACH THAT JESUS IS GOD?— THE BEGINNING OF MARK'S GOSPEL

After some research, I found that there was a famous scholar, Bart Ehrman, who was critical of Christianity and argued that John's gospel was unreliable. "Jesus, beyond doubt in John's gospel, is portrayed as divine,"[5] remarks Ehrman; but because John was written sixty years after Jesus, it need not be accurate.[6] The belief that Jesus was God was invented after his death, in the decades between Jesus and the writing of John's gospel. That is why it is not found in the other gospels. If Jesus himself had claimed to be God, why do we have to wait until the fourth gospel to hear about it?

That Jesus was deified after his death was what we believed as Muslims, and I found Islamic websites quoting Ehrman regularly. I decided to adopt his approach, arguing that, had Jesus actually claimed to be God, we would have found his deity taught in the first of the four gospels, Mark.[7] So I set out to show David that Mark presented Jesus as just a man, not God, and I immersed myself in Mark's gospel.

The more I learned about Mark, the more I realized that it was a very Jewish gospel, written with the Old Testament in mind. It refers to Jewish sources over seventy times, with a strong preference for the book of Isaiah, and never once does it explicitly refer to a Graeco-Roman source.[8] When I read Mark through that lens, the lens of Hebrew Scripture, I realized that Ehrman was terribly mistaken. Not only does Mark present Jesus as divine, but the very point of Mark's gospel is that Jesus is Yahweh.

Mark starts with a reference to a passage in the Old Testament: Isaiah 40:3–5. In that passage, "a voice calls out in the wilderness, 'prepare the way for Yahweh! Make straight a highway in the desert for our God! . . . The Presence of Yahweh will appear.'" So Isaiah prophesies that Yahweh, the God of Israel, will appear, and a voice in the wilderness will proclaim his arrival. Mark tells us in 1:4 that John the Baptist is that voice in the wilderness, and the one whose arrival John proclaimed was Jesus. In other words, Mark equates Yahweh with Jesus, saying: We have been waiting for a man to proclaim the arrival of Yahweh, our God. John the Baptist is that man, and he has proclaimed the arrival of Jesus.

In fact, Mark combines his reference to Isaiah 40:3–5 with Malachi 3:1, where the text says explicitly that the messenger (again, John the Baptist) will appear before the Lord himself comes to his temple.[9] As in the Isaiah reference, this equates the Lord with Jesus. For added emphasis, the book of Malachi ends a few verses later by saying that if the Israelites do not accept the messenger, God himself will come.[10]

Thus, at the very beginning of his gospel, Mark equates Yahweh with Jesus, using multiple Old Testament references. For the attentive Jewish reader, Mark's prologue functions very much like John: It proclaims that Jesus is God himself.

Mark continues in 2:3–10, telling us that Jesus forgave a paralyzed man his sins. The Scribes at the scene thought to themselves, "He's blaspheming. Who can forgive sins but God alone?" (NIV). For the Jews, to blaspheme against God is an accusation that someone is not giving God his due respect, most commonly by saying the name *Yahweh* or by claiming divine status for oneself.[11] Clearly, Jesus neither insulted God here nor uttered the divine name. Their charge of blasphemy can mean only that Jesus thought himself to be God by claiming the divine prerogative of forgiving sins.[12]

In response, far from denying that he claimed to be God, Jesus showed them his authority to forgive sins by healing the paralytic. Not only did this demonstrate his spiritual authority, but also it reminded the Scribes, who knew well the Hebrew Scriptures, of Psalm 103:2–3, which says, "O my soul, bless Yahweh and do not forget all his deeds! *He is the one forgiving all your sins and healing all your diseases.*"[13] When Scribes charge Jesus with claiming to be God, instead of denying it, he goes even further by healing a paralytic, thereby doing what only Yahweh does in the Psalms.

Later in the same chapter, referring to himself, Jesus says, "The Son of Man is Lord even of the Sabbath" (Mark 2:28 NIV). Unless we know the Old Testament well, it is easy to miss the fact that the Sabbath is the fourth of the Ten Commandments (Ex. 20:8). When Jesus refers to himself as Lord of the Sabbath, he is claiming lordship over the Ten Commandments, even though there is only one such Lord: Yahweh.

In Mark 4:35–41, we find the troubled disciples out on the water in the midst of a storm with waves so high they broke over the boat and began to flood it. Amid adversity they call out to Jesus. Jesus rebukes the wind and says to the waves, "Hush! Be calm!" whereupon the sea is calmed and waves are hushed (v. 39). The disciples ask themselves in amazement, "Who then is this that even the wind and the sea obey him?" (v. 41). By now, we should realize that Mark expects us to answer these rhetorical questions by turning to the Old Testament. In Psalm 107:25–30, men are on a stormy sea so perilous that their courage has melted and they are at their wits' end. "Then they cried out to the Yahweh in their distress, and he brought them out of their troubles: He calmed the storm, and the waves were hushed" (vv. 28–29).

So in the Old Testament, when men are caught in a storm at sea and fearing death, they call out to *Yahweh*, who calms the storms and hushes the waves. In Mark, when the disciples are caught in a storm at sea and fearing death, they call out to *Jesus*, who calms the storms and hushes the waves. Once again, Mark equates Jesus with Yahweh.

In another seafaring passage, Mark 6:45–52, the disciples are struggling to row against the wind. Amid the stormy waves, Jesus walks to them on the water. For those who know the Old Testament, the allusion is clear: In Job 9:8, when Job is speaking about Yahweh, he says, "He alone stretches out the heavens and treads on the waves of the sea" (NIV). What Job says only Yahweh can do, Mark shows Jesus doing.

Having discussed the highlights of Mark 1–6, we see Mark's endeavor is clear: He portrays Jesus as Yahweh. But regardless of the clarity and multiple allusions, I was not yet convinced. What convinced me that Mark portrayed Jesus as Yahweh was the climax of the gospel—Jesus' trial.

DO THE GOSPELS TEACH THAT JESUS IS GOD?— THE CLIMAX OF MARK'S GOSPEL

In Mark 14:55–64, Jesus has been brought before the high priest and the Sanhedrin. Those who brought Jesus to this trial have been seeking to destroy him since a time early in his ministry (3:6). They hope to incriminate him through his words against the temple, but without sufficient witnesses or a consistent accusation against him, the trial is going awry (14:55–59). Then the high priest stands and demands that Jesus tell them who he is. It appears the high priest hopes Jesus can be incriminated through his identity claims. When Jesus responds, he gives the Sanhedrin more than they hoped for.

Jesus' words are: "I am, and you will see the Son of Man sitting at the right hand of the power and coming with the clouds of heaven." The meaning of his words will not be clear to us if we do not know the Old Testament, but for the Jewish Sanhedrin, it was so clear that they condemned him to death for blasphemy. What exactly did Jesus say?

In Mark 14:62, Jesus makes a twofold reference to the Old

Testament, claiming the privileges and position of Yahweh for himself. The first reference is to Daniel. Jesus quotes Daniel 7:13–14, an apocalyptic vision of the prophet Daniel, which states, "In my vision at night I looked, and there before me was one like a son of man, coming with the clouds of heaven. He approached the Ancient of Days and was led into his presence. He was given authority, glory and sovereign power; all nations and peoples of every language worshiped him. His dominion is an everlasting dominion that will not pass away, and his kingdom is one that will never be destroyed" (NIV).

In this passage from Daniel, a being who looks human (one like a son of man) approaches God. Although he looks human, his entrance is on clouds—an entrance reserved for Yahweh in the Old Testament.[14] Then the one like a son of man is given everlasting dominion, glory, and a kingdom, even though only God is supposed to have dominion and glory in the everlasting kingdom. Finally, this passage says that all people will serve the Son of Man, but this word *serve*, whether in Aramaic or in Greek, always denotes a service due to God.

Thus, Daniel 7 introduces a son of man who rides the clouds, as only Yahweh can; he then receives everlasting dominion and glory over his own kingdom, as only Yahweh has; there, all people will serve him with a divine service, as only Yahweh deserves. The son of man in Daniel 7 is a divine Son of Man. Throughout the gospel of Mark, starting at 2:10, Jesus calls himself "the Son of Man," though he never explicitly defines what he means by the term. In Mark 14:62, the climax of the gospel, Jesus finally reveals to everyone who he is by quoting Daniel 7:13–14: He is the Son of Man from Daniel 7. He is Yahweh.[15]

But claiming the title "Son of Man" was not the only blasphemous act he commits before the Sanhedrin. As if to remove all doubt, Jesus also says he has the right to sit on the throne of God. When he says that they will see the Son of Man "sitting at the right hand of the power" (NIV), he references Psalm 110:1, which says, "The LORD says to my lord: 'Sit at my right hand, until I make your enemies a footstool for your feet'" (NIV).

Sitting at the right hand of God was a right that no one had dared claim, nor dared impute to anyone else, up to this point in Second

Temple Jewish history.[16] It implied sitting on the very throne of God, and it was tantamount to claiming to be God's heir, someone who shared sovereignty with God. According to a scholar of the Psalms, "'Sitting at the right hand of God,' . . . has a very definite meaning: 'the king is installed into an associate rulership; in this position of honor in the power structure of God he becomes a participant in Yahweh's strength in battle and victory.'"[17]

After learning all this, I understood why the Sanhedrin wanted to crucify Jesus for blasphemy. When Jesus claimed to be the Son of Man from Daniel 7 and the Lord of David from Psalm 110, "Both claims imply divine status, authority and power."[18] In response to the question "Who are you?" Jesus' response is essentially, "I am the One who deserves eternal worship from all mankind in My own kingdom, where I will sit on the very throne of God. I am Yahweh."

After reading Mark through the lens of Jewish scripture I could no longer avoid the obvious. From introduction to climax, Mark's gospel is an exposition of the deity of Jesus. The first biography of Jesus ever written is designed to teach that Jesus is Yahweh.

WAS JESUS GOD BEFORE THE GOSPELS?

Although I was shocked to find Jesus' deity in even the earliest of the Gospels, that was only because I was searching for the doctrine as a Muslim, and Muslims tend to focus on the Gospels. Had I paid more attention to the chronology of the New Testament, I would not have been surprised. The great majority of scholars believe that Christians had been teaching the deity of Jesus well before Mark's gospel in the very earliest Christian writings we have: the letters of Paul.[19] In 1 Corinthians 8:6, Paul splits the Jewish *shema* into two. The Jewish proclamation of one God is cast as two persons, God the Father and the Lord Jesus. Also, in Romans 9:5, Paul says Jesus is "God over all, blessed into eternity."

But the most interesting is certainly Philippians 2:

> *Have the same mindset as Christ Jesus: Who, being in very nature*
> *God, did not consider equality with God something to be used to his*

own advantage; rather, he made himself nothing by taking the very
nature of a servant, being made in human likeness. And being found
in appearance as a man, he humbled himself by becoming obedient
to death—even death on a cross! Therefore God exalted him to the
highest place and gave him the name that is above every name, that
at the name of Jesus every knee should bow, in heaven and on earth
and under the earth, and every tongue acknowledge that Jesus Christ is
Lord, to the glory of God the Father.

—verses 5–11 NIV (emphases mine)

This passage is called the *Carmen Christi*, the "Song of Christ," and
its Christology is among the highest there can be. The beginning of
the passage assumes Jesus' preexistence in the very form of God, his
ability to make decisions and act before his incarnation, and even his
own hand in being born on earth. Thus the beginning of the Carmen
Christi makes it clear that Jesus is God incarnate.

It then describes the future, when every knee will bow and every
tongue will confess Jesus' lordship. The kind of lordship Jesus has is the
very lordship of Yahweh, because these are the words Yahweh uses of
himself in one of the most powerfully monotheistic passages of the Old
Testament: "I am God, and there is no other . . . to me every knee will
bow, every tongue will swear" (Isa. 45:22–23). Once again, we find the
earliest New Testament passages substituting Jesus for Yahweh.

But how early is this passage, and is Paul really the author? The
scholarly consensus is that this passage is not one that Paul himself
wrote but one that he is quoting. Beginning chiefly with the 1928 work
of Ernst Lohmeyer, scholars have argued that this is a hymn that uses
un-Pauline vocabulary and grammatical structure.[20] The vocabulary is
so strange at points in this hymn that it is often not found anywhere
else in the New Testament; one word is not even found elsewhere in the
Greek language.[21] Lohmeyer concluded that the hymn was written in
Greek by a man other than Paul whose mother tongue was Semitic.[22]
Others have since agreed, and some have even pushed the envelope,
arguing that the hymn was originally written in Aramaic and was only
later translated into Greek.[23] These reasons and others combine to lead

scholars to conclude that the hymn was composed at the end of the thirties AD.[24] So not just Paul, but also the pre–New Testament church, perhaps as early as the Aramaic-speaking church, ascribed to Jesus the very identity of Yahweh.

CONCLUSION OF THE POSITIVE CASE FOR THE DEITY OF JESUS

When I finished investigating the deity of Jesus, I realized that every layer of Christian teaching depicts Jesus as divine. It is impossible to argue that Jesus' deity was a late invention, an evolution of Christology. Not only does John's gospel present Jesus as divine, but even Mark's gospel and Paul's writings present Jesus as Yahweh. The very earliest evidence there is, possibly from the very decade of Jesus' crucifixion, equates Jesus to Yahweh.

For the earliest Christians, Jesus is more than a prophet, more than the Messiah, and more than divine. He is Yahweh himself.

CHAPTER 30

THE ISLAMIC RESPONSE

DID JESUS REALLY SAY "I AM GOD"?

When I learned to read the New Testament in light of the Old, I was able to see the deity of Jesus clearly in its pages, but it took me years as a Muslim to get to that point. Even though the Quran affirms that both the Torah and *Injil* were inspired, Muslims are not encouraged to know either of them in any detail, so instead of reading the Bible on its own terms we read it through the lens of the Quran and Islamic teaching.

That is why I rejected the deity of Christ for as long as I did. Not only was I predisposed against it, highlighting verses that seemed to challenge the doctrine, but also I expected Jesus to say certain things and speak certain ways if he really claimed to be God. Those two challenges were my main arguments against Christians: There are many verses in the Bible that seem to deny Jesus' deity, and Jesus never clearly says "I am God." Together, these were my most compelling reasons to doubt that Jesus claimed to be God, and these are the same arguments that I find most Muslims using today.

VERSES THAT DENY THE DEITY OF JESUS

Thanks to the work of Ahmed Deedat and other Muslim apologists, there are many verses isolated from the Gospels readily used by Muslims to argue that Jesus explicitly denied divine status.

One of my favorites was John 17:3 because it seemed very Islamic in its proclamation: "Now this is eternal life: that they know you, the only true God, and Jesus Christ, whom you have sent" (NIV). Just like the *shahada*, this verse proclaims the existence of only one God and a messenger whom he sent. Clearly, the one sent is inferior and separate from the one sending. As far as I was concerned, this verse showed that Jesus' teachings were very similar to Islam's, and that he denied being God, saying that the Father is the "only true God."

Another verse I commonly used on account of its stark clarity was John 14:28: "The Father is greater than I" (NIV). How could Jesus be God if the Father is greater than he is? This shows that Jesus is both separate from God and inferior to him. Another verse with a similar impact was Mark 10:18: "Why do you call me good? . . . No one is good—except God alone" (NIV). Jesus again distinguishes himself from God and clarifies that he is inferior.

Just as we would expect as Muslims, there are texts in the Gospels that show Jesus praying to God (Mark 1:35) and saying that people should worship God alone (Matt. 4:10). Mark 14:36 appears to show Jesus praying in desperation to the Father, saying, "Everything is possible for you. Take this cup from me" (NIV). Not only is Jesus praying to God, but he seems to be emphasizing that everything is possible for the Father, not for Jesus, and that Jesus is utterly dependent on him.

Regarding this dependence, Jesus says that he can do nothing apart from God: "The Son can do nothing by himself; he can do only what he sees his Father doing" (John 5:19 NIV). His inability to do anything by himself was apparent again in Mark 6:5, when he returned to Nazareth and "could not do any miracles there" (NIV). Indeed, Jesus could not even prophesy without God's intervention, as he said, "But about that day or hour no one knows, not even the angels in heaven, nor the Son, but only the Father" (Mark 13:32 NIV).

We very frequently argued that Jesus was portrayed as a human and that the term "Son of God" did not imply a divine status. Adam had been called a "son of God" (Luke 3:38), as had David (Ps. 2:7), Solomon (1 Chron. 28:6), and even unnamed strangers (Gen. 6:2). In fact, the Bible taught that even we could become children of God (Rom. 8:14, Gal. 3:26). Therefore, Jesus was a "son of God" in the same sense, a human sense.

Finally, Jesus must have been just a human because he ate (John 21:12), wept (John 11:35), slept (Mark 4:38), hungered (Matt. 4:2), thirsted (John 4:7), and even tired (John 4:6). Could God really hunger, thirst, and grow tired? Of course God cannot, and therefore Jesus is not God. Also, he called himself a prophet (Luke 4:24), not God. The matter is settled when we consider his preferred term for himself: "Son of Man." By using this title, Jesus emphasized that he was just a human, not God.

JESUS NEVER CLEARLY SAYS "I AM GOD"

In addition to pointing out the verses that seemed to deny Jesus' deity and establish his humanity, I often challenged Christians by pointing out that he never actually says, "I am God." If Jesus were God, why does he not just come out with it and say it? God certainly proclaims his divinity boldly in the Old Testament, with verses such as "I am the LORD, and there is no other; apart from me there is no God" (Isa. 45:5 NIV). Christians argue that Jesus is that very God, the one making the bold proclamation in Isaiah 45. Why does Jesus talk so differently about himself, never clearly saying he is God?

In fact, there seems to be a specific occasion when some Jews interpreted Jesus as saying he is God, but Jesus clears up this misinterpretation (John 10:33–36). The Jews said, "You, a mere man, claim to be God," to which Jesus responded, "Is it not written in your Law, 'I have said you are "gods"' . . . Why then do you accuse me of blasphemy because I said, 'I am God's Son'?" (NIV). When people think Jesus is claiming to be God, he tries to clarify the situation, explaining that many people were called "gods" in the Old Testament and therefore there is nothing wrong when Jesus calls himself "God's Son."

If he really were God, why did he not just say in that instance, "Yes, I am claiming to be God?" Why does he never say anything of that sort? Clearly, he was not claiming to be God.

THE CLAIM TO DEITY AND THE HISTORICAL JESUS

Those were the initial arguments I provided against the deity of Jesus, the ones that had been taught to me by the Muslim community, and I was confident that they were powerful. Later, as I progressed in my understanding of the responses to these arguments, I provided another challenge which was more nuanced and sophisticated: Even if it can be shown in the Gospels that Jesus does claim to be God, what reason do we have to think that this goes back to the actual Jesus?

In other words, even if John depicts a divine Jesus, can we really think that Jesus claimed to be God himself? The same goes for the earlier writings of the New Testament, such as Mark and Paul. Even if they were to show that Jesus claimed to be God, maybe they invented it?

Given the evidence at hand, and given the very notion itself, it is simply preposterous to believe that Jesus claimed to be God.

CONCLUSION OF THE MUSLIM RESPONSE

As Muslims, this was an arena in which we felt very confident: Jesus never claimed to be God. Never did he claim it, and there are many verses where he denies it, teaching that there is only one God. There is no God but one, and Jesus is just his messenger.

CHAPTER 31

ASSESSING THE ISLAMIC RESPONSE

LETTING THE CONTEXT SPEAK

Taken in isolation, some of the verses presented would pose a challenge to the belief in Jesus' deity, but that is the problem: The verses are not supposed to be taken in isolation. Much more than in Quranic exegesis, verses in the Bible depend on their context for proper interpretation. Considering the context of the verses and taking a closer look at the doctrine of Jesus' deity resolves most of the Muslim challenge. To address the entire response, we will also consider Mark's Messianic Secret and the likelihood that Jesus' claim to be God goes back to the person of Jesus himself.

CONSIDERING CONTEXT

While a Muslim, I used many verses from the gospel of John to challenge the deity of Jesus, such as "the Father is greater than I" and "the Son can do nothing of himself." As I became more acquainted with the Gospel, I began to see a major problem: John introduced his gospel by announcing that Jesus is God, as we discussed in chapter 30, and he concluded his gospel with a climactic pronouncement from a disciple that Jesus is God (John 20:28). In between, there were many verses that exalt Jesus and give him the honor due to God alone. This is why even skeptical scholars like Bart Ehrman say that Jesus is portrayed as divine in John's gospel.

How could I use verses from John's gospel to deny the deity of Jesus when that Gospel as a whole certainly proclaimed that Jesus was God? That would be disingenuous, extracting verses out of their context to suit my purposes rather than seeing what they actually say.

It was this realization that led me to change the way I approached the Bible. Instead of searching for verses from the text that I could use to support my Islamic position, I started reading each verse carefully for the meaning it intended to convey. This meant understanding verses in light of one another and having to put the puzzle pieces together. How could John's gospel call Jesus Lord and God (John 20:28) and say that the universe was created through him (John 1:3), while also saying that "the Father is greater" than Jesus (John 14:28 NIV) and that Jesus can do nothing apart from the Father (John 5:19)? A proper understanding of John's gospel must account for all these verses, not just some.

The way to account for them, the way that the Christians of Nicaea and Chalcedon accounted for them, is by understanding that Jesus is God, that the Father is God, that the two are not the same person, yet there is only one God. In other words, the only way to account for the teachings of John's gospel is through a monotheistic model with multiple persons: a Trinitarian model.[1] In this model, the Father is greater than Jesus and Jesus does not do anything apart from the will of the Father, but both the Father and Jesus are God.

An appropriate question that Muslims often ask is, "How can Jesus be God if the Father is greater than he is?" The question is easy to answer with an illustration. When I consider myself compared to the president of the United States, I would not hesitate to say that the president is greater than I. He is in charge of the entire nation and is one of the most powerful men in the world, whereas I am just a normal citizen. So the president is greater than I, far greater; but we are both equally human. In his essence, the president is just a human being, as am I, and in that sense we are equal. So when I say, "The president is greater than I," I am referring to his office, not his essence. In office, he is greater than I; in essence, we are equal. Similarly, when Jesus says, "The Father is greater than I," that does not mean Jesus is not God. The Father has a different role, a higher office than Jesus, but that does not mean the Father is greater in essence. They are both equal in essence. They are both God.

REVISITING THE DOCTRINE OF JESUS' DEITY AND THE TRINITY

A proper understanding of the doctrine of Jesus' deity resolves many of the Islamic arguments, even the ones using the texts of Mark, Matthew, and Luke. That Jesus hungered and thirsted does not challenge Jesus' deity, because Christians believe in the hypostatic union that we discussed in chapter 10—that Jesus has a divine nature and a human nature, which means he really was a human and he really did hunger and thirst. For the same reason, God really could be a prophet. Since God can come into the world according to the Judeo-Christian teachings, he can take a human nature and be both God and man. There is nothing mutually exclusive about his humanity and his deity.

I remember when I encountered this argument for the first time as a Muslim, I resisted it. Surely, to be God is to be unlimited, whereas to be human is to be limited. How can someone be limited and unlimited at the same time? For example, God knows all things, and Jesus did not know all things (Mark 13:32). How can Jesus be God?

The Christian response, found in Philippians 2, is that God voluntarily limited the expression of his deity when he became human. Yes, theoretically Jesus could have known all things while on this earth, but he chose not to because he "did not consider equality with God something to be used to his own advantage; rather, he made himself nothing by taking the very nature of a servant" (Phil. 2:6–7 NIV). He limited himself voluntarily, becoming a real man, so that as a man he could atone for the sins of man.

For that reason, he was a real human. Jesus was born. He could grow in wisdom and in stature. He was dependent on the Father, and as such he could pray to the Father. This is not "God praying to himself," as some allege, because the Son is not the Father. There are two persons here, two selves.

Although there are many verses that I used to challenge the deity of Jesus as a Muslim, these two clarifications resolve almost all of them: the context of the verses and understanding the doctrine of the hypostatic union.

WHY DID JESUS NOT SAY "I AM GOD"?
UNDERSTANDING THE MESSIANIC SECRET

Muslims ask a good question when they ask why Jesus did not boldly and publicly proclaim his deity, but a good answer is readily available: He did not want to announce his identity right away. This is stated explicitly at the beginning of Mark's gospel. When Jesus was casting out demons, "He would not let the demons speak because they knew who he was" (Mark 1:34 NIV). Mark makes it explicit: Jesus wanted to keep his identity a secret for a time.[2]

There were a variety of reasons why. When people came to learn about Jesus, they crowded around him so much that he was no longer able to go into towns (Mark 1:45). Also, as the Pharisees and Herodians began to see what Jesus was doing and claiming, they began to plot how they might kill him (Mark 3:6), but Jesus did not want to be killed until it was the right time.[3] When Jesus and the disciples discussed the issue, he explained to them why he wanted to keep his identity secret: because "the Son of Man must suffer many things and be rejected by the elders, the chief priests and the teachers of the law, and that he must be killed and after three days rise again" (8:31 NIV).[4]

So Jesus did not want to publicly proclaim his identity. This is known among scholars as the "Messianic Secret." When the days of his death and ascension were approaching, he headed straight for Jerusalem (Luke 9:51). That is when he was arrested and taken before the Sanhedrin to reveal his identity.

As a Muslim, I did not concede this point until I realized something surprising. Both Muslims and Christians agree Jesus is the Messiah, but in the Gospels Jesus only publicly proclaimed that he is the Messiah one time.[5] That one location is at his trial before the Sanhedrin, the very passage where Jesus claims to be God.

To repeat, *the one time in the Gospels that Jesus publicly claimed to be the Messiah was the same time he publicly claimed to be God.* Since Muslims believe Jesus was the Messiah even though he publicly proclaimed it only once, we cannot demand he proclaim his deity more often or more boldly. He was not in the business of proclaiming his identity over and over again. He chose to wait for the right moment.

Also, though Jesus did not often proclaim his identity publicly, the Gospels inform their readers of his identity through the narrative of the text. For example, Mark 1:1 identifies Jesus as the Son of God;[6] Mark 1:11 shows God himself declaring that Jesus is his Son; verse 3:11 shows a demon declaring Jesus is the Son of God. By showing spiritual beings declaring Jesus' sonship, Mark is able to inform his readers that Jesus is no mere mortal, letting the readers in on the secret even before Jesus' public proclamation at the trial.

Mark uses other means to inform the perceptive reader that Jesus is beyond human, as discussed in the previous chapter. He uses controversies, such as his public remission of the paralyzed man's sin (2:5); he uses claims of sovereignty, such as his sovereignty over one of the Ten Commandments (2:28); he shows Jesus performing miracles that only God should be able to, such as calming the seas (4:38–39) and walking on the water (6:48).

Throughout his gospel, Mark is preparing the reader for the moment that the Messianic Secret will be revealed, when Jesus will tell everyone who he really is, tying together all his words and deeds. This makes 14:62, the climax and divine revelation, all the more powerful and important to understand. It is there that Jesus claims to be the divine Son of Man from Daniel 7 and the One sitting on the throne of God from Psalm 110:1.

These two claims, Jesus' most powerful proclamations of deity in the Gospels, are also our anchor of confidence that Jesus actually did use these terms.

ASSESSING HISTORICAL ACCURACY

What is powerful about Jesus' claims before the Sanhedrin, historically speaking, is that they pass the most stringent scholarly criteria for historical accuracy. The title "Son of Man" is used more than eighty times in the four gospels, almost always by Jesus himself, in multiple settings.[7] Scholars are confident that Jesus actually used this phrase for himself because there was no widespread expectation that the Messiah would be the Son of Man. In addition, the Christians in the early church did not really refer to Jesus as the Son of Man. Why would all four gospels show Jesus calling himself the Son of Man when no one expected the Messiah to speak that way and when people did not really refer to him in those terms later? The most plausible reason is that he actually used the title himself. Thus it passes the most stringent criterion of historical investigation, the criterion of dissimilarity.[8] That Jesus called himself the Son of Man is virtually certain.

Similarly, there can be little doubt that Jesus was considered the Lord of David who sits on the throne of God at a very early point in Christian history. It is the most commonly quoted Old Testament passage in the New Testament, deeply ingrained in the Christian conscience well before the New Testament was written.[9] The best explanation for this early Christian unanimity regarding Psalm 110:1 is that Jesus himself taught and proclaimed that he is the one sitting at the right hand of the Power, worthy to rule the universe with the Father.

Thus we can be confident that Jesus' boldest proclamation of his identity, the one time he publicly proclaimed that he was the Messiah and God, are words that Jesus himself actually proclaimed.

CONCLUDING OUR ASSESSMENT OF THE MUSLIM RESPONSE

The fact is not just John's gospel but all the Gospels teach that Jesus is God. Though there are some verses in the Gospels that might appear to challenge Jesus' deity, understanding them in their context and understanding the Christian doctrine of Jesus' deity resolves them. Even Ehrman, the skeptical scholar most favored among Muslims, has now changed his mind and says: "The idea that Jesus is God is not an invention of modern times, of course. As I will show in my discussion, *it was the view of the very earliest Christians* soon after Jesus's death."[10] The best explanation for this immediate belief that Jesus is God, as the evidence shows, is that Jesus himself claimed to be God.

CHAPTER 32

CONCLUSION

JESUS CLAIMED TO BE GOD

The very earliest Christian records are unanimous: Jesus is God. All four gospels teach that Jesus is divine, and even before they were written, Christians had firmly established God's incarnation as the core of their faith. This was not a teaching that evolved over time but one that was present at the inception of the church and has its roots in Jesus' proclamation. It makes sense when we study Jesus' life through the lens of first-century Judaism, including the Old Testament records of Yahweh visiting man and the expectation that he would come again. The common Islamic response, that there are verses that contravene the teaching of Jesus' deity, usually does not take into consideration the context of those verses and at other times misunderstands the Messianic Secret or the doctrine of the hypostatic union.

When I was studying the Gospels as a Muslim, I was shocked to discover these facts. Having always believed that the doctrine of Jesus' deity was invented decades if not centuries after Jesus' death, I realized that the Islamic explanation for Christian beliefs does not work. The very first Christians believed that Jesus is God, including the disciples themselves. How could the disciples have concluded this, especially considering the Jewish emphasis on monotheism and on worshiping God alone?

The best conclusion is that Jesus himself claimed to be God. The Gospels are telling the truth. As a Muslim my mind rebelled against this, but considering the perspective of an objective investigator I had to admit that it was the best explanation of the evidence. Nothing else accounted for the origins of the church without strain.

Putting together the components for the case for Christianity, there was little room for me as a Muslim to object. The historical evidence was so contrary to Islamic teaching that there was no ground for me to stand on.

ASSESSING THE CASE FOR CHRISTIANITY AND ISLAM'S EFFORTS TO ACCOUNT FOR CHRISTIAN ORIGINS

After studying the historical origins of the Christian faith, I came to these conclusions: that Jesus died on the cross is as certain as anything historical can be; that he rose from the dead is by far the best explanation of the events surrounding his death; and that Jesus claimed to be God is the best explanation for the immediate Christian proclamation of Jesus' deity.

Putting it all together, the historical evidence for Christianity is very strong: Jesus claimed to be God, and he proved it by rising from the dead. The case for Christianity is powerful.

Despite my ardent desire to believe Islam, I had to admit that history was in favor of Christian claims, and even more reluctantly, that it challenged Islamic teachings. In order to believe the Quran when it says Jesus did not claim to be God, we have to ignore the best explanation of early Christian beliefs; and to believe the Quran's teachings about Jesus' death, we would have to dismiss all the historical evidence. So the records of Christian origins testify against Islam.

But the evidence is actually even more problematic for Islam than it might initially appear. Far more problematic. Islamic teachings about Jesus are utterly incompatible with history.

THE UTTER INCOMPATIBILITY OF ISLAM WITH JESUS' IDENTITY

For Islamic teaching to be true, it is not enough for Jesus to simply deny deity; Jesus has to proclaim that he is merely a human prophet. But the earliest records are categorically against Islam on this point.

Even a cursory glance at the Gospels shows us that Jesus sees himself as greater than a mere human. Of course, as we have already seen, Jesus considers himself able to forgive sins, receive worship, heal people in his own authority, demand the honor that is due to God, hear and answer prayers, ransom mankind by his death, and exist even before Abraham was born. But Jesus also commended people who called him God (John 20:28), claimed to be the king of another realm (John 18:36–37), descended from heaven (John 3:13), and claims to be the judge on the day of judgment (John 5:22–23). Such teachings are not just found in John's gospel; the Synoptic Gospels agree that Jesus is the king over an eternal kingdom (Matt. 25:34), that he is the one who will judge mankind (Matt. 25:32), that he has the authority to grant people salvation (Luke 23:43), that he has elected people who will go to heaven (Mark 13:27), and that his return to earth will be as the return of the master to his own house (Mark 13:35). Of course, this is all in the context of Jesus' claim to be heir of God's throne from Psalm 110, sitting on the throne of God, and as the divine Son of Man from Daniel 7 who is worshiped by all men in his eternal kingdom.

These are the teachings of the Gospels, the earliest biographies of Jesus' life, produced during the lifetimes of Jesus' disciples. There is absolutely no early Christian record of a merely human Jesus. All evidence indicates that Jesus' followers uniformly believed him to be divine, unquestionably more than a mere human.

How can the Islamic model account for this? Why is it that the followers of Jesus preached a superhuman Jesus, in fact God himself? Without dismissing the history, there is no alternative explanation. Islam requires us to believe that Jesus was so incompetent as a teacher and prophet that he was not able to instill this most simple fact in his followers' minds: that he was merely a human. Given that Islam's central proclamation is *tawhid*, this means Jesus was an abject failure. In fact, he was worse than a total failure, since he left his disciples believing the exact opposite of *tawhid*.

Could I really conclude that the Messiah was so woefully incompetent? Of course not, but that is what Islam requires us to believe if we are to take the historical evidence seriously. The records of Jesus' identity are not just slightly mismatched with Islamic teachings; the records of Jesus' identity are categorically incompatible with Islam. If Jesus truly taught *tawhid*, he was an entirely incompetent Messiah, worse than an abject failure.

THE UTTER INCOMPATIBILITY OF ISLAM WITH EARLY CHRISTIAN PROCLAMATION

Similarly, Islam teaches that the disciples were godly men, but the entire body of evidence testifies that the proclamation of the early church was the death and resurrection of Jesus—something Islam denies. How could I account for this discrepancy as a Muslim?

The only option that accounted for the historical evidence was that the disciples simply got the facts wrong; but upon consideration, this posed a serious problem for my Islamic belief. If Allah saved Jesus from the cross while making it look like Jesus died, as most Muslims believe, then Allah is responsible for the disciples' proclamation of Jesus' death and resurrection. Therefore, Allah started Christianity, a false religion that has kept billions away from Islam. Worse, Christians believe Jesus is God because of their faith in his resurrection, yet the Quran tells us that people who believe Jesus is God will go to hell (5.72). Could I really believe that, just to save Jesus from the cross, God deceived the disciples, letting them proclaim that Jesus is the risen Lord and thereby sending billions of people to hell?

Again, there is absolutely no record of a disciple who preached anything other than the death and resurrection of Jesus. Why did Allah not adequately communicate to them that Jesus had not died on the cross and had not risen from the dead? Allah could easily have stopped them from preaching the death and resurrection of Jesus. But the history is incontrovertible: The foundation of the disciples' preaching was the proclamation of Jesus' resurrection. Therefore, if it is true that Allah saved Jesus from the cross, the deception of Allah is responsible for the establishment of the Christian church and billions of people committing *shirk*, the unforgivable sin.

Could I really conclude that Allah committed such a massive blunder? Of course not, but that is what Islam requires us to believe if we are to take the historical evidence seriously. The records of the early Christian proclamation are not just slightly mismatched with Islamic teachings; *the records of the early Christian proclamation are categorically incompatible with Islam.* If Allah saved Jesus from the cross and did not inform the disciples, he is a deceptive God who is responsible for the damnation of billions.

For these reasons, if we are Muslim and we take the historical evidence of Christian origins seriously, we have to conclude that Jesus was an incompetent Messiah and Allah is a deceptive God.

ISLAM'S REJECTION OF HISTORY

Of course, Muslims do not believe that, and neither did I. I took the only remaining alternative: Reject all of the historical evidence of Christian origins, regardless of how much there is, how widespread it is, and how firmly grounded it is. The historical records are incredibly vast, including dozens of sources from dozens of authors—Christian, Jewish, and Graeco-Roman alike. Could I really just dismiss everything, turning a blind eye to all the evidence, to maintain my Islamic beliefs?

I also knew something I could no longer overlook: Scholars are virtually unanimous that Jesus died on the cross, that the early church believed he rose from the dead, and that the earliest Christians believed he was superhuman, even divine. Not just Christian scholars but even skeptical scholars are virtually all on the same side on these issues, against the teachings of Islam. As a Muslim, I had a great deal of respect for scholars, but now I knew their conclusions were against my faith. The people who spend their lives studying these matters disagree with Islam.

While pondering all this, my mind continually returned to that question I forced myself to ask: "Would an objective investigator throw out all the evidence? Would an objective investigator side with Islam on these issues?" The answer was obvious: of course not. To believe Islam on the history of Christian origins is to dismiss all evidence ad hoc, and no objective investigator would do that.

A TENTATIVE CONCLUSION

After spending three years investigating the case for Christianity as a Muslim, I tentatively concluded that Christians had good historical reason to believe in their faith. This was a paradigm shift in my mind, utterly incompatible with what I had been taught as a Muslim, but it was unavoidably true.

And because the evidence also challenged my Islamic beliefs, I had to either ignore it all (which my mind could not do), become a Christian (which I could not even imagine), or believe that, despite how strong the evidence for Christianity was, the evidence for Islam must be stronger.

The last option was the only viable option for me, so I found myself assuming that the case for Islam must be stronger than the case for Christianity. But my friend David would not allow me to operate on such an assumption without providing evidence.

That is why I delved into our investigation of Islam: to prove that the case for Islam is stronger than the case for Christianity. My first step was to corral the evidence that Muhammad was a prophet of God. After spending some time preparing, David invited me to argue my case at a discussion group of people from many religious backgrounds that met monthly at Mike Licona's house. It was there that I presented my positive case that Muhammad was a prophet of God.

PART 9

IS MUHAMMAD A PROPHET OF GOD?

CHAPTER 33

THE POSITIVE CASE

THE FORETOLD PARAGON

I bear witness that Muhammad is the messenger of Allah." This is the proclamation of a devout Muslim, announced multiple times a day from every minaret before the daily prayers and recited in the heart of every Muslim during the prayers. The proclamation that "there is no God but Allah, and Muhammad is his messenger" is enough to welcome a person into the fold of Islam. There really can be no doubt that Muhammad's status as a messenger of God, his prophethood, is a central pillar of Islamic faith.

Growing up Muslim, Muhammad's prophethood was a given, an integral part of our world, and sharing Islam meant compelling hearts toward him. It is for that reason, when my friend David asked me to share Islam with a room full of non-Muslims, I chose to present and defend the prophethood of Muhammad.

Seated in Mike Licona's living room and speaking to Christians, Buddhists, atheists, and agnostics, I made my case for Muhammad's prophethood. I presented three arguments: that Muhammad's life and character testified that he was a prophet; that Muhammad was prophesied in the Bible; and that Muhammad had God-given insight into science.

MUHAMMAD'S LIFE AND CHARACTER

Providing a portrait of Muhammad's life that had passed down to me through generations, I started by telling everyone that Muhammad lived a very meek and humble childhood. His father died before he was born, his mother died shortly thereafter, and he lived most of his childhood as an orphan. He grew to become a trusted and respected young merchant, ultimately marrying a widow fifteen years his elder instead of a youthful maiden. Muhammad was thus a very noble young man uninterested in worldly attractions even before receiving his prophetic call.

It was only with reluctance that he accepted the mantle of prophethood. Within the pagan environment of Mecca, Muhammad boldly proclaimed monotheism with no concern for his personal well-being. Understanding the plight of widows, orphans, and the poor, he fought for their rights.

Despite his peaceful message, the hatred of the Meccans against the message of monotheism led to persecutions. Although Muhammad was protected by his uncle, he faced ridicule and threats, even having camel entrails placed on him while he was prostrate in prayer. His followers, who had no protectors, fared worse, some even being martyred. The persecutions increased over the years, and the Meccans ultimately boycotted the Muslims, resulting in such harsh conditions that Muhammad's uncle and wife died. When a plot was underway to assassinate Muhammad, he fled to Medina, and it was there that he finally had enough support to defend the fledgling Muslim people.

From that point on, Muhammad invited the tribes of Arabia to accept Islam, and many became allies of the Muslims on account of the beauty of the message. All the while, the Meccans kept coming to Medina to destroy the Muslims, but Allah miraculously defended them. After ten years of having to fight such defensive wars, Muhammad made a treaty with the Meccans that allowed him to travel to Mecca and perform a pilgrimage to the sacred mosque, the Kaaba. Unfortunately, the Meccans broke their treaty, so Muhammad marched on Mecca with ten thousand followers. The Meccans could not withstand the might of the Muslim armies, so they surrendered.

Although these were the very people who had persecuted and killed Muslims—the ones who caused the death of Muhammad's beloved uncle and first wife, and the very ones who dragged the Muslims into war time and again at the cost of many lives—Muhammad granted them clemency by forgiving all of them. The fame of Muhammad's message spread throughout Arabia, and by the time Muhammad died two years later, the whole Arabian Peninsula had embraced Islam.

Such was the character of Muhammad: In addition to being a champion for women and orphans, he was a resilient proclaimer of monotheism, a great leader, and a merciful conqueror. His life and character are proof that he is a prophet of God.

MUHAMMAD IN THE BIBLE

An even more common argument among Muslims than the compelling character of Muhammad is the case that Muhammad is prophesied in the Bible.

The Quran teaches that Muhammad was prophesied in the Torah and the gospel: "The messenger, the unlettered prophet whom they will find with them written in the Torah and the Gospel" (7.157).[1] For this reason, Muslims are willing to use Bible verses to defend the prophethood of Muhammad. There were two such biblical passages that we used more than any other, usually quoting the King James Version: Deuteronomy 18:18–19 and John 16:12–14.

Deuteronomy 18

In Deuteronomy 18:18–19, God says, "I will raise them up a Prophet from among their brethren, like unto thee, and will put my words in his mouth; and he shall speak unto them all that I shall command him. And it shall come to pass, that whosoever will not hearken unto my words which he shall speak in my name, I will require it of him" (KJV). In this passage, God is addressing Moses, saying a prophet like Moses will come, one who will come from among the brethren of the Jews and speak in the name of God.

Muslims commonly argue that, even though Christians believe this passage refers to Jesus, it speaks of Muhammad. Who is more "like unto" Moses: Jesus or Muhammad? Moses was born naturally, came with a law, led his people for many years, was a statesman as well as a prophet, had to lead his people out of oppression, married and had children, and ultimately died a natural death; none of this is true of Jesus, yet all of it is true of Muhammad. Undoubtedly, Moses is more like Muhammad than Jesus.

In addition, the prophecy says that the prophet will be "from among their brethren," that is, the brethren of the Jews. The Jews are Israelites, and their brethren are the Ishmaelites. Therefore, the prophecy speaks of a prophet like Moses from the lineage of Ishmael. That must be Muhammad.

Finally, the passage says that the prophet will reveal "words which he shall speak in my name." In the Quran, every chapter begins with, "In the name of Allah." Thus, more than anyone else, Muhammad spoke in the name of God, and every chapter of the Quran testifies to this.

Thus I presented the common argument that, through Moses in the Old Testament, God prophesied the coming of Muhammad.

John 16

In John's gospel, the sixteenth chapter also speaks of a prophet who will come, I argued. The text reads, "I have yet many things to say unto you, but ye cannot bear them now. Howbeit when he, the Spirit of truth, is come, he will guide you into all truth; for he shall not speak of himself; but whatsoever he shall hear, that shall he speak: and he will shew you things to come. He shall glorify me: for he shall receive of mine, and shall shew it unto you" (vv. 12–14 KJV).

Here, Jesus speaks of a prophet, the Spirit of truth (v. 13), who will come and finish Jesus' message. Who else could this be but Muhammad, the only prophet of a major religion to come after Jesus? As in the Deuteronomy prophecy, this text describes one who will not speak of himself, but only what he hears. The Quran is revelation that was given to Muhammad, not composed by him whatsoever, so he spoke only what he heard, just as the prophecy says.

In addition, John 16 says the Spirit of truth will glorify Jesus. Unlike the Jews who said Jesus was an illegitimate child, Muhammad proclaimed that Jesus truly was born of a virgin, thereby glorifying him when others were not and fulfilling the prophecy.

To top off the argument, the Greek of John 16:7 uses the word *parakletos* to describe this "Spirit of truth." This word is very similar to the Greek word *periklutos*, which means "the praised one." In Arabic, the word *Muhammad* means "the praised one." Thus, Jesus used the Greek word for Muhammad when prophesying the coming Spirit of truth.

For all these reasons, we could be confident that, through Jesus, God prophesied the coming of Muhammad in the New Testament. These were just two prophecies I chose to present that night out of over a dozen such prophesies that Muslims commonly argue establish Muhammad's authority and prophethood.

MIRACULOUS SCIENTIFIC KNOWLEDGE

The final argument I presented to the attendees of our meeting was Muhammad's miraculous scientific knowledge. This argument was usually provided in defense of the Quran, but I and many other Muslims presented it to defend the prophethood of Muhammad as well. While delivering the Quran and while answering questions recorded in hadith, Muhammad showed insight into science that he could not have possibly known as a man living in the seventh century. This could mean only that God was giving Muhammad supernatural wisdom, and therefore that he was a prophet of God.

For example, in 23.12–14, the Quran describes the development of an embryo in stages. Describing zygotic development from fertilization to differentiation, the Quran shows familiarity with a scientific field that was unknown in Muhammad's day. It was not until the development of modern medicine that we find mankind discovering what was already revealed in the Quran.

Another common argument we used was that the Quran relayed miraculous geological truth about mountains. In 78.6–7, the Quran describes mountains as "pegs," indicating that they have roots which go beneath the surface of the earth. Only in modern times has science uncovered the existence of such roots. In addition, the Quran teaches that these mountain roots stabilize the earth, which the science of plate tectonics has only recently established.

Since Muhammad was the one who received these miraculous scientific teachings, he must be a prophet of God.

CONCLUDING THE POSITIVE CASE
FOR MUHAMMAD'S PROPHETHOOD

After presenting my argument to the discussion group for forty-five minutes, I felt confident that I had argued the case for Muhammad's prophethood strongly. His life and message are inherent proof that he is a prophet of God; his coming was prophesied by the messengers before him like Moses and Jesus; and the advanced scientific knowledge that was revealed through him proves that he is a prophet of God. Together, these are compelling reasons to believe that Muhammad is a prophet and that Islam is the truth sent by God.

But then came the questions, issues I had not seen that challenged the prophethood of Muhammad.

CHAPTER 34

THE RESPONSE

DON'T FORGET THE COUNTEREVIDENCE

When I finished my presentation on the historical Muhammad, the very first question was from Mike. Since he had studied Islam for his debate with Shabir Ally, he knew that there were holes in my presentation, evidence I had not provided before concluding that Muhammad's character is peaceful. "Nabeel," he asked, "there are other verses in the Quran, like, 'Slay the infidel wherever you find him.' How do we know that what you quoted takes precedence?"

Although I was very often offended when people questioned Muhammad's character, it was fair to ask. If I am presenting Muhammad's excellent character as evidence that he is a prophet of God, that means I have to allow counterevidence that might lead us to conclude Muhammad's character was not that of a prophet of God. The same holds true for the prophecies pertaining to Muhammad and Muhammad's scientific knowledge; we must weigh potential counterexamples. When we consider the full body of evidence, is the prophethood of Muhammad still the best conclusion?

CRITICALLY CONSIDERING MUHAMMAD'S CHARACTER

When we read about the life of Muhammad, there is no doubt that Muhammad taught many good things. This goes beyond the simple proclamation of monotheism and submission to God. Muhammad taught people to feed the poor;[1] to love others for God's sake;[2] to abstain from theft, fornication, and infanticide;[3] to release slaves, help the weak, and serve those who cannot work for themselves;[4] and much more. When considering the historical record of Muhammad's life, one has to conclude that he taught many things that were very moral and noble.

But before concluding that he is a prophet of God, one has to consider the counterevidence, and we will consider only that evidence which is found in the sources most Muslims consider most trustworthy: the Quran and the hadith of Sahih Bukhari and Sahih Muslim.

The best place to start is at the beginning. When he received his very first revelation, Muhammad reacted very strangely: He became suicidal. "He intended several times to throw himself from the tops of high mountains and every time he went up the top of a mountain in order to throw himself down," an angel would appear to him and urge him not to kill himself.[5] Is this the behavior of a prophet? No prophet in the Old Testament or New Testament ever became suicidal after seeing an angel.

Muhammad's initial encounter with a spiritual being sounds little like an angelic encounter at all. According to the same hadith, this spiritual being was called Namus.[6] Namus grabbed hold of Muhammad and squeezed him so vehemently that he could not bear it.[7] Three times Namus squeezed Muhammad unbearably hard until Muhammad ultimately complied with his command. To the objective observer, this sounds like a violent episode, not at all like an angelic encounter. The beginning of Muhammad's ministerial career sounds little like that of a prophet.

When we consider whether he was a man of peace, we must recognize that though Muhammad's ministry was fraught with battles, that in itself is not evidence against his divine commission. Joshua and others in the Old Testament had been commanded to fight.

What is striking, though, is how enthusiastically Muhammad embraced warfare. He said that fighting is literally the best thing in the world.[8] Nothing earns a Muslim more reward than fighting in jihad, and it is better than praying without ceasing and fasting perpetually.[9] Muhammad taught that dying in battle is so great that it is the only thing that would make a man want to leave heaven.[10]

As far as his conduct with enemies, at times Muhammad would invoke curses upon them[11] and encourage his men to compose insults and abusive poetry.[12] On one occasion, he asked Allah to fill peoples' homes with flames simply because they delayed the Muslims in their daily prayers.[13] At other times, Muhammad sent assassins to kill his enemies in their sleep,[14] and even to deceive and abuse trust in order to assassinate.[15] He punished some enemies by cutting off their hands and feet, branding their eyes with a heated iron, and causing them to lick the dust until they died.[16] He led battles against unarmed cities.[17] He allowed even women and children to be killed during nighttime raids.[18] On more than one occasion, Muhammad decimated tribes by killing all their men and teenage boys while distributing their women and children as slaves.[19] This is quite contrary to the image of a Muhammad who reluctantly fought only defensive battles.

It also does not appear that Muhammad fought only those who were attacking him. Muhammad said, "I have been ordered to fight against the people until they testify that none has the right to be worshiped but Allah and that Muhammad is Allah's Messenger . . . then they save their lives and property from me."[20] Muhammad clarifies in another hadith, "I will expel the Jews and Christians from the Arabian Peninsula and will not leave any but Muslim."[21]

There can be no denying, based on these records, that Muhammad fought people and wished to expel them from Arabia based on their beliefs. Only if they became Muslim would they "save their lives and property from" Muhammad. How could we argue that Muhammad was so peaceful that it proved his prophetic status?

In assessing Muhammad's character, we have considered only two matters in any depth: the beginning of his ministry and his teachings regarding warfare. These alone are enough to question Muhammad's character and prophethood, but in case more is needed, there is much, much more that skeptics commonly bring to the table, such as concerns about his spiritual aptitude, his teachings about women, his troubling theological teachings, his incorrect understandings of Judaism and Christianity, his unfulfilled prophecies, his commands to perform idolatrous rites, and his special allowances for himself. We will briefly touch on just the first two.[22]

As far as his spiritual aptitude and authority, apart from considering suicide on several occasions, Muhammad said that he had been a victim of black magic;[23] he had delusional thoughts of doing things he had not done;[24] and he confused demonic inspiration with divine inspiration, saying Satan had put Quran verses into his heart which he then used in prayer.[25]

Regarding his estimation and treatment of women: Muhammad allowed for prostitution through the institution of temporary marriage;[26] when fifty-two years old he consummated his marriage with his nine-year-old bride Aisha, who was still playing with dolls;[27] Muhammad allowed his men to have sex with female captives and slaves, unconcerned if they became pregnant or were to be sold;[28] Muhammad declared women to be mentally deficient compared to men;[29] and Muhammad said women will be the majority of hell's inhabitants because they are ungrateful to their husbands.[30]

The issues we have covered should suffice for our present point. Though Muhammad may have taught many good things and been a man of mercy at times, given the extensive counterevidence, we cannot conclude that his character is excellent enough to prove he is a prophet of God.

LOOKING MORE CAREFULLY FOR MUHAMMAD IN THE BIBLE

Though there are many suggested prophecies of Muhammad in the Bible, the ones from Deuteronomy 18 and John 16 are the ones we considered strongest and therefore the ones we most frequently advanced. A common problem with the way we handled them, though, was that we tried to make the text conform to our expectation. Instead of understanding what the words meant and what they intended to convey, we did our best to read them as prophecies about Muhammad.

For example, while reading Deuteronomy 18, we never bothered to consider the Old Testament notion of a prophet, always just assuming the Islamic notion. In the Old Testament, a prophet is anyone who prophesies because the spirit of Yahweh rests upon him (or her!). The Old Testament speaks of prophetesses (Judg. 4:4) and whole groups of prophets at once (1 Sam. 10:5), and neither of these cases aligns with the Muslim notion of prophethood.

Where our interpretation of words became a real problem in Deuteronomy 18, though, was the way we interpreted "from among their brethren." This phrase cannot mean from among the Ishmaelites. Whenever the Bible uses this phrase it means "countrymen," always referring to either close kinsmen or clansmen. It never means anything as distant as an entirely different people group related only through a distant ancestor.

One does not need to be all that familiar with the biblical use of the term to conclude this because the previous chapter defines the term for us. In Deuteronomy 17:15, the Bible says, "You shall set over yourselves a king whom Yahweh your God chooses, from among your brethren. You shall not set a foreigner over yourselves, who is not your brother." So the text defines the word for us: A brother from among the Hebrews is a Hebrew. He cannot be a foreigner, and the Ishmaelites were foreigners. This text cannot be about Muhammad.

Similarly, in John 16, we used to do whatever we could to read Muhammad into the text, ignoring the counterevidence that simply did not allow it. The Greek word was *parakletos* and not *periklutos*, no matter how much we wanted Jesus to use the Greek equivalent to Muhammad. And just as *brethren* had been defined in the paragraphs preceding the Deuteronomy passage, *parakletos* had been defined earlier in the same passage of John. In 14:26, the text tells us the *parakletos* is the Holy Spirit. There is no room for conjecture; the prophecy was about the Holy Spirit living inside Christians. It was not about the coming of any man, let alone a prophet.

This is why the text says about the Spirit of truth, "The world cannot accept him, because it neither sees him nor knows him. But you know him, for he lives with you and will be in you" (John 14:17 NIV). The disciples already knew the Spirit of truth because the Holy Spirit was with them and would soon be in them. How could this be Muhammad? Muhammad was not already with them, nor could he possibly be in them. In context, it is impossible to conclude that the Spirit of truth from John 14–16 is Muhammad.

The same turns out to be the case when we consider any of the so-called "Muhammad in the Bible" prophecies. In most of them, the

Bible is not prophesying the coming of anyone at all. In others, the full context brings in counterevidence that prohibits us from concluding that it is about Muhammad. There simply is no compelling prophecy about Muhammad in the Bible.

MUHAMMAD AND SCIENCE

Counterevidence and context have proven problematic for arguments proposing Muhammad's prophethood, and the same is the case when we examine the argument from miraculous scientific knowledge, that Muhammad knew science so advanced it must have come from God.

Consider the example of Quranic embryology. Before even looking at the text of the Quran, we should consider what mankind had already discovered in order to properly calibrate what might be miraculous knowledge. About a thousand years before Muhammad, Aristotle had published a treatise on embryology, *On the Generation of Animals*. It is far more scientific and detailed than anything Muhammad suggests, being a whole book on the topic of embryology. In section 734a, Aristotle explicitly discusses embryological development in stages.[31] In section 745b, he mentions that an embryo is attached to the uterus via an umbilicus.[32] Galen, a Greek scientist living about five hundred years after Aristotle and five hundred years before Muhammad, also wrote a treatment on embryology, *On the Natural Faculties*. Agreeing that development happens in stages, he says, "Now Nature constructs bone, cartilage, nerve, membrane, ligament, vein, and so forth, at the first stage of the animal's genesis, employing at this task a faculty which is, in general terms, generative and alterative."[33] Both Aristotle and Galen had very carefully defined terms and concepts, positing in great detail the process of embryological development.

Turning now to the Quran, let us quote the passage in question, 23.12–14: "And indeed we made man from an essence of clay; then we placed him as a drop in a safe lodging; Then we made the drop a hanging (thing), then we made the hanging into a chewed (thing), then we made the chewed into bones, then we clothed the bones with flesh, then we developed it into another creation, so blessed be Allah, the best of creators."

At the outset, we must conclude that there is no possibility of anything miraculous here. In no way can it be argued that Muhammad would not have known details of embryology when whole books had been written by Aristotle a thousand years prior and Galen five hundred years prior. In addition, the Quran uses poorly delineated terms and concepts, nowhere near the scientific precision of Galen. Many Muslim explanations of this passage assume "hanging" and "chewed" have specific embryological referents; and they may assume this *if they already believe* the Quran has miraculous scientific knowledge, but they cannot assume *this in order to prove* it has such knowledge. Such a deduction would be circular. The unrefined language makes this passage undecipherable, not miraculous.

What can be ascertained through the rudimentary wording is the notion of development in stages, but this is certainly not miraculous as it was well-known by Muhammad's time. Similarly, Aristotle had already described the tethering of an embryo to the uterus via an umbilical cord (i.e., a hanging thing). Regarding a chewed thing, women in Arabia suffered miscarriages as do women today, and they would have seen fetuses such as the Quran describes.

Regarding details, we can only guess as to what was meant by that section of the passage. As far as understanding the text with clarity, the only section of this Quranic passage that makes a plain assertion is that bones are developed first and that they are then clothed with flesh. Unfortunately, this is false. Modern science has taught us that a single embryological layer, the mesoderm, differentiates into bones and flesh at the same time.

Thus, the one section of this passage that is stated clearly is scientifically inaccurate, and the whole passage is far less sophisticated than texts that had been written a thousand years prior. This is simply not a miraculous passage whatsoever.

Regarding the allegedly miraculous insight about mountains, that they stabilize the earth and have roots, much can be said, but it would be helpful just to point out the patterns. Here again, the scientific assertion is false. Mountains do not create stability in the earth's crust; instead, they are a result of tectonic instability. Although the assertion that mountains have roots beneath the earth's surface is correct in a sense, the Quran was certainly not the first book to posit this. We see that assertion made at least three times in the Bible: Job 28:9, Psalm 18:7, and Jonah 2:6.

As a Muslim, I believed there were dozens of examples of miraculous scientific knowledge in the Quran, but when I started investigating them carefully, I found that each and every one succumbed to at least one of three critiques: First, the verses were being made to say things they did not assert (much like the "Muhammad in the Bible" prophecies); second, the science was actually well-known before Muhammad's day (such as embryological development in stages); or third, the science was false (such as the bones developing before muscles).

There are many examples of the third criticism, which really is the nail in the coffin for this argument. These incorrect statements are found in both the Quran and hadith. For example, just in the field of embryology, the Quran is incorrect regarding spermatogenesis, asserting that semen is produced between a man's backbone and his ribs (86.7). In the hadith, we find a case that is very telling: A man asked Muhammad to prove that he is a prophet by correctly answering questions.[34] One of the questions inquired why a child might look like his father more than his mother, or vice versa. Muhammad responded that Gabriel had informed him of the answer to his question: The first parent to have discharge during intercourse determined the appearance of the child.

It goes without saying that this is scientifically false, because genetics determine the appearance of a child. We ought not blame a man in the seventh century for being unfamiliar with Mendelian genetics, but in this case, Muhammad actually was trying to prove that he was a prophet of God through his scientific insights, and he was very wrong. That stark reality was enough to give me pause as a Muslim.

There were many more times when Muhammad was incorrect in his science, and examples can be found in the Quran as well as the hadith. For example, apart from what we have already seen, the Quran says that the sun sets in a pool of muddy water in the west (18.86),[35] and it assumes stars are the same thing as meteorites (67.5). In the hadith, apart from what we have already seen, Muhammad teaches that flies carry diseases on one wing and antidotes on the other,[36] that cumin heals all diseases,[37] and that camel urine cures stomach aches.[38] These are but a few examples of many of Muhammad's scientific inaccuracies.

CONCLUDING THE RESPONSE TO THE CASE FOR MUHAMMAD'S PROPHETHOOD

It is worth remembering that we have not tried to *disprove* Muhammad's prophethood. We have considered arguments that are used to *prove* Muhammad's prophethood, and we have concluded that they are quite problematic.

Though other Muslims and I often said that Muhammad ought to be followed because of his excellent character, I could not sustain that argument in the face of the counterevidence. Although Muhammad gave plenty of moral teachings and exhibited merciful and peaceful character at times, there are many other accounts of Muhammad's brutality and exultation in war, his spiritual shortcomings, and his troubling treatment of women, among other concerns.

Also, there are no prophecies regarding Muhammad in the Bible. Reading the full context of the proposed passages and considering the meaning of their words carefully demonstrates that none of these passages are prophecies.

Similarly, there is no miraculous scientific knowledge in either the Quran or the hadith. On the contrary, historical and textual context show every example to be flawed. In addition, many counterexamples of faulty science can be found in the texts of the Quran and the hadith that prohibit us from concluding that the text is miraculous.

CHAPTER 35

ASSESSING THE RESPONSE

HADITH VERSUS HISTORY

The three reasons most commonly given by Muslims to accept Muhammad as a prophet—his character, prophecies in the Bible, and miraculous scientific insights—are all very problematic. As a result, we are left with no reason to believe that Muhammad was sent by God. This reasoning is incredibly straightforward.

In simply setting out the arguments for Muhammad's prophethood and considering them carefully, we have done something most Muslims never do. Generally speaking, most Muslims inherit a fulsome image of Muhammad from their parents and teachers during childhood and then assume that the stories they have always heard are true. That was the case for me, and since I had never really considered the arguments rationally, I did not respond to counterarguments rationally. Even though I had invited my friend David to study the matter with me, we often got into heated arguments while discussing Muhammad. I remember charging him with "dragging our prophet through the mud" more than once, when in actuality, I knew in my heart that I did not know how to handle what I was learning about Muhammad.

The fact is most Muslims simply have not read the primary sources on Muhammad's life, instead only hearing overviews that have filtered out the more problematic accounts. When they first hear these stories, they do not know how to react. When I began reading these accounts with my own eyes, I tried to resolve each one individually, searching out explanations and ways to account for or dismiss each account that challenged the image of the peaceful, noble Muhammad I knew.

Individual problematic accounts quickly became dozens of such stories, and within a matter of months I was trying to account for over a hundred traditions of Muhammad's life that I simply could not believe were true. This is when I began to approach the life of Muhammad more systematically. How could I know which accounts of Muhammad's life were reliable and which were not?

HADITH SCIENCES AND THE HISTORICAL METHOD

As Muslims, we knew it was a long time after Muhammad died before anything substantial was written about his life, but people did not cease talking about him. For over two hundred years, stories about the Islamic prophet were passed orally from person to person, and among the true accounts proliferated many fabrications. By the time a systematic effort was made to sort through them, over five hundred thousand accounts of Muhammad's life were in popular circulation, and it is commonly estimated that the vast majority of them were false.

How can we know which accounts of Muhammad's life are trustworthy?

At first, I assumed the classical Islamic method for assessing the authenticity of hadith. In the field of *uloom al-hadith*, translated "the science of Muhammad's sayings," Muslim scholars grade individual accounts of Muhammad's life based on criteria such as how well-known an account was and who the people relaying it were. The most trustworthy hadith are ultimately graded *sahih*, which means "true" or "authentic," whereas the weakest hadith are labelled *daeef* ("weak") or even *maudu* ("fabricated").

Imam Bukhari and his student Imam Muslim were two highly respected scholars in the third century after Muhammad, and they collected only those hadith which they considered *sahih* and beyond dispute. Most Muslims consider their collections above reproach. In using only the hadith that they approved, I hoped that we could see Muhammad was the noble and peaceful man that I had always been taught, and that there were no problematic accounts in his life.

But this did not happen. Problematic accounts existed even amid the *sahih* collections; in fact, every single account in the previous chapter was either from the Quran or from the *sahih* collections of Imam Bukhari and Imam Muslim.

I began asking imams to resolve these problematic accounts found in the *sahih*, and I also searched online to see how other Muslims responded to the criticisms. What I learned was that many were willing to accuse even the *sahih* collections of containing fabricated accounts, finding ways to dismiss those accounts that were considered authentic by the great Muslim scholars of old.

It was then I realized they were playing a dangerous game. *They were essentially finding ways to pick and choose from the ancient records which accounts were reliable and which were not, creating a Muhammad that they felt comfortable with.*

I did not want to do that. I wanted to know who Muhammad really was and whether I should follow him as my prophet, not to create a Muhammad in my mind that was worth following. I decided to reconsider my approach and study Muhammad using the historical method instead of *uloom al-hadith*. What were the earliest accounts written about Muhammad, and how soon were they written?

It was then that I discovered some shocking facts about early Islam. First, people were not writing books in Arabic during Muhammad's time. *The first Arabic book to have been written was the Quran*, and even that was turned into a written book only after Muhammad died. There was no such thing as written Arabic literature, only oral. This is because, second, *people were still figuring out how to write Arabic*. Arabic script was far from standardized, having been invented only a century or two before Muhammad's time. For these reasons and others, third, *no one wrote a biography of Muhammad's life until about 140 years after Muhammad died.* By that time, there were certainly no eyewitnesses of Muhammad's life, and people were generations removed from the events they discussed. Could we trust such an account to be an unfiltered and accurate depiction of Muhammad?

The first biography, *Sirat Rasul Allah*, was written by a man named Ibn Ishaq, but the book itself has actually been lost. Ibn Ishaq taught a man named al-Bakkai, who made his own edition of Ibn Ishaq's book, and al-Bakkai taught a man named Ibn Hisham, who edited al-Bakkai's edition, and it is this edition that we have today. Why did these men each make their own editions? Ibn Hisham tells us in his introductory remarks: "Things which it is disgraceful to discuss, matters which would distress certain people, and such reports as al-Bakkai told me he could not accept as trustworthy—all these things I have omitted."[1] In other words, the earliest biography of Muhammad's life was reputed to contain fabrications, disgraceful material, and distressing facts.[2] What we have today has been filtered many times, both for fabrications and for difficult truths.

It is because of such intentional editing that historians do not consider late accounts as trustworthy as early accounts, all else being equal. The earlier accounts have not been as filtered, and therefore are more likely to be true. Also, people are more prone to forget information over time, especially information that does not fit with the narrative at large. When it comes to the records of Muhammad's life, we simply do not have such early or unfiltered data. Everything has been filtered through multiple generations.

Even though the earliest biography went through layers of filtering, it still contains shocking material. Muhammad personally oversaw the beheadings of up to nine hundred men on a single day, digging trenches in the marketplaces so that their corpses could fall into mass graves upon being decapitated;[3] he ordered the assassination of an old man who had composed poetry complaining about Muhammad;[4] a woman lamented the old man's death in poetry, so Muhammad ordered her assassination, and her blood splattered on her children as she breastfed;[5] Muhammad ordered the torture of a city treasurer to extract the location of the money, so his men kindled a fire with flint and steel on the treasurer's chest until he was nearly dead, ultimately beheading him;[6] when Muhammad was about to execute a man, the man pleaded, "Who will look after my children?" to which Muhammad responded, "Hell!"[7] Just by scratching the surface of the earliest biography we find many troubling accounts of Muhammad.

By the time hadith were written under men like Imam Bukhari and Imam Muslim, many of these accounts were filtered out of Muhammad's biography, just as Ibn Hisham and al-Bakkai had filtered the accounts that they received. *For this reason, selective filtration, the whole body of hadith is inherently flawed: They contain only those accounts that multiple generations of early Muslims each chose to save.* As we have seen, even those that were kept are often considered flawed and fabricated.

WHAT CAN WE REALLY KNOW ABOUT MUHAMMAD?

For this reason, non-Muslim scholars of early Islam are very hesitant to trust the information about the life of Muhammad. Almost none accept the science of hadith criticism as it stands, most just hoping to extract historical kernels of truth from the hadith. Some scholars have even abandoned hope of that much success, saying virtually nothing can be known about Muhammad. These scholars are from a variety of religious and nonreligious backgrounds. *One Muslim scholar concluded that, given the nature of the evidence, Muhammad may not have even existed.*

Muhammad Sven Kalisch completed his PhD in Islamic jurisprudence in 1997 and became Germany's first professor to hold a chair in Islamic theology. When he arrived at Münster University in 2004, he struck some as too conservative on account of his zeal for sharia. But then, according to the *Wall Street Journal*, Kalisch "wanted to subject Islam to the same scrutiny as Christianity and Judaism."[8] At first he defended the historicity of Muhammad in print, but the more he studied, the more he realized there were significant problems with the record. The word *Muhammad* appears only four times in the Quran, and it is unclear whether it is a name or a title. Quran 61.6 appears to say that the Prophet's name was Ahmad, not Muhammad.[9] There is no other evidence of Muhammad's existence until the turn of the eighth century, when coins bearing his name were produced. "The more I read, the historical person at the root of the whole thing became more and more improbable," says Muhammad Kalisch.

Other scholars are coming to similar conclusions on account of the holes in the historical records. Their concerns are more than an argument from silence; if the traditional understanding of Islam is true, it is indeed very problematic that we do not find more about Muhammad in the earliest historical records. If Muhammad was the prophet of the Arabs, and if they were energized and motivated by his teachings, why is it that the Arab conquests of the Middle East, North Africa, and Persia never mention his name? These conquests occurred in the middle of the seventh century, immediately after Muhammad's death, yet none of the contemporary records mention Muhammad. In fact, none mention a holy book or even the word *Muslim*. It is not that there are no records; considering the communications of the conquerors and the writings of the conquered, there are abundant records, yet Muhammad is never named, a holy book is never discussed, and the conquerors are never called Muslims.

Other evidence also has historians scratching their heads: Although Mecca is reputed to be a trade center, it never appears in any trade routes until the turn of the eighth century; none of the earliest mosques faced toward Mecca (all faced toward either Jerusalem or Petra until about the turn of the eighth century); Mecca is mentioned only once in the Quran; the descriptions of the land in the Quran sound very little like Mecca, much more like northern Arabia; and the list goes on.

For these reasons, not just one Muslim scholar but many scholars doubt the traditional origins of Islam and even the existence of Muhammad, at least as the early Islamic records describe him. According to them, the truth about the origins of Islam is unfortunately veiled. There is almost nothing we can know with certainty about the historical Muhammad.[10]

CHAPTER 36

CONCLUSION

THE DILEMMA OF THE
HISTORICAL MUHAMMAD

Both as a Muslim and now ten years later, I did not conclude that Muhammad did not exist. Given the sheer volume of stories and accounts, as well as their relative coherence, it seems more probable than not to me that Muhammad existed. But I do have to agree with the basic consensus of non-Muslim scholarship: We cannot know much about Muhammad with certainty.

The alternative, of course, is to trust the Islamic records of Muhammad's life, the hadith and *sirah*. But if we consider their accuracy according to the standards of *uloom al-hadith*, we still find a Muhammad who is not compelling as a prophet of God. Perhaps he was a great seventh-century general and one who adhered to the cultural standards of his day, but he certainly was not the greatest moral exemplar of all time nor one to whom I would declare my allegiance. If we abandon the *uloom al-hadith* and use the historical method of assessing the earliest biographies and accounts of Muhammad's life, we find an even more brutal and problematic picture of Muhammad.

This is the dilemma I had as a Muslim: *Either I could trust the historical sources of Muhammad's life and find a man I would never want to follow as a prophet, or I could question the sources and have no reason to consider him a prophet.* Either way I could not conclude, based on the evidence, that Muhammad was a prophet of God.

A DISTURBANCE IN THE *SHAHADA*

Much like Professor Muhammad Sven Kalisch, I was confident in my Islam and in following Muhammad until I used the same critical standards to study his life as I did to study the life of Jesus. While critically studying Jesus' claim to be God, I had been willing to discard John's gospel because it was written fifty-five or sixty years after Jesus' death, even though eyewitnesses of Jesus' life would still have been alive at that time and in that community. If I treated the accounts of Muhammad's life the same way, I would have to throw out absolutely everything, and I would have no basis to consider him my prophet.

But the records of his life left me with a dilemma: If I did believe the records to be reliable, then there was no way I could follow Muhammad as a prophet. His character was certainly not so excellent that it compelled us to believe he was a prophet. He had many spiritual shortcomings, and he was very violent throughout his ministry, among other concerns. Nor did the records indicate that God had sanctioned his ministry: He was not prophesied in the Bible and he did not have any remarkable depth of insight into science.

Crestfallen, I came to the conclusion that there was simply no way I could declare Muhammad a prophet of God based on the historical record. I could no longer recite the *shahada* without a sharp pang of doubt, and it haunted me.

The only way for me to continue following Muhammad was through the Quran. If it could be shown that the Quran is the Word of God, then the one who delivered it would have to be a messenger of God. I clung to the hope that my investigation of the Quran not only would vindicate Muhammad but also would completely outshine the evidence for Christianity.

PART 10

IS THE QURAN THE WORD OF GOD?

CHAPTER 37

THE POSITIVE CASE

THERE IS NO OTHER BOOK LIKE IT

The Quran is the jewel of Islam. The "why" of Muslim belief, it is the prize of Muhammad and the foundation of the faith. Its place in Islamic theology is that of Jesus in Christian theology, and as a Muslim, my confidence was built on nothing less than the text of the Quran and its excellence.

We inherited our high view of the Quran from the Muslims around us and our world of tradition. I grew up memorizing its chapters by hearing portions read aloud during the daily prayers and by being quizzed on it by my mother daily. That is how I had the last seven chapters of the Quran memorized by the age of five, and the last fifteen chapters memorized by the age of fifteen. While I was more acquainted with the Quran than most Muslims I knew, I certainly was not out of the ordinary. Some in our Islamic community had the entire Quran memorized by their teenage years.

We regarded the Quran more highly than any other physical object in the world. After all, we believed it was the Word of God.

When I began losing my historical confidence in the prophethood of Muhammad, I placed all my hope on the pillar of the Quran, believing it would stand firm enough to authenticate Muhammad's prophetic status. In all honesty, I truly was convinced it would stand firm because I had heard many arguments for its inspiration.

THE LITERARY EXCELLENCE OF THE QURAN

A deeply held belief of devout Muslims is that the excellence of the Quran is unsurpassed, that it is inimitable in its literary quality. This is inherently true not only because it is an expression of Allah, the Word of God on earth, but also because the Quran says so. When people charged Muhammad to prove that the Quran was inspired by God, the response came: "This Quran could not be produced by any other than Allah . . . Do they say, 'he has invented it'? Say, 'then bring a surah like it'" (10.37–38).

Thus, the Quran challenges skeptics to try their hand at making something equal or better, asserting that no one but Allah could compose a recitation so excellent. They will never be able to do it, not even if they had the help of every man and every demon: "If mankind and jinn gathered to bring something similar to this Quran, they could not" (17.88). The basic challenge is repeated multiple times in the Quran.[1]

According to Muslims, this challenge was made to skeptical Arabs who were experts in poetry. They were never able to produce anything as excellent and compelling as the Quran, and the challenge thus stands to this day.

THE FULFILLED PROPHECIES OF THE QURAN

If the Quran can be shown to contain fulfilled prophecies, then we have good reason to believe it is from God. One of the clearest prophecies is found in sura 30, the chapter on the Romans. In it, the Quran mentions a recent loss of the Roman Empire, predicting that the Romans would ultimately regroup, defeating their enemies within the next few years (30.2–4). This is exactly what happened. The Persians defeated the Romans in 614, but Emperor Heraclius ultimately defeated the Persians in 622.

Other prophecies, more long-term in their predictions, have also come true. For example, the Quran says, "Their skins testify against them as to what they used to do" (41.20). Reading the verse, one would wonder how skin can testify against a man. Muhammad could never have known about fingerprint analysis, that people's skin could testify against them. This verse is therefore a prophecy that has come true in modern times.

Many more prophecies such as these two, prophecies of events in both ancient and modern times, confirm that the Quran is the Word of God.

THE MIRACULOUS SCIENTIFIC KNOWLEDGE IN THE QURAN

Muslims often argue that there is miraculous scientific knowledge in the Quran. In addition to the examples in chapter 33, Muslims often argue that the Quran speaks of the big bang in 21.30, which says, "Have the disbelievers not known that the universe was a singularity, and we tore it apart?" In addition to the miraculous astronomic insight, the verse goes on to show miraculous biological insight: "We made every living thing out of water."

Muhammad could not have known about the big bang nor about the fact that water is essential to all forms of life. The best explanation of this miraculous scientific knowledge is that the Quran must have come from Allah.

THE MATHEMATICAL MARVELS OF THE QURAN

Although it was not an argument that I ever used, many Muslims argue that the Quran displays mathematical marvels that could only be the result of God's authorship. One kind of mathematical marvel is numerical parallels: the word *month* appears twelve times in the Quran, the word *day* appears 365 times, the words *man* and *woman* appear an equal number of times, the words *angels* and *Satan* appear an equal number of times, and the words *this world* and *the hereafter* appear an equal number of times. Such numerical parallels could only be the result of a divine mind behind the text.

In addition to these patterns, there is a hidden code in the Quran. In 74.30, the Quran says "over it are nineteen." When we analyze the text of the Quran for patterns, we start finding the number nineteen everywhere. For just a few examples, the total number of chapters in the Quran is divisible by nineteen; the first revelation of the Quran had nineteen words; and the first chapter chronologically revealed has nineteen verses and a total number of words divisible by nineteen. Dozens of such examples can be found, and the number nineteen is not a small prime number, making it very difficult for a text to exhibit this as a common pattern. Given the Quranic verse about the number nineteen, the oddity of the number, and the prevalence of the pattern, we can be confident that Allah is the author of this text.

THE PERFECT PRESERVATION OF THE QURAN

One argument more essential to Muslim faith than all the others is the perfect preservation of the Quran. Every single word, every single letter, every single stroke of the Quran remains exactly as it was revealed, from Allah to Muhammad down to our day. It is an essential belief because of the view of the Quran in Islam: It is the eternal expression of Allah, so it can never change. Its immutability is also necessary because it is the foundation of sharia, a law for all time.

This is miraculous proof of the Quran's inspiration because it was prophesied in the Quran: "Surely we have revealed the Reminder (Qur'an) and we will surely be its guardian" (15.9). And since we believed that every other holy book has been corrupted by its followers, this miracle is all the more potent.

CONCLUDING THE POSITIVE CASE

In our circles, the Quran really was above dispute. For multiple reasons, the Muslim community is convinced beyond any doubt that it is the Word of God: Its text is inimitably excellent, it foretells prophecies that have been fulfilled, it holds hidden scientific truths waiting to be discovered, its marvelously calculated text could only be the product of a divine mind, and the text has been preserved perfectly, down to the very stroke of the scribes' pens.

Such were the arguments in which we had always placed our faith, and I had been convinced of their strength my entire life. When it became the only remaining pillar of my faith, though, I had to scrutinize these arguments with much more precision than ever before. They were now the sole foundation of my faith, and I had to be certain whether they could bear the weight of my entire Islamic worldview.

CHAPTER 38

THE RESPONSE

IN WHAT WAY IS THAT MIRACULOUS?

When I began my investigation of the Quran, I was more than convinced that it was the Word of Allah, but I needed to be able to show that an objective investigator would also find the case convincing.

That is where the case started crumbling.

THE LITERARY EXCELLENCE OF THE QURAN: A FLAWED TEST

One of the first things that became apparent was that the Quran's own defense of its inspiration—the challenge to write a revelation like it—is virtually impossible to assess.

I vividly remember Mike Licona's response when I told him of the Quran's challenge. "I've seen better writing than the Quran," he responded nonchalantly. "Have you ever read Psalm 23?" Shocked at his brazen assertion, I retorted that Psalm 23 was not of the caliber of the Quran, but he simply disagreed with me, saying it was one of the most powerful passages ever composed, more moving than anything he had read in the Quran.

That is when I took a step back and reassessed the test. What is it really asking? I began to think that it must be the Arabic of the Quran that was inimitable, not the English translation or interpretations. But did that mean that this test was limited to Arabic speakers?

That could not be the case either. People who had specifically set out to respond to the Quran's challenge had already composed a book of Christian teachings in Arabic called the *Furqan al-Haqq*, "The True

Discernment." They included many teachings of the Psalms in this Arabic book, writing them in the style of the Quran. Their results were so convincing that they read the text aloud, chanting it in Quranic style, in the middle of Arab Muslim cities. Many who passed would hear the recitation and, confusing it for the Quran, thank the readers for reciting it. Clearly, then, the test did not work for Arabic speakers either, not even Arab Muslims.

Researching the issue online, I found Muslim apologists arguing that the Arabs who had mistaken the *Furqan al-Haqq* were probably unlearned, so they had not grasped the lofty beauty of the Quran. An expert in Arabic would find the text of the Quran inimitable.

It was then that I found the assessment of a scholar, Gerd Puin, whose expertise is on the Arabic orthography of the Quran. Puin argued that "every fifth sentence or so simply doesn't make sense."[1] Preemptively defending his assertion, Puin adds, "Many Muslims—and Orientalists—will tell you otherwise, of course, but the fact is that a fifth of the Koranic text *is just incomprehensible.*"[2] To this, Muslim apologists responded that Gerd Puin was not a native Arabic speaker; the Quran needed to be assessed by an expert in Arabic who is himself an Arab and has grown up speaking Arabic.

With every step, it seemed that the test was being redefined to somehow protect it from scrutiny, but this leads us to ask the question: In what way is this challenge pertinent to us? If it is only for Arabic speakers, it serves no proof for the vast majority of people in the world today; if people have to be experts in classical Arabic, then it is relevant only to a very small number of people in human history.

Of course, all this is apart from the subjectivity of the test and its ultimately non-sequitur nature: Who is to say whether one composition is more excellent than another? By what measure? The Quran certainly does not set the parameters the apologists do. And even if it were ascertained that the Quran is the best writing mankind has ever seen, that does not mean it is inspired. Stradivarius, a man who lived from the mid-1600s to the 1700s, is reputed to have made the most acoustically perfect violins the world has ever heard; not even with our modern technology have we been able to reproduce their perfection.[3] Were he to have said that his violins were made by God and offered their matchless quality as evidence, we would have thought him a lunatic or a liar. In what way does an excellent product prove divine origin?

For these reasons, the literary excellence of the Quran is a flawed test, and as I found with Mike, it is unconvincing to non-Muslims—the very people for whom it is intended. An objective investigator would not be convinced.

THE PROPHECIES OF THE QURAN: NOT REALLY PROPHECIES

When we consider the prophecies of the Quran carefully, we conclude there are virtually none to even test. As an example, let us consider the claim that 41.20 is a prophecy about fingerprints. The full context of the verse reads, "And (make mention of) the day when the enemies of Allah are gathered unto the Fire, they are driven on till, when they reach it, their ears and their eyes and their skins testify against them as to what they used to do. And they say unto their skins: Why testify ye against us? They say: Allah hath given us speech, Who giveth speech to all things" (41.19–21).

By reading the context we find that the Quran is actually speaking about the day of judgment, that skin will speak with a voice, along with eyes and ears. It is not a prophecy of something that will happen on earth but an apocalyptic description of judgment. Only by wrenching this verse from its context and forcing a contrived meaning upon it can this verse be made to sound like a prophecy for our time.

Of course, we can do this with just about any text if we try hard enough, and it is easier with apocalyptic texts such as this one. For example, I have just now opened the Bible to a random section of the book of Revelation, and my finger landed on 11:8, which says, "Their bodies will lie in the public square of the great city—which is figuratively called Sodom and Egypt." I can argue that this was a miraculous prophecy of the Arab Spring that describes the aftermath of the Tahrir Square demonstrations that took place in January 2011, leading to over eight hundred people killed. Moreover, the city of Cairo, where Tahrir Square is located, is often referred to figuratively as Egypt in the Arabic language (*Misr*). Thus, eight hundred bodies laid in Tahrir Square, a public square in the great city that is figuratively called Egypt. Revelation 11:8 prophesies the event with extreme precision almost two thousand years ahead of time.

Of course, that is not what the text is prophesying, and I have just made all this up on the spot, but I could make the case appear convincing if I really wanted to, especially if I take the verse out of context. This is exactly what we see with the vast majority of so-called prophecies in the Quran. There is no reason to think the Quran is making any of these so-called prophecies. That is not to say there may not be hidden prophetic meaning in the text of the Quran, but in order to be a prophecy that convinces an objective investigator, it needs to meet the minimum criterion that it is obviously a prophecy, not text that can be turned into one.

For example, the passage about the Roman victory in 30.2–4 actually does appear to be a prophecy, the clearest example of a prophecy in the Quran, so it is worth considering more carefully. There are two minor problems with considering this a fulfilled prophecy, and two major problems. Briefly, the first minor problem is the nature of the prophecy; it is not much of a prediction. Given the ongoing nature of the Byzantine-Persian conflicts at the time, there was bound to be a Byzantine victory at some point. It is almost like saying, "The Chicago Bulls have just lost to the LA Lakers, but the Bulls will be ultimately victorious."[4]

The second minor problem is the number of years it took for the Byzantines to be victorious; the verse of the Quran uses a word that implies ten years or less, but it took seventeen years for the Romans to ultimately defeat the Byzantines.

There are two much more significant problems with using this as prophetic fulfillment. First, Quranic verses were regularly abrogated, and the Byzantine victory came during Muhammad's lifetime. Had it looked as if it were not going to happen, the text could easily have been abrogated.[5]

Second, and along the same vein, the Quran was not collected in a book until even later. Had this prophecy failed, it could have been left out of the final collection of the text, as other verses had.[6]

So this example of a Quranic prophecy, the best that the text has to offer, is not convincing. It is essentially a 50/50 prediction that could have easily been taken back, and if we consider the text literally, it appears that it did not come true anyway, as the Byzantines did not defeat the Persians until after the prophesied time had elapsed.

THE MIRACULOUS SCIENTIFIC KNOWLEDGE: CONSIDERING TEXT AND CONTEXT

While considering the prophethood of Muhammad, we already saw that the Quran contains scientific inaccuracies—such as the setting of the sun in water and the production of sperm between the backbone and the ribs—which are enough to cause serious doubt that the Quran is scientifically miraculous. As before, simply investigating the text and the context of such supposed miraculous knowledge is usually enough to conclude that this is not a convincing argument.

That rule of thumb turns out to be true here as well. Looking again at 21.30 of the Quran, the text actually reads, "Have not those who disbelieve known that the heavens and the earth were of one piece, then We parted them." It does not say that the universe was a singularity, but rather that the heavens and earth were joined and God separated them. This is actually just an approximation of what God was doing in Genesis 1:6—nothing new or specific to the Quran. Similarly, the notion that all living creatures are made of water is not that difficult to postulate, as humans and animals all drink water, and very little survives in the desert where there is not much water. Finally, it might be worth knowing that the Quran frequently asserts that *jinn* were made from fire, not water, and some would consider this a contradiction within the Quran.[7]

So these examples, as before, are shown to be far from convincing when we consider the actual text of the verse, the historical context of the science claims, and the accuracy of what the Quran asserts. There is no miraculous scientific knowledge in the Quran.

MATHEMATICAL MARVELS:
IN WHAT WAY ARE THEY SPECIAL?

Although many Muslims find the argument from mathematical patterns compelling, I honestly never did. All sorts of amazing patterns can be found in the world around us if we simply look for them. This is true of the natural world, as anyone who has considered the golden ratio will attest, and it is true of manmade products as well. Searching for patterns in *Moby Dick*, for example, one can find predictions of the future, including the assassinations of Leon Trotsky, Martin Luther King Jr., John F. Kennedy, Abraham Lincoln, and Princess Diana.[8] If you look hard enough, and if you can fudge the parameters, you will find patterns.

And we know that the person who "discovered" the pattern of the number nineteen in the Quran was doing just that. Rashad Khalifa, the person who first published the pattern of the number nineteen, used about 250 pages to defend fifty-two different ways that the number nineteen was found in the text of the Quran. According to a popular Muslim scholar, Bilal Philips, "Most Muslims readily and unquestioningly accepted Khalifa's claims as they had the aura of 'scientific fact' about them." But some Muslims emphatically decried the argument from the number nineteen, pointing out the great flaws in Khalifa's arguments and reasoning. Philips himself penned an entire treatise against it, called "The Qur'an's Numerical Miracle."[9]

In it, Philips says, "The Theory of Nineteen is a shoddily concocted hoax unable to withstand serious scientific scrutiny."[10] Part of Philips's response to Khalifa pertains to the Quranic verse Khalifa quotes, 74.30–31. Reading the full text in this case clarifies that the number nineteen refers to the number of angels who are wardens over the hellfire, not at all to miraculous patterns in the text of the Quran. As we have seen others do with Quranic "prophecies," Khalifa simply wrenched the words out of their context and tried to fit them to his theory.

Another part of Philips's response relates to the inconsistent method and arbitrary selections required to argue for the number nineteen. "By Using Dr. Khalifa's inconsistent method of concocting multiples," argues Philips, "it is also possible to establish 8 as the axis of the Qur'an's miraculous numerical code," and he goes on to give eight reasons why.

The majority of Philips' response to Khalifa's argument, though, is systematically analyzing Khalifa's publications and calculations, concluding that Khalifa had "fabricated data in order to artificially create letter totals which are multiples of nineteen." Not only does Khalifa inconsistently count letters and verses, following "a haphazard system of word identification that totally contradicts both classical and modern rules of Arabic grammar," but also he is willing to go as far as discarding two verses from the Quran in order to make his calculations work. Philips's arguments against the "miraculous pattern" are convincing, as is his conclusion that Khalifa was willing to tamper with the Quranic text simply to make the data fit.

In a similar way, the arguments of marvelous numerical parallels appear to treat the text inconsistently and tamper with the wording. The Quran does not use the word *day* 365 times, for example. It uses it 360 times, and to make the other five work, proponents of the argument have to fudge the data, allowing words to count that are not exactly the word *day*. The same is true for the number of times *month* is used, and the supposedly parallel occurrences of *man/woman* and *this world/ hereafter*. Since Arabic is a Semitic language and uses a triliteral root system for its words, different words are very similar to one another in spelling, and this is often used to the advantage of those who would be willing to "massage the data" to make their argument work.

To summarize our response to the argument from marvelous mathematical patterns, I will quote Philips's final words: "It may be concluded that the theory of nineteen as a miraculous numerical code for the Qur'an has no basis in the Qur'an itself and the few instances where nineteen and its multiples do occur are merely coincidences which have been blown out of proportion."[11] The same can be said for all the mathematical marvels found in the Quran.

PERFECT PRESERVATION OF THE QURANIC TEXT: IN WHAT WAY HAS IT BEEN PERFECTLY PRESERVED?

Finally, though we had firm faith in the perfect preservation of the Quran, the fact is that it is impossible to prove. When Uthman produced an official, edited copy of the Quran and destroyed all the other copies, he left future historians no means to determine whether today's Quran actually goes back to Muhammad.[12] Uthman destroyed all the evidence, and it appears he did so precisely because there were variants.[13]

Despite the fact that perfect preservation cannot be *proven*, it can be *disproven* to a significant degree. In the first place, the Quranic text was not always written but sometimes just known by memory. It was for this reason that Umar convinced Abu Bakr to collect a copy of the Quran in the first place. Many *Qurra* (reciters of the Quran) were dying on battlefields, and Umar said, "I am afraid that more heavy casualties may take place among the Qurra' on other battlefields, whereby a large part of the Qur'an may be lost."[14] If the Quran had been written, why would he fear its loss by the death of its reciters?

The fact is that portions of the Quran were not in writing, and it had to be collected from people's memories. This is said explicitly in Sahih Bukhari: The Quran was collected from "palmed stalks, thin white stones and also from the men who knew it by heart." The same hadith tells us that at least two verses were known by only one person: "I started searching for the Qur'an till I found the last two Verses of Surat at-Tauba with Abi Khuza'ima Al-Ansari and I could not find these Verses with anybody other than him."[15] In other words, two verses of the Quran have been included on the testimony of just one individual.[16] Had he not remembered those verses, they would have been lost, and we would all have been none the wiser.

Sahih Bukhari mentions that a verse was missed the first time the Quran was written, and it had to be found later: "A verse from Surat Ahzab was missed by me when we copied the Qur'an and I used to hear Allah's Messenger reciting it. So we searched for it and found it with Khuza'ima bin Thabit Al-Ansari."[17] It appears that verses kept being forgotten and lost, just barely being recovered.

Muhammad himself used to say that Muslims tended to forget Quranic verses very easily. "Keep on reciting the Qur'an because it escapes from the hearts of men faster than camel do."[18] He was not exaggerating, as even he forgot verses of the Quran. Upon hearing a man reciting the Quran at night he said, "May Allah bestow His Mercy on him, as he has reminded me of verses which I forgot."[19]

If, according to the most trustworthy traditions, parts of the Quran were known by only one person, and other parts were missed, and indeed Muslims forgot verses, could it not be that some parts of the Quran were left out altogether? Can we really say such a precarious text has been perfectly preserved?

Unfortunately, we cannot. Sahih Bukhari puts the nail in the coffin by recording this hadith: "Umar said, 'Ubay was the best of us in the recitation of the Qur'an yet we leave out some of what he recites.' Ubay says, 'I have taken it from the mouth of Allah's Messenger and will not leave it out for anything whatever.'"[20] So the very best reciter of the Quran was adamant that verses of the Quran have been left out.[21] Muhammad himself chose Ubay as one of the best teachers of the Quran,[22] and yet he disagreed with today's Quran.

To summarize, not only is there no way to prove that the Quran has been perfectly preserved, but it appears to have been disproved: Portions are missing, and one of the greatest teachers of the Quran, hand selected by Muhammad, disagreed with today's edition of the Quran. There is much, much more to be said against the argument from perfect preservation, but we have confined ourselves to just that evidence present in Sahih Bukhari, and not even all of that.[23]

Finally, as we saw in chapter 14, the text of the Quran was undergoing abrogation. Muhammad would cancel certain older verses and replace them with newer verses. The Quran itself testifies to this in 2.106 and 16.101. Muslims may be able to accept this phenomenon as a divine mandate, and they are well within their rights to do so, but to an objective investigator it strongly challenges the case of perfect preservation. Rather, the phenomenon of abrogation makes the text of the Quran appear very artificial and man-made.

Of course, even if the Quran were perfectly preserved, that is not necessarily a miracle. Many texts have been unchanged throughout the ages. But given the abrogation of its text, the missing sections, the portions that had been forgotten, and the controlled destruction of all variants, an objective investigator is forced to ask, "In what way is the preservation of the Quran miraculous?"

CONCLUDING THE RESPONSE TO THE POSITIVE CASE

The arguments for the divine inspiration of the Quran all prove unconvincing when we begin to dig beneath the surface. The literary excellence of the Quran proves to be untestable, subjective, and non-sequitur; the prophecies of the Quran are not compelling; the science of the Quran is actually problematic; the numerical patterns are often distorted data combined with exaggerated interpretations; and the Quran has not been preserved in any miraculous sense.

Because there is no compelling argument, there is no reason to accept the Quran as the Word of God.

CHAPTER 39

ASSESSING THE RESPONSE

WHAT KIND OF BOOK IS THE QURAN?

When assessing these counterarguments as a Muslim, my immediate response was to bring more evidence to the table, and to provide more examples of fulfilled prophecies and more examples of miraculously scientific knowledge. We had heard dozens of such examples at the mosques throughout our lives. Surely if the first few examples were not convincing, then one of the many others would compel.

It took months of bringing example after example to the table before I finally realized that, indeed, they all succumb to the same basic critiques.

It was a different process altogether when I came to learn about the history of the Quranic text. In that case, it was not a series of examples that was called into question, but a foundational narrative of my Muslim faith. We had learned from everyone, not just imams in the mosque but our parents and elders and books that we had read, that the Quran was absolutely perfect in its transmission. Muhammad had relayed it to his scribes, the scribes had written it down and memorized it, the Muslim people treasured it in their hearts and recited it regularly during the prayers, and it was readily written down and preserved. All copies today are exactly the same.

That is what we had been told. But as I read Sahih Bukhari, specifically the book titled *The Virtues of the Quran*, it became clear to me that a great deal of the evidence had been left out of the narrative I inherited.

The truth about the Quranic text and its history is shocking to Muslims when I share it with them today, but it is well documented. Arabic writing was far from perfected during the time of Muhammad, which is why there was no such thing as a written Arabic book.[1] When initially writing the text of the Quran, letters and vowel markings were still being standardized, which led to confusion. For these reasons, what the scribes wrote were memory aids for the oral text. This is actually a fairly uncontroversial fact even among Muslim Quran scholars.

What is controversial is the result of this: The text of the Quran was fluid during the time of Muhammad. He would recite the same verse multiple ways, saying he could do so up to seven ways.[2] If at any point a text needed to be canceled, it could simply be abrogated and replaced with another text. Since the text of the Quran was not seen as a written text, this caused little problem: All that was required was to stop reciting certain verses and to "forget" what had been revealed.[3]

An advantage of a written text is that clear boundaries must be delineated; the book starts with a certain verse and ends with a certain verse. With an oral text that is being recited in portions, repeated in different ways, abrogated at times, and never publicly read in full from start to finish, it is difficult to determine what the exact contents are. For this reason, when the Quran was finally written down, there were many disagreements about its canon. We have already seen that the final version of the Quran was problematic to Ubay, who said portions were missing, and Ubay was one of the best teachers of the Quran. According to early Islamic sources, Ubay had two chapters at the end of his Quran that are not in the modern Quran: surat al-Hafd and surat al-Khal.[4] Ubay was not alone in including these chapters, as at least two other companions of Muhammad believed them to be a part of the Quran.[5]

But Ubay was not the best teacher of the Quran. When giving a list of the four best teachers of the Quran, Muhammad named Abdullah ibn Masud first.[6] He disagreed with Ubay, saying that Ubay's final two chapters were divine revealed prayers, not scripture. On that very same basis, though, he disagreed with the modern Quran, insisting that sura 1 as well as suras 113 and 114 are divinely revealed prayers, not portions of the Quran. He left them out of his final version, limiting his canon to 111 suras.[7]

Today's Quran, which was not put together by one of the teachers

Muhammad named, is but one of multiple Quranic canons, the one that received official approval by the caliphate and became the standard text when the rest were burned.

When that happened, the Quran went from a primarily oral text to a primarily written text, and what was recited from memory before was read from a page now. The Arabic script, unperfected as yet, needed to be standardized and finalized. The Quran is what drove the development of this standard Arabic script.

Three hundred years after Muhammad died, Arabic script had been more or less standardized, so a scholar with significant authority, Ibn Mujahid, ordered that all but seven different readings be made illegal. Some of his elders disagreed with him, as they had been reading the Quran from their childhood in a reading that was now deemed illegal, and they continued reading the Quran the way they always had. One of these, Ibn Shanabudh, was beaten until he publicly recanted.[8] This is how the proliferation of different Quranic readings was controlled.

However, those seven readings each proliferated once more as they were read according to different receivers, until around 1924, when the Muslim world produced its first Arabic Quran. The Royal Cairo Edition picked one of eighty readings for mass production, the reading of Hafs according to Asim; and this is the Quran that most of the world knows today. Some of the Muslim world, however, still has Qurans according to other readings, such as the reading of Warsh according to Nafi. There are some significant differences in meaning between these Qurans, but the vast majority are insignificant—usually just differences in vocalization. Regardless, few Muslims realize that only one hundred years before, there were about eighty different readings of the Quran in the Muslim world, and that there are significant differences in Qurans even today.

That is the true history of the Quran, not at all what we had been told by our elders and at mosques. The Quran started as an oral text, was transformed into a written text that was not unanimously agreed upon, and has been shaped and crafted by human authority even into the twentieth century.

The Quran's textual transmission is pockmarked by human artifice and intervention, and none of the other arguments for the Quran's inspiration bear the weight of scrutiny. Truly, there is no argument that compels the objective investigator into believing that the Quran is divinely inspired.

CHAPTER 40

CONCLUSION

THERE IS NO COMPELLING REASON TO THINK THE QURAN IS THE WORD OF GOD

As I studied each of the arguments for the Quran's inspiration, a pattern became clear: I could find reason enough to defend my faith in the Quran, but it was beyond doubt that not a single one of the arguments could stand on its own merit and compel a careful investigator who did not already believe Islam.

Could I continue believing the Quran was literarily excellent beyond any other book? Of course I could, dismissing assessments like that of my friend Mike or the scholar Gerd Puin. Could I believe that the Quran has miraculous prophetic knowledge? Yes, I could find such knowledge in the text, even if it was not apparent to others. Could I believe the Quran was miraculously preserved? Yes, I could assume that Allah had guided the Quran in all its shaping and evolving to keep it true to its original text.

But not a single one of the arguments is compelling to an objective investigator. The Quran cannot be used as miraculous proof to convince someone who has carefully scrutinized the evidence.

And that was me: someone who wanted to believe in the inspiration of the Quran but would do so only if the evidence was strong. After carefully considering the five most common arguments, I saw that, far from being so strong that they can vindicate the faith, they actually need to be vindicated by faith.

ISLAM OR CHRISTIANITY? THE EVIDENCE IS CLEAR

ASSESSING THE CASE FOR ISLAM AND ITS EFFORTS TO ACCOUNT FOR ISLAMIC ORIGINS

To be a Muslim, one must confess the *shahada*: "There is no God but Allah, and Muhammad is his messenger." The best way to assess the truth of the *shahada* is by investigating the prophetic status of Muhammad and the claim that Allah inspired the Quran. Even though my heart's deepest desire was to defend the Islamic faith and remain Muslim, the truth became unavoidable: There was no argument I could use to defend Muhammad's prophetic status, and there was no compelling reason to think the Quran was from God.

Once again, it was not just that history did not support the traditional narratives of Islam, but rather that *history proved to be entirely incompatible with Islamic origins*. When using the same standards to assess the origins of Islam as are used to assess the origins of Christianity, we find a gaping hole in the historical record. The contemporary records of the mid-seventh-century Arabs, supposedly the very earliest Muslims after Muhammad's time, show that they were not referred to as Muslims and that they never referred to their holy book, never mentioned Muhammad's name, never referred to Mecca, and did not pray toward Mecca. Given the vast array of records from that time, especially those of the many nations conquered by Arabs, this is not an argument from silence. The contemporary historical record is simply incompatible with the traditional narrative of Islam.

Similarly, the history of the Quran is incompatible with the narrative we were taught as Muslims. We had been told that the Quran had never been changed, every letter remaining exactly the same from Muhammad's time until today. On the contrary, the Quran had been fundamentally altered, being very fluid originally as an oral text and then evolving into a written text that remained in various degrees of flux even to this day.

The traditional Islamic narratives of Muhammad and the Quran are fundamentally incompatible with the historical records. These are the pillars of Islamic confidence, and their foundations are ungrounded.

This meant that if I wanted to remain Muslim, I would have to do so based on some reason other than objective truth. I could remain Muslim because I liked the Islamic message, because I desired the discipline of *sharia*, or because I just wanted to keep my family happy.

But if there was one thing Islam had taught me, it was that I must submit to God and not to man. That meant following the truth, no matter where it led.

Of course, the very reason I had been investigating the case for Islam was to respond to the case for Christianity. Now I had explored every recourse, and I had to be honest with myself and assess for the last time the case for Christianity and the case for Islam.

THE EVIDENCE FOR CHRISTIANITY OVER ISLAM

After thoroughly investigating the truth claims of Islam and Christianity, even while a Muslim, there was no avoiding the obvious truth: The evidence in favor of Christianity was far, far stronger than the evidence for Islam.

The three core claims of Christianity, that Jesus died by crucifixion and rose from the dead proving he was God, are very firmly grounded in history. Even though Islam denies these points, I concluded that the historical evidence for Jesus' death on the cross was as strong as anything historical could be, that his resurrection from the dead was by far the best explanation of the facts surrounding his crucifixion, and that his claiming to be God was the best way to account for the proclamation of the early church.

These conclusions were not idiosyncratic but were based on the consensus of scholars across the theological spectrum.[1] In other words, the truth of the Christian message makes the most sense of the historical evidence.

By contrast, neither of the core truth claims of Islam, that Muhammad is a prophet and that the Quran is the Word of God, are compelling. Muhammad's character does not make one think he was a man chosen by God, nor was he prophesied in the Bible. He had no miraculous scientific insights either recorded in hadith or in the Quran. The Quran, for that matter, cannot be shown to be inspired by its literary quality, by fulfilled prophecies, by mathematical patterns, or by miraculous preservation.

The traditional Islamic narrative is incompatible with both the history of Christianity and even with its own historical records. To believe in the Islamic account of Christian origins while taking the historical records seriously, we would have to conclude that Jesus was an utterly incompetent Messiah and Allah is a deceptive God. The historical record of Islamic origins makes many scholars wonder whether Muhammad existed, and it makes scholars think the Quran was originally far more fluid and indeed a very different kind of book than it is today.

The Islamic narratives of Christian origins, and even of Islamic origins, are incompatible with history. In other words, to believe the truth of Islam is to ignore the historical evidence.

As a Muslim, I wanted to base my beliefs not on blind faith, not on what appealed to me, and not even on my family's heritage. I wanted to ground my faith in reality. If I wanted to take the records of history seriously, I had to abandon my Islamic faith and accept the gospel.

But that would come at a tremendous cost, essentially everything I had ever known. Is it worth sacrificing everything for the truth? Is the truth worth dying for?

IS THE TRUTH WORTH
DYING FOR?

Leaving Islam can cost you everything: family, friends, job, everything you have ever known, and maybe even life itself. Is it really worth sacrificing everything for the truth? The answer is simple: It depends on the value of the truth.

When we consider the gospel, we find the deep secrets of the world unfolded. We find a triune God because of whom love is eternal and absolute, who did not need the world but created it out of an overflow of his love. In him, Yahweh, we have the Father who loves us unconditionally, who offers us extravagant grace, who runs to us when we turn to him, who makes us with a purpose and orchestrates all things for the good of those who love him. In Yahweh we find the Son who is willing to shoulder our pains, who leads us in exemplary humility by suffering for us, makes our burdens light, and forges a way for us to live life to the full even though we die. In Yahweh we receive the Holy Spirit, our Comforter, who fills us with grace, transforms our hearts, renews our minds, and sends us into the world as God's hands and feet to serve others as he served us. The gospel is the answer to our individual pains, to the world's sufferings, and to life's mysteries.

There is no God but one, and he is Father, Spirit, and Son. There is no God but one, and he is Jesus.

It is worth all suffering to receive this truth and follow him. God is more beautiful than this life itself, and the one who loves him is ready to die when death comes, not just to glorify him but to hasten to his arms. Though we will die, we will live.

Sara Fatima al-Mutairi knew this when her brother locked her in her room. She knew that there was a great difference between the way of Muhammad and the way of the Messiah, and she was confident of the gospel's truth. She chose not to repent for her faith in Christ.

On August 12, 2008, a story in the Saudi newspaper *Al-Akhdood* appeared with this title: "A member of Al-Hasba assassinates his sister over her conversion to Christianity." The article shares these details: "A Saudi citizen working for the Commission for the Promotion of Virtue and the Prevention of Vice in the Eastern Province killed his sister for allegedly converting to the Christian religion. According to sources close to the victim, the murderer attacked the girl by burning her and cutting her tongue."

Our sister, twenty-six-year-old Sara Fatima, was certain of the grace of our God, that it was worth giving up everything to have him. She chose Jesus over this life.

It turns out, she did not spend her last minutes reconsidering her faith. Instead, her heart was overwhelmed with anguish for Muslims. In the final moments before her brother returned to take her life, she posted a poem online.[1] Though he cut out her tongue and took her life, her living voice reaches us now. Here are the words that Sara Fatima left this world:

> My tears are on my cheek and, Oh! the heart is sad.
> On those who become Christians, how you are so cruel!
> The Messiah says: "blessed are all the persecuted"
> And we, for the sake of the Messiah bear all things.
> What is it to you that we are apostates?
> You will not enter our graves or be buried with us.
> Enough, your swords do not matter to me at all!
> Your threats do not concern me, and we are not afraid.
> By God, I am to death a Christian!
> O, my eye, cry for what has passed as a sad life,
> For I was far from the Lord Jesus for many years.
> O history, record! And bear witness, O witnesses!
> We are Christians walking on the path of the Messiah.
> Take from me this knowledge and note it well!
> Jesus is my Lord, and he is the best protector.
> I advise you to pity your state of being
> Gaze upon your look of hatred, how hideous it is.
> Man is brother of man, O learned ones!

Where is the humanity and love? And where are you?
My last words I pray to the Lord of the worlds,
Jesus the Messiah, the Light of Clear Guidance:
Change their hearts and set right their discernment.
May he spread love among you, O Muslims.

Amen, amen. To my sister, Sara Fatima, I say this: You were a Christian for mere months, yet your faith is an example to us all. May your voice echo forever, and may we follow your example as an inspiration, even unto death. We are confident we will be with you soon, in the arms of Jesus.

NOTES

Chapter 5: The Islamic Inquisition

1. Along with Jesus' deity and the Bible.

Chapter 6: Comparing *Tawhid* and the Trinity

1. We find out through verses like Philippians 2:10, where a reference to Yahweh in Isaiah 45:23 is substituted with "Jesus," that the name they share is Yahweh.
2. There is something to be said for this common Muslim response. Christians excommunicated for heretical beliefs such as polytheism often did relocate to areas like Arabia, so this hypothesis is not implausible. However, I have found no actual evidence of such Christians living specifically in Muhammad's context.
3. I do not use the word *threat* lightly, but the Arabic word for threat surrounds the verse in question, in 50.14 and 50.20.
4. Technically, *Allahu-Akbar* is in the comparative form, translating to "God is greater." For more, see question 14 in my book *Answering Jihad: A Better Way Forward* (Grand Rapids: Zondervan, 2016).

Chapter 7: Questioning Complexity

1. John Polkinghorne, *Quantum Theory: A Very Short Introduction* (Oxford: Oxford Univ. Press, 2002), 21.
2. Ibid., 21–22.
3. To be clear, I am not saying that *echad* necessitates a compound unity, but it certainly allows for it. The word *echad* itself has many potential meanings.
4. Zohar, Bo, 2:43b; found in *The Zohar*, ed. M. Berg (New York: Kabbalah Centre International, 2003), 121.
5. Alan F. Segal, *Two Powers in Heaven: Early Rabbinic Reports about Christianity and Gnosticism* (Waco, TX: Baylor Univ. Press, 2012), 150.

6. Daniel Boyarin, *Border Lines: The Partition of Judaeo-Christianity* (Philadelphia: Univ. of Pennsylvania, 2004), 89–111.

Chapter 8: Do Muslims and Christians Worship the Same God?

1. For a more thorough answer to this question, see question 13 in *Answering Jihad: A Better Way Forward*.

Chapter 9: The Council of Nicaea

1. Tacitus, *Annals* XV.44.
2. Tertullian, *Apologeticum* L.

Chapter 11: Questioning the God-Man

1. Brennan Manning, *The Ragamuffin Gospel* (Sisters, OR: Multnomah, 2005), 107.

Chapter 12: Libya's Best Friend

1. Anita Smith, "An Open Letter from the Widow of Ronnie Smith to the Libyan People," December 12, 2013, http://www.RonnieSmithLibya.com.

Chapter 14: Comparing the Quran and the Bible

1. Of course, the analogy breaks down when we consider that there are many copies of the Quran and only one incarnate Jesus, but this is perhaps the closest approximation to describing the symbolic impact of burning the Quran.
2. Although a small number of scholars argue that portions were composed in orality, such as sections of Genesis and the book of Mark, this is strongly contested. And even if these portions were orally composed, the vast majority of the Bible was undoubtedly written.
3. Cf. 16.101.
4. I present here, of course, the Protestant position. There are more parallels between the Catholic and Muslim views of Scripture and authority.

Chapter 15: Questioning Texts

1. "Contradictions in the Qur'an," http://www.answering-islam.org/Quran/Contra.
2. See chapter 34 for further discussion.

Chapter 16: The First Burning of the Quran

1. Included in those who testify to the inspiration of the Bible are, of course, Muhammad and the Quran.

Chapter 17: The First Crusade

1. See *The First Crusade: The Chronicle of Fulcher of Chartres and Other Source Materials*, ed. Edward Peters (Philadelphia: Univ. of Pennsylvania, 1971), as well as Robert the Monk, *The Historia Iherosolimitana of Robert the Monk*, ed. D. Kempf and M. G. Bull (Woodbridge, UK: Boydell, 2013).

2. *Select Documents of European History, 800–1492*, ed. R. G. D. Laffan (New York: Henry Holt, 1929). Available as an ebook: https://archive.org/stream/selectdocumentso000965mbp/selectdocumentso000965mbp_djvu.txt.

3. "Daimbert, Godfrey and Raymond, Letter to the Pope (1099)," *Hanover College Department of History*, October 1997, https://history.hanover.edu/texts/1stcru3.html.

4. Robert Louis Wilken, "Rescuers, Not Invaders," *Wall Street Journal*, March 13, 2010, http://www.wsj.com/articles/SB10001424052748703915204575103791369415182.

5. Joseph Michaud, *History of the Crusades*, vol. 3, trans. W. Robson (London: George Routledge and Co., 1852), 17–18. Please note that I have modernized the language.

6. The one exception was the Umayyads, who were still in the process of systematizing the use of slave warriors. See Daniel Pipes, "Military Slaves: A Uniquely Muslin Phenomenon" (presentation, conference on "The Arming of Slaves from the Ancient World to the American Civil War," New Haven, CT, November 16–18, 2000). Full text available at http://www.danielpipes.org/448/military-slaves-a-uniquely-muslim-phenomenon.

7. Felix Fabri testifies to Christian *mamluks* in the fifteenth century.

8. John, Bishop of Nikiu, *The Chronicle of John (c. 690 A.D.), Coptic Bishop of Nikiu* (Amsterdam: Philo, 1916), chapter CXVI.12.

9. Ibid., chapter CXVIII 4–10.

10. Thomas F. Madden, "Crusade Propaganda: The Abuse of Christianity's Holy Wars," *National Review*, November 2, 2001, http://www.nationalreview.com/article/220747/crusade-propaganda-thomas-f-madden.

11. Found in Katharine J. Lualdi, *Source of the Making of the West, Volume I: To 1740: Peoples and Cultures* (Boston: Bedford/St. Martin's, 2009), 196.

12. Jonathan Simon Christopher Riley-Smith, *The Crusades, Christianity, and Islam* (New York: Columbia Univ. Press, 2011), 69.

13. Christopher Tyerman, *The Crusades: A Very Short Introduction* (Oxford: Oxford Univ. Press, 2005), 59.

14. Riley-Smith, *The Crusades, Christianity, and Islam*, 71.

Chapter 18: Comparing the Traditions of the Founders

1. "SAW" represents the common Muslim prayer recited whenever Muslims say the name of Muhammad: "May peace and blessings be upon him." It is inserted here because my friend said the prayer immediately after saying Muhammad's name.

2. Sahih Bukhari, Book 84 (or 88, depending on the numbering system), is the Book of Apostates. In it are found hadith like, "Whoever changes his Islamic religion, kill him" (9.84.57).

3. "Attempts to rewrite history occur solely in Western-authored presentations of jihad, or those with Western audiences as the primary focus . . . Perhaps because early Muslim history is heavily emphasized in the Islamic educational curriculum, those who write in Arabic or other Muslim majority languages realize that it is pointless to present jihad as anything other than militant warfare." David Cook, *Understanding Jihad* (Berkeley: Univ. of California, 2005), 43.

4. *Tafsir al-Qurtubi*, the commentary of a thirteenth century imam, comments on 2.256 with a detailed list of the various views of the abrogation of this verse.

5. *Tafsir ibn Kathir*, though this entry appears inconsistently in printings I have seen. Consider also consulting Qurtubi's commentary.

6. See Sahih Muslim 3432, 3371; Sunan Abi Dawud 11.2150; and Sahih Bukhari 3.46.718.

7. "Open Letter to Al-Baghdadi," *Letter to Baghdadi*, September 14, 2014, http://www.lettertobaghdadi.com.

8. Sunan Abi Dawud 39.4390.

9. Guibert of Nogent, quoted in Riley-Smith, *The Crusades: A History*, 13–14, emphasis added.

10. Sahih Bukhari 4.56.2924.

11. Sahih Bukhari 4.52.50.

12. Sahih Bukhari 4.52.44.

13. For more, see *Answering Jihad: A Better Way Forward*, question 17. Alternatively, see Jonathan Riley-Smith's *The Crusades, Christianity, and Islam*.

Chapter 19: Questioning Christian Peacefulness

1. Notice the martial terms in which this word is used: "Repent therefore! Otherwise, I will soon come to you and will fight against them with the sword [*rhomphaia*] of my mouth" (Rev. 2:16 NIV). Also see Revelation 6:8.

2. Luke 22:35–38 NIV: "Then Jesus asked them, 'When I sent you without purse, bag or sandals, did you lack anything?' 'Nothing,' they answered. He said to them, 'But now if you have a purse, take it, and also a bag; and if you don't have a sword, sell your cloak and buy one. It is written: "And he was numbered with the transgressors"; and I tell you that this must be fulfilled in me. Yes, what is written about me is reaching its fulfillment.' The disciples said, 'See, Lord, here are two swords.' 'That's enough!' he replied."

3. The only potential challenge to this is the temple cleansing, so this deserves some attention. All four gospels describe the event (Matt. 21:12–17; Mark 11:15–19; Luke 19:45–48; and John 2:13–17), but the only account that appears violent is John's. It describes Jesus seeing cattle sellers, dove sellers, and moneylenders, and then making a whip and driving out all from the temple. But a careful reading of the Greek shows that Jesus expelled all three of these groups differently, none with violence against people. First, he only struck the sheep and oxen: He "drove all from the temple courts, both sheep and cattle" (NIV). The cattle having been driven out, their sellers followed. Jesus then turned over the tables of the money changers, causing them to leave. Finally, Jesus did not release the doves as this would amount to stealing them, but he told their sellers in his zeal to depart. So Jesus systematically purged the temple, having struck no man and not in a blind rage.

4. Ibn Kathir, tafsir.

5. Sahih Muslim 1767a.

6. See Suyuti's *Itqan fi Ulum al-Quran*.

7. Sahih Muslim 1910; 33.226; 20.4696; Book on Government #47.

Section: Question 2

1. A Muslim might object, saying that "Jesus is Lord" might simply mean "Jesus is a lord" or "Jesus is a prophet," but the context of Romans precludes this interpretation. Not only does such a reading usually impose an anachronistic Islamic understanding of lordship and prophets on the text, but also verse 13 clarifies which Lord is in mind. It quotes Joel 2:32 NIV: "Everyone who calls on the name of the LORD will be

saved," where LORD is a rendering of the divine name, Yahweh. In its context, Romans 10:9 is saying Jesus is the LORD Yahweh, the God who saves. It is also insightful to remember that this is the exact meaning of the name "Jesus": "God saves."

2. This is most clearly found in Matthew 12:39–40.

3. An objection here may be that "Allah" refers to a generic concept of God, not a specific one, and the *shahada* just proclaims monotheism. This is a common rhetorical move, but the answer is apparent upon consideration: The message of Muhammad teaches specific doctrines about God (e.g., he is not a Father, he is not a Son, he helped Muslims in the Battle of Badr, he chose Muhammad as a prophet, etc.). Together, the message of Muhammad forms a notion of God that is implicit in the word *Allah*. Therefore in the *shahada*, "Allah" refers to the God that Muhammad preached, the God of Islam.

4. Quran 2.23; 10.37–38; 11.13; 17.88; 52.33–34.

5. Acts 1:22; 2:24, 29–32; 3:15; 5:29–32; 10:39–41; 13:26–37; 17:30–32; 23:6; 24:15–21; 26:6–8, 23.

Chapter 21: The Positive Case

1. Gerd Lüdemann, "The Decline of Academic Theology at Göttingen," *Religion* 32, no. 2 (2002), 87–94.

2. Gerd Lüdemann, *What Really Happened to Jesus: A Historical Approach to the Resurrection*, trans. John Bowden (Louisville: Westminster John Knox, 1995), 17.

3. Paula Fredriksen, *Jesus of Nazareth: King of the Jews* (New York: Vintage, 1999), emphasis mine.

4. John Dominic Crossan, *The Historical Jesus: The Life of a Mediterranean Jewish Peasant* (San Francisco: HarperSanFrancisco, 1991), 375.

5. John Dominic Crossan, *Jesus: A Revolutionary Biography* (San Francisco: HarperCollins, 1991), 145.

6. I must point out here, though, that unlike the other scholars to whom I referred, Reza Aslan is not a scholar of New Testament or historical Jesus studies but a scholar in sociology of religion and a professor of creative writing.

7. Interview with Lauren Green.

8. In fact, some scholars say that this teaching was formulated less than a year after Jesus' death: "This tradition, we can be entirely confident, was formulated as tradition within months of Jesus' death." James D. G. Dunn, *Jesus Remembered* (Grand Rapids: Eerdmans, 2003), 855.

9. It should be understood here, though, that the implications of "converting" or becoming a Christian from a Jewish background at this point in Christian history are not fully known, and the term *Christian* when juxtaposed with *Jew* or even *non-Christian* is unavoidably problematic. But terminology aside, the point stands: They were not simply defending what they already believed.

10. Matthew 28:12–15.

11. Marcus Tullius Cicero, *Pro Lege Manilia. Pro Caecina. Pro Cluentio. Pro Rabirio Perduellionos*, trans. H. Grose Hodge (Cambridge: Harvard Univ. Press, 1990), 467.

12. Seneca, *Epistles 93–127*, trans. Richard M. Gummere (Cambridge: Harvard Univ. Press, 1925), 167.

13. Josephus, *Antiquities* 12.256.

14. Martin Hengel, *Crucifixion in the Ancient World and the Folly of the Message of the Cross* (Philadelphia: Fortress, 1977), 31–32.

15. Josephus, *Jewish War* 6.304 and 2.612.

16. Seneca, *Epistles*, 167.

17. Hengel, *Crucifixion in the Ancient World and the Folly of the Message of the Cross*, 9.

18. The only possible exception is found in Josephus's autobiography. He tells of seeing three personal acquaintances in the process of being crucified. Being a friend of the soon-to-be emperor, he tearfully told Titus about this. Titus "commanded immediately that they be taken down, and to have the greatest care taken of them that they might recover." Two of the three died regardless, though one friend survived. That is the only recorded account of anyone in Roman history surviving crucifixion: a partial, interrupted crucifixion victim who was given an emperor's best medical treatment. There is no one on record to whom the full punishment has been meted who has survived. Josephus, *Life*, 420–21.

19. Hengel, *Crucifixion in the Ancient World and the Folly of the Message of the Cross*, 3.

Chapter 22: The Islamic Response

1. It is important to know, while reading this verse, that the early Christians understood Jesus' resurrection as being saved from death. See Acts 2:31–32.

Chapter 23: Assessing the Islamic Response

1. I do not think an "objective observer" is *ipso facto* a naturalist. Naturalism is itself a conclusion that entails its own biases. I think an objective observer must allow for the existence of God without asserting it.
2. I am not here arguing that this is a sufficient condition for concluding a miracle has occurred, but that it is a necessary condition. Many phenomena that are inexplicable for a time are later explained by additional knowledge. Further reason for believing a miracle has happened should be adduced. See chapter 25 for further discussion.
3. Josephus, *Antiquities* 18.85–88.
4. Josephus, *Jewish War* 2.175–177.
5. That is also the case in the other reference to this account, 3.49.
6. Alexander Roberts, James Donaldson, and A. Cleveland Coxe, eds., "The Arabic Gospel of the Infancy of the Saviour," in *The Ante-Nicene Fathers: Fathers of the Third and Fourth Centuries; The Twelve Patriarchs, Excerpts and Epistles, the Clementina, Apocrypha, Decretals, Memoirs of Edessa and Syriac Documents, Remains of the First Ages*, trans. Alexander Walker, vol. 8 (Buffalo: Christian Literature Company, 1886), 405.
7. Thus K. Aland, W. Bauer, W. Foerster, G. May, E. Procter, and A. Gregory; for a fuller discussion on whether the book should be called a 'gospel,' see J. A. Kelhoffer, "Basilides's Gospel and 'Exegetica (Treatises)'" *Vigiliae Christianae* 59, no. 2 (2005), 115–34.
8. Irenaeus of Lyons, "Irenæus against Heresies," in *The Ante-Nicene Fathers: The Apostolic Fathers with Justin Martyr and Irenaeus*, ed. Alexander Roberts, James Donaldson, and A. Cleveland Coxe, vol. 1, (Buffalo: Christian Literature Company, 1885), 349.
9. Ibid., emphasis mine.

Chapter 24: Conclusion

1. This is true apart from the vindication of this message by the resurrection, of course—though the incredibility of the resurrection might compound the unappealing nature of the message in the eyes of some audiences, as well.

Chapter 25: The Positive Case

1. Acts 1:22; 2:24, 29–32; 3:15; 5:29–32; 10:39–41; 13:26–37; 17:30–31; 23:6; 24:15–21; 26:6–8, 23.
2. 1 Corinthians 15:19.

3. This debate can be watched online: ThomisticTheist (YouTube user), "Did Jesus Rise from the Dead? Michael Licona vs. Shabir Ally," YouTube.com, uploaded August 19, 2013, https://www.youtube.com/watch?v=FTyqQlBGX_4.

4. Of course, what mattered was not the scholarly consensus so much as the reason for the consensus: The evidence was so strong that virtually everyone who studied the matters agreed.

5. James D. G. Dunn, *Jesus Remembered* (Grand Rapids: Eerdmans, 2003), 855.

6. It is striking that Peter's verbiage begins in a manner very similar to the creed of 1 Corinthians 15:3–8.

7. A. J. M. Wedderburn, *Beyond Resurrection* (Peabody, MA: Hendrickson, 1999), 13.

8. See 2 Corinthians 11:24–26 and Acts 14:19. The record of Paul's execution is found in 1 Clement 5, a few short years after his death. Paul's manner of execution is recorded in Eusebius' *Historia Ecclesiastica* 2.25.5.

9. The four are: Josephus, Hegesippus, Clement of Alexandria, and Eusebius. Unfortunately, the accounts of Clement and Hegesippus are only preserved in Eusebius' *Ecclesiastical History*; the former in 2.1.3–5 as well as 2.23.3, the latter in 2.23.3–19. Eusebius' account of Josephus is found immediately following, 2.23.20–25, though there are some discrepancies between his record and the record of our manuscripts of Josephus, which records the account beginning in *Antiquities* 20.200.

10. Since there is no narrative account of James seeing the risen Jesus, only the report from 1 Corinthians 15, the reason for James' conversion has less scholarly consensus. Regardless, Habermas tells us that the majority of critical scholars concede that James was converted as 1 Corinthians 15 reports, on account of a resurrection appearance. Habermas and Licona list the following as examples of scholars who hold this view: Allison, Betz, Byrskog, Conzelmann, Craig, Davis, Derret, Ehrman, Funk, Hoover, Kee, Koester, Ladd, Lorenzen, Ludemann, Meier, Oden, Osborne, Pannenberg, Sanders, Spong, Stuhlmacher, Wedderburn and Wright. M. Licona, *The Resurrection of Jesus: A New Historiographical Approach* (Downers Grove, IL: InterVarsity Press, 2010), 460–61.

11. E. P. Sanders, *Jesus and Judaism* (Philadelphia: Fortress, 1985), 334.

12. Please note that the phrase "and later Paul" was in parentheses in the original, but for the sake of clarity in this text I have placed the phrase in commas. E. P. Sanders, *The Historical Figure of Jesus* (London: Penguin, 1993), 280, emphasis mine.

13. David R. Catchpole, *Resurrection People* (Macon, GA: Smyth and Helwys, 2002), 158.

14. Hershel Shanks and Ben Witherington, *The Brother of Jesus: The Dramatic Story and Meaning of the First Archaeological Link to Jesus and His Family* (London: Continuum, 2003), 107–9.

15. E. P. Sanders, *The Historical Figure of Jesus*, 280.

Chapter 26: The Islamic Response

1. See also 5.111 and 61.14.

Chapter 27: Assessing the Islamic Response

1. Hyam Maccoby, *The Mythmaker: Paul and the Invention of Christianity* (New York: Harper and Row, 1986).

2. Karen Armstrong, *The First Christian: Saint Paul's Impact on Christianity* (London: Pan, 1983), 12.

3. For an excellent treatment of the topic, see David Wenham, *Paul: Follower of Jesus or Founder of Christianity?* (Grand Rapids: Eerdmans, 1995). See also E. P. Sanders, *Paul and Palestinian Judaism: A Comparison of Patterns of Religion* (Philadelphia: Fortress, 1977).

4. Thomas J. Herron has given strong arguments for dating 1 Clement before AD 70 in his book *Clement and the Early Church of Rome: On the Dating of Clement's First Epistle to the Corinthians*, though others disagree and date it circa AD 90. Even the latter date is still within the lifetime of those who knew Paul, but the former date is nigh immediate by historical standards.

5. F. F. Bruce, *The New International Greek Testament Commentary: The Epistle to the Galatians* (Exeter: Paternoster, 1982), 117.

6. Galatians 2:12 NIV says "certain men came from James," and some take this to mean that everything these men did was sanctioned by James, and by taking issue with them, Paul was taking issue with James himself. None of that is found in the text itself; there is no indication that James sanctioned their activities nor that Paul ever had an argument with James.

7. It might be useful to also note that Antioch had about fifteen times the population of Jerusalem at this time in the first century, and a church schism here could have been dangerous. It was Paul's duty to remind Peter of the disciples' earlier decision.

8. Acts 15:7–11 NIV says, "Peter got up and addressed them: 'Brothers, you know that some time ago God made a choice among you that the Gentiles might hear from my lips the message of the gospel and believe.

God, who knows the heart, showed that he accepted them by giving the Holy Spirit to them, just as he did to us. He did not discriminate between us and them, for he purified their hearts by faith. Now then, why do you try to test God by putting on the necks of Gentiles a yoke that neither we nor our ancestors have been able to bear? No! We believe it is through the grace of our Lord Jesus that we are saved, just as they are.'"

9. Some assume that Matthew 5:18 means the law will always apply. But again, the Law here refers to the Pentateuch, and regardless, the verse clearly says "until everything has been accomplished" (NIV), meaning there will be an end, and there is good reason to think that the end is the cross. Some point to verse 19 to say that people need to follow the law to be saved, but that cannot be what Jesus means because the verse explicitly says that even those who do set aside the commands and teach others to do so will still be in the kingdom of heaven.

10. Jews were required to take certain oaths as part of the ceremonial laws. By telling His followers not to, Jesus was telling them to break Jewish law.

11. An assumption that Stanley Porter challenges in his recent book, *When Paul Met Jesus: How an Idea Got Lost in History* (New York: Cambridge University Press, 2016).

12. C. H. Dodd, *The Apostolic Preaching and Its Developments* (London: Hodder and Stoughton, 1944), 16.

13. 1 Corinthians 4:11–13; 7:10–11; 9:14; 11:23–25; 13:2–3; 15:3–5.

14. Of course, the epistle to the Romans is the exception that proves the rule. It is the one Pauline letter sent to a congregation where Paul had not been, and it is also the one letter that is most systematic and careful in explicating its theology.

15. Cf. Quran 61.14: "O ye who believe! Be Allah's helpers, even as Jesus son of Mary said unto the disciples: Who are my helpers for Allah? They said: We are Allah's helpers. And a party of the Children of Israel believed, while a party disbelieved. *Then We strengthened those who believed against their foe, and they became the uppermost.*"

16. See Tafsir al-Qurtubi 61.14, as well as Tabari's *History*.

Chapter 29: The Positive Case

1. That both words refer to Jesus is firmly established by the Granville Sharp Rule. See Daniel Wallace, *Sharp Redevivus? A Reexamination of the Granville Sharp Rule*, https://bible.org/article/sharp-redivivus -reexamination-granville-sharp-rule.

2. "In the Gospel of John, Jesus says, 'Before Abraham was, I Am'; 'I Am'

is the name of God in the book of Exodus . . . Jesus' listeners know full well what he's saying. They pick up stones to stone him because they think he's committed a blasphemy, claiming himself to be God." Bart Ehrman, "The Earliest Gospels" (lecture, "History of the Bible: The Making of the New Testament Canon," the Great Courses).

3. These are the exact words used to in the Greek Old Testament to address God in Psalm 35:23.

4. For a more detailed treatment, see Richard J. Bauckham, "Monotheism and Christology in the Gospel of John" in *Contours of Christology in the New Testament*, ed. R. N. Longenecker (Grand Rapids: Eerdmans, 2005), 148–66.

5. Ehrman, "The Earliest Gospels."

6. The consensus dating for John is circa AD 90, though this date has been challenged because it relied on a scholarly assumption which is now defunct (i.e., John's reliance upon the synoptics). Cf. J. A. T. Robinson, who dates the gospel of John between the fifties and sixties. See Robinson, *Redating the New Testament* (Eugene, OR: Wipf and Stock, 2000), 307. Regardless of its correctness, my reason for rejecting John was because it was written sixty years after Jesus' death.

7. Although the consensus dating for Mark is AD 65–70, this dating, like the consensus on John, relies upon obsolesced assumptions. Maurice Casey dates Mark near AD 40 in his work *Aramaic Sources of Mark's Gospel*. For different reasons yet with a similar result, James Crossley has suggested in his monograph *The Date of Mark's Gospel* that Mark was written sometime between the midthirties and midforties. I presently find a date in the early forties more compelling than any alternative, though my set of reasons are not exactly the same as either Casey or Crossley. With differing degrees of likelihood, it is possible that: Mark presupposed his hearers knew Pilate, Caiaphas, Bartimaeus, Rufus, and Alexander; that he did not want his hearers to know the identity of the boy fleeing naked and the apostle striking the high priest's ear for purposes of protective anonymity; that his account predates the early church discussions about the law; that he was concerned about the impending statue of Caligula standing in the temple; that the gospel was spurred by Peter's departure from Jerusalem; and that he wrote early enough to supply a standard text about Jesus' ministry for those who had seen the risen Jesus themselves. Combined, these features would indicate a date around AD 40–44. Though that specific date is my position, it is consensus that Mark's gospel is the first of the four.

8. Rikk Watts, "Mark," in *Commentary on the New Testament Use of the Old Testament*, ed. G. K. Beale and D. A. Carson (Grand Rapids: Baker Academic, 2007).

9. The word used for "Lord" here is *adonai*, a word commonly used for Yahweh but also applicable to humans. However, in context, this is the Lord of the temple, which is Yahweh.

10. Malachi 4:6 says God will "come and strike the land with total destruction" (NIV). Of course, Christians understand the latter portion of the prophecy to relate to Jesus' second coming.

11. Cf. Philo, *On the Embassy to Gaius* 368 and *On Dreams* 2.131.

12. A charge we also find in John 10:33.

13. The antecedent of the participles is Yahweh, and I have included the antecedent in my translation as "he."

14. Deuteronomy 33:26; Psalm 104:3, Isaiah 19:1.

15. It should be remembered that this is not the first time in the Old Testament that Yahweh is depicted as two persons, or as being in two separate places. See chapter 6.

16. The potential exception is the *Exagoge of Ezekiel*, a Hellenistic Jewish drama in which Moses has a vision of a throne on Mt. Sinai, where a noble man sitting on the throne gestures to Moses with his right hand that Moses take his place on the throne, giving Moses his crown and scepter with his left hand. The noble man could be God, and Moses might actually sit on the throne, though neither is said explicitly. *Exagoge*, lines 68–76.

17. Hans-Joachim Kraus, *Psalms: A Commentary*, trans. Hilton C. Oswald (Minneapolis: Augsburg, 1988–89), 2.348–49.

18. Adela Yarbro Collins, "The Charge of Blasphemy in Mark 14:64," *Journal for the Study of the New Testament* 26, no. 4 (2004): 379.

19. As stated in a previous note, I prefer a date for Mark in the early forties, and therefore I am not one of those who believe Paul writes earlier than Mark. But I am in the great minority.

20. Ernst Lohmeyer, *Kyrios Jesus: Eine Untersuchung zu Phil 2, 5–11* (Heidelberg: Winter, Universitätsverlag, 1961), 4.

21. Colin Brown, "Ernst Lohmeyer's *Kyrios Jesus*," in *Where Christology Began: Essays on Philippians 2*, eds. Ralph P. Martin and Brian J. Dodd (Louisville: Westminster John Knox, 1998), 10.

22. Lohmeyer, *Kyrios Jesus*, 8.

23. J. M. Furness, "The Authorship of Philippians ii.6–11," *Expository Times* 70 (1958), 240–43.

24. Ralph P. Martin, "*Carmen Christi* Revisited," in *Where Christology Began: Essays on Philippians 2*, eds. Ralph P. Martin and Brian J. Dodd (Louisville: Westminster John Knox, 1998), 2.

Chapter 31: Assessing the Islamic Response

1. Or at least a theology of multiple persons within one Godhead.
2. A few verses later, Jesus cleansed a leper *in his own authority*, a miracle that no prophet from the Old Testament had ever done and one which could give away his identity. So "Jesus sent him away at once with a strong warning: 'See that you don't tell this to anyone'" (Mark 1:43–44 NIV).
3. John 7:30.
4. Parallels in Matthew 16:16–20 and Luke 9:21.
5. Mark 8:30 and 9:41 imply that Jesus is the Messiah, but neither verse shows explicit admission, the kind that Muslims often seek for a claim to deity. In addition, both are private conversations, not public proclamations. Matthew 16:16–20 is the exception that proves the rule; here, in private, Jesus admits that he is the Christ, but insists that he himself did not tell them this, nor does he want them to tell anyone. (Parallel in Luke 9:21 without clear admission.) The same can be said of John's gospel; the clearest admission is John 4:26, when he agrees that he is the Messiah, but it is a private conversation. Publicly, many continue to be upset that he has not clearly said who he is (see John 10:24). Also, if John 4:26 suffices as a claim to be the Messiah, so should John 20:29 suffice to be a claim to deity.
6. There is textual contention as to the original form of the verse.
7. The title is used in didactic, apocalyptic, and historical settings.
8. The criterion of dissimilarity suggests that a historical datum must be sufficiently dissimilar from its context if we are to be certain that it was not imposed onto history. In the case at hand, Jews were not expecting the Messiah to be the Son of Man, so we would not expect such a claim to be imposed upon Jesus; perhaps more important, the early church virtually abandons the title, thus making it unlikely that the gospel authors would have retroactively projected the words onto Jesus. The only likely reason that they portray Jesus using this title so regularly is because he actually did use it for himself.
9. Approximately twenty-two times. Richard Bauckham, *God Crucified: Monotheism and Christology in the New Testament* (Grand Rapids: Eerdmans, 1999), 29.

10. Bart D. Ehrman, *How Jesus Became God: The Exaltation of a Jewish Preacher from Galilee* (New York: HarperOne, 2014), 3. Kindle ebook. Emphasis mine.

Chapter 33: The Positive Case

1. Quran 61.6.

Chapter 34: The Response

1. Sahih Bukhari 1.2.12.
2. Sahih Bukhari 1.2.16.
3. Sahih Bukhari 1.2.18.
4. Sahih Bukhari 3.46.694.
5. Sahih Bukhari 9.87.111.
6. He is later identified as Gabriel.
7. This is the translation of the word *ghatt* provided by *Lane's Lexicon*, the standard English lexicon for classical Arabic. Vol II, 2269.
8. Sahih Bukhari 4.52.50.
9. Sahih Bukhari 4.52.44.
10. Sahih Bukhari 4.52.72.
11. Sahih Bukhari 5.59.297.
12. Sahih Bukhari 5.59.449.
13. Sahih Bukhari 4.52.182.
14. E.g., Sahih Bukhari 5.59.370.
15. Sahih Bukhari 5.59.369.
16. Sahih Bukhari 7.71.589.
17. Sahih Bukhari 1.11.584.
18. Sahih Bukhari 4.52.256.
19. E.g., Sahih Bukhari 5.59.362 with Banu Quraiza; Sahih Bukhari 5.59.512 with the inhabitants of Khaibar.
20. Sahih Bukhari 1.2.25.
21. Sahih Muslim 1767.
22. See more at David Wood, "50 Reasons Muhammad Was Not a Prophet," *AnsweringMuslims.com*, April 6, 2014, http://www.answeringmuslims.com/2014/04/50-reasons-muhammad-was-not-prophet.html.
23. Sahih Bukhari 7.71.661.
24. Sahih Bukhari 4.53.400.
25. There is a passing reference to the satanic verses in Sahih Bukhari 2.19.177, in which Muhammad recites Sura Najm, causing *jinn* and pagans to prostrate with him. This is part of a much larger account,

found in thirty-seven early Islamic records. Shahab Ahmed, a Muslim scholar who graduated from Princeton University and taught at Harvard University, submitted his 1999 doctoral dissertation on this topic, arguing that Muhammad actually did proclaim the satanic verses.

26. Sahih Bukhari 6.60.139; Sahih Muslim 3248.

27. Sahih Muslim 3481; see also Sahih Bukhari 7.62.64.

28. Quran 23.1–6; Sahih Bukhari 5.59.459; Sahih Muslim 3371 and 3384.

29. Sahih Bukhari 3.48.826.

30. Sahih Bukhari 2.18.161.

31. "How, then, are the other parts formed? Either they are all formed simultaneously—heart, lung, liver, eye, and the rest of them—or successively . . . As for simultaneous formation of the parts, our senses tell us plainly that this does not happen." Aristotle, *Generation of Animals*, trans. A. L. Peck (Cambridge: Harvard Univ. Press, 1979), 147.

32. "The embryo obtains its growth through the umbilical attachment. Since the nutritive faculty of the Soul, as well as the others, is present in animals, it immediately sends off the umbilicus, like a root, to the uterus." Galen, *On the Natural Faculties*, trans. Arthur John Brock (London: W. Heinemann, 1916), 239.

33. Ibid., 21.

34. Sahih Bukhari 4.55.546; 5.58.275.

35. As a Muslim I found it unbelievable that the Quran would say this, but it is verified in hadith as well. Sunan Abi Dawud 4002: "I was sitting behind the Messenger of Allah who was riding a donkey while the sun was setting. He asked: Do you know where this sets? I replied: Allah and his Apostle know best. He said: It sets in a spring of warm water."

36. Sahih Bukhari 7.71.673.

37. Sahih Bukhari 7.71.592.

38. Sahih Bukhari 7.71.590.

Chapter 35: Assessing the Response

1. Found in Ibn Hisham's notes. *The Life of Muhammad: A Translation of Ibn Ishaq's Sirat Rasul Allah*, trans. Alfred Guillaume (Oxford: Oxford Univ. Press, 2002), 691.

2. We can be sure the disgraceful material and distressing facts are related to Muhammad, since Ibn Hisham had already discussed excising material that was not related to Muhammad earlier in his list of omissions.

3. *The Life of Muhammad*, 494.

4. Ibid., 675.

5. Ibid., 675–76, with supplemental details from Ibn Sa'd: "Umayr Ibn Adi came to her in the night and entered her house. Her children were sleeping around her. There was one whom she was suckling. He searched her with his hand because he was blind, and separated the child from her. He thrust his sword in her chest till it pierced up to her back. Then he offered the morning prayers with the prophet." Muhammad Ibn Sa'd, *Kitab al-Tabaqat al-Kabir*, trans. S. Moinul Haq, vol. 2 (Karachi: Pakistan Historical Society, 1972), 30–31.

6. *The Life of Muhammad*, 515.

7. Ibid., 308.

8. Andrew Higgins, "Professor Hired for Outreach to Muslims Delivers a Jolt," *Wall Street Journal*, November 15, 2008, http://www.wsj.com/articles/SB122669909279629451.

9. Some may respond by objecting that Ahmad is a title for Muhammad, but that is begging the question.

10. For more on Western scholastic approaches to studying early Islam, read F. M. Donner, *Narratives of Islamic Origins: The Beginnings of Islamic Historical Writing* (Princeton: Darwin Press, 1998). For a more popular-level, engaging read, consider Tom Holland's *In the Shadow of the Sword: The Birth of Islam and the Rise of the Global Arab Empire* (New York: Random House, 2012).

Chapter 37: The Positive Case

1. Quran 2.23; 10.37–38; 11.13; 17.88; 52.33–34.

Chapter 38: The Response

1. Quoted in Toby Lester, "What Is the Koran?" *Atlantic*, January, 1999, http://www.theatlantic.com/magazine/archive/1999/01/what-is-the-koran/304024.

2. Italics original to the article. Puin adds, "This is what has caused the traditional anxiety regarding translation. If the Koran is not comprehensible—if it can't even be understood in Arabic—then it's not translatable. People fear that."

3. This is disputed on grounds of subjectivity, but that serves to further exemplify the matter at hand: Who is to say whether something is actually the best?

4. An astute observer might deduce that I have not watched major league basketball since the mid-1990s. He would be correct.

5. A Muslim might object that Muhammad did not abrogate the Quranic verses so arbitrarily, but that is begging the question. Unless we have good reason to think that he was a prophet, he may very well have done so. That would not necessitate a subversive character; he could have had the best of intentions while abrogating a text such as this hypothetical example.

6. We will consider this phenomenon explicitly in the upcoming chapter.

7. Quran 7.12; 15.27; 38.76; 55:15. As a reminder, I do not consider such apparent "contradictions" problematic, either in the Quran or in the Bible. Please see chapter 15.

8. Brendan McKay, "Assassinations Foretold in Moby Dick!" 1997, https://cs.anu.edu.au/people/Brendan.McKay/dilugim/moby.html.

9. Abu Ameenah Bilal Philips, *The Qur'an's Numerical Miracle*.

10. Ibid.

11. Philips continues: "It may be further concluded that the Doctor's record of data falsification, textual changes and figure manipulation clearly indicate his dishonesty as a researcher and expose the low levels to which he stooped to invent support for his hoax. Hence, nineteen and its multiples may not be used to interpret anything of the Qur'an or Islam and all those sincere Muslims who have publicly propagated this theory in ignorance are Islamically obliged to publicly disown and discredit it, and immediately cease the publication, distribution and sale of books and tapes which support it."

12. Sahih Bukhari 6.61.510.

13. Some Muslims argue here that the variants were only in the vocalization of the Quran, but the vocalizations were not yet recorded in the text. In other words, there would be no reason to destroy the manuscripts because of variant vocalizations. The differences must have been in the *rasm*, the consonantal text itself.

14. Sahih Bukhari 6.61.509.

15. Sahih Bukhari 6.61.511.

16. In response, some Muslims argue that he had the only written evidence to support what Zaid and others had memorized, but the hadith and earliest Islamic sources simply do not say that. They say only one man had these two verses.

17. Sahih Bukhari 6.61.510. Some argue that Zaid would not have known to search for it had he not had it memorized, and therefore Khuzaima must have had a written record. That is not what the hadith says, though, and it could just as easily be that Zaid had a vague recollection of it and needed to find someone who was much more familiar with it.

18. Sahih Bukhari 6.61.550.

19. Sahih Bukhari 6.61.558. I have removed the words "such and such" from the translation to make the hadith more readable.

20. Sahih Bukhari 6.61.527.

21. Some would try to argue that the verse had been abrogated, unbeknownst to Ubay, but that actually proves the ultimate point of this section: The Quran was a fluid composition, and to say it has been perfectly preserved takes faith, not an objective assessment of the evidence.

22. Sahih Bukhari 6.61.521.

23. For example, Sahih Bukhari 6.61.512 indicates that a blind man was able to influence a verse of the Quran after it had been revealed, having an exception added to the text. These sorts of phenomena are also disconcerting to those who are not already Muslim.

Chapter 39: Assessing the Response

1. Any reference to an Arabic *kitab*, the word for "book," was actually an oral text that was handed down through poets and reciters. It was not a written book.

2. Sahih Bukhari 6.61.513.

3. This is exactly what 2.106 and 16.101 say: Allah can "cause people to forget."

4. There are many records of this, perhaps the best being one that was recently rediscovered: *Kitab al-Masahif* by ibn Abi Daud. One can also refer to Ibn Nadim's *Fihrist* and Suyuti's *Itqan fi Ulum al-Quran*.

5. Ibn Abbas and Abu Musa. See Suyuti's *Itqan fi Ulum al-Quran*.

6. Sahih Bukhari 6.61.521

7. The details are also found in the sources quoted above: *Kitab al-Masahif, Fihrist*, and *Itqan fi Ulum al-Quran*.

8. Christopher Melchert, "Ibn Mujahid and the Establishment of Seven Qur'anic Readings," *Studio Islamica* 91 (2000), 5–22.

Conclusion to Question 2

1. To clarify, non-Christian scholars do not believe Jesus rose from the dead, but they concede the facts that are best explained by His resurrection; similarly, scholars do not all concede that Jesus claimed to be God, but the current consensus is that the earliest Christians did believe Jesus to be divine, which I only take one step further by saying that the best explanation for this is that Jesus claimed to be divine.

Section: Conclusion

1. The details of Sara Fatima's final moments differ from account to account, as people can only piece together her story from her online posts and the news reports. My understanding is that, in the days leading up to her martyrdom, she was working on a poem that was a response to a Muslim who was cursing apostates. She finished that poem in her last moments in light of her impending sacrifice.

Seeking Allah, Finding Jesus

A Devout Muslim Encounters Christianity

Nabeel Qureshi

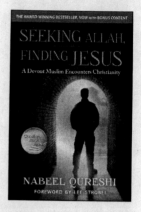

In *Seeking Allah, Finding Jesus*, now expanded with bonus content, Nabeel Qureshi describes his dramatic journey from Islam to Christianity, complete with friendships, investigations, and supernatural dreams along the way.

Engaging and thought provoking, *Seeking Allah, Finding Jesus* tells a powerful story of the clash between Islam and Christianity in one man's heart and of the peace he eventually found in Jesus.

Answering Jihad

A Better Way Forward

Nabeel Qureshi, Author of
The New York Times *Bestseller,*
Seeking Allah, Finding Jesus

From *New York Times* bestselling author
and former Muslim Nabeel Qureshi
comes this personal, challenging, and respectful answer to the
many questions surrounding jihad, the rise of ISIS, and Islamic
terrorism.

San Bernardino was the most lethal terror attack on
American soil since 9/11, and it came on the heels of a coor-
dinated assault on Paris. There is no question that innocents
were slaughtered in the name of Allah and in the way of jihad,
but do the terrorists' actions actually reflect the religion of
Islam? The answer to this question is more pressing than ever,
as waves of Muslim refugees arrive in the West seeking shelter from the violent ideology of ISIS.

Setting aside speculations and competing voices, what
really is jihad? How are we to understand jihad in relation
to our Muslim neighbors and friends? Why is there such a
surge of Islamist terrorism in the world today, and how are
we to respond?

In *Answering Jihad*, bestselling author Nabeel Qureshi
(*Seeking Allah, Finding Jesus*) answers these questions from
the perspective of a former Muslim who is deeply concerned
for both his Muslim family and his American homeland.

Available in stores and online!